# MORNING HAS BROKEN

*A biography of Eleanor Farjeon*

Eleanor Farjeon in her room

# MORNING HAS
# BROKEN

*a biography of*
*Eleanor Farjeon*
*by Annabel Farjeon*

Julia MacRae

A DIVISION OF FRANKLIN WATTS

First published in Great Britain 1986 by
Julia MacRae Books, a division of Franklin Watts
12a Golden Square, London WIR 4BA
*and* Franklin Watts Australia
14 Mars Road, Lane Cove, N.S.W. 2066

*TO IGOR ANREP*

*British Library Cataloguing in Publication Data*

Farjeon, Annabel
Morning has broken : a biography of Eleanor Farjeon.
1. Farjeon, Eleanor – Biography    2. Authors,
English – 20th century – Biography
I. Title
823'.912   PR6011.A67

ISBN 0-86203-225-3

Typeset by Ace Filmsetting Ltd, Frome, Somerset
Printed in Great Britain at The Bath Press

# CONTENTS

✥

# ILLUSTRATIONS

꙳ﾂﾞ.ﾂﾞ꙳

# PREFACE

IN GETTING TOGETHER the biography of somebody who is twenty years dead there will be gaps. The disappearance of papers, the inaccuracies of memory, the prejudices of those interviewed, as well as the prejudices of the biographer, all contribute to muddle and mistake. But if, at the end, the essence of a character can be conveyed, with the extraordinary individuality which all human beings exhibit, and powerful individuals exhibit in excess, then the gaps may be acceptable, like the chancy pattern of living.

In the helter-skelter of Eleanor Farjeon's days so many people were coming and going, each slotted in to his special place, so that within the honeycomb of her interests and affections each had his own compartment. But in this biography some have been neglected, left out either for lack of information or because it seemed that the story was becoming a hotch-potch of names. Her brother Bertie said, "Nellie is the best friend of everyone who knows her." And she was friends, real friends, with more people than any person I have ever known or heard of.

One regret is not knowing more of her relationship with the eccentric lonely poet, William Ibbert, who wrote so prolifically that one's heart sinks at the sight of the cardboard box topped by a black book where, with painful legibility, he wrote out his poems. These he gave into my aunt's keeping. How she bore the burden of those piles of mediocre verse and his patronising attitude to her own writing reveals the magnitude of her cheerful charity. Another regret is that there is so little written material to be found in Eleanor's papers about her last love, the actor Denys Blakelock. In the final months of her life she commanded my sister to tear up and burn great quantities of manuscript and letters. She watched narrowly to see that her orders were carried out.

All the conversations that I have recorded are taken from Eleanor's memoirs, both published and unpublished, or from my personal recollections. That a good deal is quoted from her writing has been done not only because I wish to show her off as an artist and a personality, but because no paraphrase has the same spirit that emanates from the spontaneously composed sentence. And she was the most spontaneous person.

# ACKNOWLEDGEMENTS

I WANT TO THANK Anne Harvey whose particular intelligence and enthusiasm so often made it a delight to struggle with this book. Also I would thank all those who magnanimously gave information, letters and papers relating to Eleanor Farjeon. They are: Jessica Albery, Nicky Archer, John Bell, George Benson, Pamela Benson, Bertha Bettesworth, Bridget Coffey, Eileen Colwell, Jean Davis, Giles de la Mare, John Donat, Nora Earle, Gervase Farjeon, Grace Farjeon, Joan Farjeon, Joan Jefferson Farjeon, Violetta Farjeon, John Fernald, George Fradd, Joscelyn Frank, Leslie French, Christopher Fry, Livia Gollancz, Chloe Green, Elizabeth Hawkins, Martin Hawkins, Christian Hardie, Grace Hogarth, Tony Kraber, Willy Kraber, Dorothy Lampel, Cyril Luckham, Violet Luckham, Ann MacEwan, David March, Jessica Morton, Isobel Morton-Sale, John Morton-Sale, Ena Neill, Clifton Parker, Yoma Parker, Anthony Popham, A. H. Reed, James Roose-Evans, Steve Race, Stanley Scott, Myfanwy Thomas, Sarah Thomas, Francis Thompson, Cherry Watson, Kaye Webb and Teresa Wilkinson.

Gratitude is due to Laurence Pollinger Ltd and the Frieda Lawrence Ravalgi Estate for permission to quote D. H. Lawrence's letter; to the *Evening Standard* to quote Beverly Baxter's review; to the Carcanet Press to quote from *As it Was* by Helen Thomas; to Victor Gollancz Ltd to quote from *Eleanor, Portrait of a Farjeon*, by Denys Blakelock. Finally, to the Leverhulme Trust for its one year award to Anne Harvey, enabling her to research Eleanor Farjeon both on her own and my behalf.

To those who have not been traced, but who unwittingly assisted, my apologies as well as thanks.

A.F.

# POSTSCRIPT TO A LETTER

I'M SORRY, WILLIAM, but I will *not* let you whitewash my smoky ceiling. I know whitewash is fun for the one who's doing it, but you'd be the one. Then you'd go away, and I would be left staring up at glaring dead-white boards instead of the lovely cobwebby rafters of two hundred years ago, when this loft was full of hay instead of my books and me. That's how I like it. I'm sorry, William.

# THE FARJEON–JEFFERSON FAMILY TREE

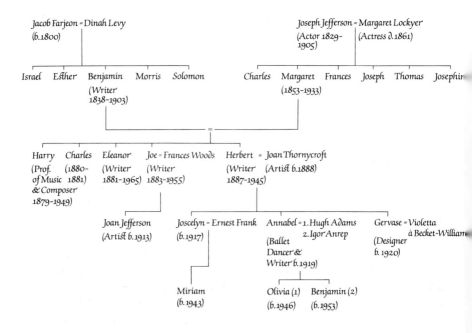

Jacob Farjeon = Dinah Levy
(b.1800)

Joseph Jefferson = Margaret Lockyer
(Actor 1829–          (Actress d.1861)
1905)

Israel    Esther    Benjamin    Morris    Solomon         Charles    Margaret    Frances    Joseph    Thomas    Josephin
                    (Writer                                          (1853–1933)
                    1838–1903)

Harry        Charles    Eleanor    Joe = Frances Woods    Herbert = Joan Thornycroft
(Prof.       (1880–     (Writer    (Writer               (Writer    (Artist b.1888)
of Music     1881)      1881–1965)  1883–1955)            1887–1945)
& Composer
1879–1949)

            Joan Jefferson         Joscelyn = Ernest Frank    Annabel = 1. Hugh Adams         Gervase = Violetta
            (Artist b.1913)        (b.1917)                            2. Igor Anrep                    à Becket-William
                                                             (Ballet                        (Designer
                                                             Dancer &                       b. 1920)
                                                             Writer b.1919)

                                   Miriam                    Olivia (1)    Benjamin (2)
                                   (b.1943)                  (b.1946)      (b.1953)

# Benjamin Farjeon

BENJAMIN FARJEON and his daughter Eleanor had the same kind of abounding energy, the same love of words, wit and food, the same passionate interest in people, theatre, music and, above all, literature.

'It would have been more natural to live without clothes than without books,' Eleanor wrote of her childhood, as her father filled nurseries, study, bedrooms, dining-room and the overflowing little bookroom with eight thousand volumes of plays, histories, romances, legends, poetry and other publications.

Ben Farjeon was born in 1838. His Jewish parents kept a second-hand clothes shop in London's Mile End Road. The family was poor, and by the age of thirteen he was working as a printer's devil, or errand boy, for a Christian newspaper, *The Nonconformist*. This was no pious or paltry publication, but a large, well-printed weekly, with full reports of debates in Parliament, general news and serious discussion of how the impure water supply to Manchester encouraged intemperance. Among its many advertisers were Mudie's Library, Mill Hill Grammar School and Jujube Cough Lozenges.

The employment of his third child on such a newspaper cannot have been much to the taste of Jacob, the father, who was rigorous in his observance of the Jewish faith; but money was important. Ben Farjeon earned four shillings a week for a twelve hour day, which was less than Charles Dickens, who had received six shillings a week for his label pasting thirty years earlier. Only, unlike Dickens, the child would not have suffered exquisitely, having no pretensions to being a gentleman.

Ben's interest in writing began early, for as soon as he had mastered the difficulties of the alphabet he began to spell out stories. Later an enduring enthusiasm for books was fostered by a bookseller, past whose shop he had to walk every day on the way to the newspaper office. One day there lay in the window an open volume of F. H. K. de la Motte Fouqué's *Undine* whose pages the boy stopped to read. Next morning the page had been turned, so that he enjoyed another romantic instalment. On the third occasion when he arrived somewhat earlier in order to have more time, the old bookseller came out and asked him in. The result of this meeting was an invitation to read in the shop when he pleased. With such a library at his disposal, the printer's devil spent every lunch hour absorbed in poetry, novels, Shakespeare, Dickens, and fairy stories. He devoured literature with that amazed and greedy excitement which can overwhelm the young on a sudden discovery of what imaginative miracles may be found within the cover of a book.

Besides this haphazard education, there were lessons from a schoolmaster, Mr Hands, whose daughter in later years reported that her father had never had such a boy to teach, with his love of reading and his head for figures, for when faced with a mathematical problem he would invent his own swift formula.

At thirteen, young Farjeon was writing an epic poem which opens with the following self-portrait:

*A poet in his chamber sat with melancholy brow,*
*His book was spread before him, he took no heed I trow,*
*For though his eye was constant fixed, his thoughts were far away,*
*Tracing through dim futurity the bright and coming day,*
*The day when through his genius grand his name should mighty be,*
*When titled lords and jewelled dames to him should bend the knee.*

Such dreams were not fostered by the hard-pressed family, although Ben was his mother's favourite and encouraged by her in all he did. For her and his sister he felt strong affection, but he was on bad terms with his father. That strict observance of Jewish rites, on which Jacob insisted, was not readily accepted by the son when he discovered that, although tearing paper was forbidden on the Sabbath, his father always seemed to know the contents of a letter delivered that day. In fact he ordered one of his other children to perform the sinful act. However, there was a favourite uncle, an atheist, 'one of the best men I ever knew', and it seems likely that it was he who influenced Ben Farjeon towards agnosticism, and a sense of honour, enforced by moral disapprobation of his father's hypocrisy. This uncle once said to his nephew, "If ever you need fifty pounds for a particular purpose, Ben, come to me."

That day came when the boy was sixteen.

In 1854 the Australian gold-rush was inspiring and inciting both rich and poor with visions of wealth and adventure. Farjeon decided to go and make his fortune, in order to bring home money with which to lift his family out of the poverty they endured. He was an optimist always. So he asked his uncle for the fifty pounds, and a steerage passage to Melbourne was bought on the sailing ship, *The Ocean Wave*.

At that time a journey to Australia took from three to four months, and the confined travellers had no occupation but that which they could devise for themselves. From the crowded steerage of speculators and emigrants, Farjeon edited his first newspaper. He already had the experience and skills learnt on *The Nonconformist*, and now composed two handwritten sheets : articles, news, jokes, a serial and advertisements. Putting one copy aside for the steerage passengers, he took the other to the captain and asked permission to distribute it in the saloon. According to Farjeon's story, the captain was so impressed and amused that he moved him into a saloon cabin from which *The Ocean Record* was produced weekly, to the entertainment of all, including the crew, until the last day came and the ship docked. Then he walked into Melbourne, penniless.

The immediate problem of finding work was settled by a notice which offered twelve shillings a day for labour in a brickyard. However, after the first hours sweltering in the sun, the boss, noting Farjeon's poor physique, inquired whether he was any good at figures. Once they were in the office the young man was handed a mass of papers dealing with contracts and given three hours in which to get out estimates. After half an hour Farjeon reappeared.

"Got you beat, heh?"

"No, sir, they're done."

Although his head for figures was remarkable, one suspects that these stories gained in the telling, for Farjeons have always felt a lively enthusiasm for their own talent.

After a month it was possible to buy a blanket and pannikin and set out for the gold-fields. The story of how he got lost in the bush when taking a short cut at the end of a ninety mile tramp, searching for the Dunolly diggings, is the only truly autobiographical piece of Farjeon's writing to be found. It is called *Christmas Day in the Bush*, and this extract gives the flavour of his writing: its serious, simple nineteenth century sentimentality and its dramatic style. At this moment he had been lost for two days, had eaten every scrap of food and, in the night, unconsciously drunk the last of his bottle of tea. In the appalling heat his mind had begun to wander, while he struggled to write one final note to his mother.

> But I started up. I would not, would not die! There must be a way – there must, there must! Why should I bring my sweet Mother in the dear old country the agony of reading that the boy she doted on was lost in the bush? There *must* be a road out of this dead eternal stillness. Yes, there it was! The gold-field of Dunolly was not five hundred yards away. I saw it, saw the white tents of the diggers, saw the men at the windlasses, saw them stooping over the creek with their tin gold-dishes, saw the picks at work, and the diggers signalling to each other. One standing on top of a great heap of pipeclay, beckoning to me to come on. "I am coming – I am coming!" I cried with joy. "It is all right, Mother!" My voice was hoarse, my parched lips were rubbing together convulsively. And then as I walked towards the man on the pipeclay mound I began to sing in a cracked undertone, "For Bonny Annie Laurie!" But as I staggered on the man faded, the white tents, the miners at the windlasses, the fortunate ones swinging their gold-dishes round at the creek, all, all melted away! No objects met my sight except the horrible gum trees, this side of me, that side of me, all around me, thousands and thousands of them, staring down at me, and mocking me![1]

Farjeon was found unconscious by a farmer searching for strayed cattle on Christmas Day.

Eleanor wrote that 'it was a strange life for a boy, born and bred in the poor streets of London, with no experience and no physique, but

---

1. *A Nursery in the Nineties*, autobiography. London, Gollancz, 1935, as *Portrait of a Family*, N.Y., Stokes, 1936. Referred to hereafter as [NN].

*The Emigrant* by Nicholas Chevalier (See p. 8.)

the spirit of a bantam cock! Plunging into the rough, coarse, dangerous fellowship of the camps, learning to make a damper [primitive
bread], smoke his cutty pipe, to bluff with a straight face at poker, to
light a fire with three sticks (he was a terror to our housemaids,
demanding their bundle of firewood per grate): and writing, writing, writing, wherever he went.' At every digging he started a news
sheet.

One of Farjeon's short stories, *In Australian Wilds*, describes
another occasion, travelling on horseback with a convict, Lilly Trot,
and without any histrionics gives a very real picture of the gold-
diggers' world in the 1850s. Hour after hour they passed through a
forest along a faint track under the white staring sky. 'The lynx eyes
of Lilly Trot were busy in all directions and every now and then he
pointed to some gully or hillsiding as a likely place to find gold, if a
man searched for it . . . I had fallen into a kind of listless dejection,
when suddenly I found myself listening delightedly to a gush of the
sweetest melody that ever flowed from mortal lips. It was simply
Lilly Trot, whistling divinely, if such a term may be applied to what
is usually considered a vulgar accomplishment. As I gazed at Lilly
Trot and heard him breathe beautiful melody from a pair of the
coarsest lips that ever deformed a human mouth, my amazement
grew very strong. He was whistling the principal airs from *La
Sonnambula*, and I never heard them more artistically rendered. The
softest-toned flute could not have produced sweeter music, and, as I
listened, the skill of the whistler raised about me the village where
Elvino and Amina lived and loved, the mill, the stream, and the
pleasurable traditional associations with which all simple love stories
are surrounded. The pleasant effect remained long after Lilly Trot
ceased whistling, but when the rusty cawing of the crows forced
itself again upon my attention, I noticed that the sun was sinking
behind the distant ranges.'

Farjeon did not take readily to manual labour and made no fortune
of any sort until he went to New Zealand, landing up in Dunedin in
1861. There he began to work for *The Otago Daily Times* as manager,
sub-editor, contributor, and sometimes even compositor.

He had grown into a short, thick man with curly black hair, a
heavy end to his nose and twinkling brown eyes full of vitality and
fun. He was not good-looking, but his lively humour, his enthusiasm
for others as well as himself, his integrity and romantic sense of

honour, his hot temper and generosity drew friends. That he had been driven to, and always expected to live by, his wits was apparent.

One Saturday a fire burnt out the press of *The Otago Daily Times* and ruin seemed inevitable. But Farjeon led his compositors to the premises of their rival, a weekly paper, and broke in. This was possible because the people of Dunedin were mainly strict Scottish Sabbatarians, so that business buildings remained undisturbed all Sunday. Behind locked doors the gang worked for twenty-four hours and the paper was printed. Then Farjeon went to the owners of the weekly and offered them £100 for the use of their press and paper. They refused.

"You'd better take it," he responded.

"Why?"

"Because the paper is set up already."

The owners were taken aback at first, then impressed. They not only accepted the money, but gave Farjeon the use of their premises until others could be re-established.

In an article[1] he described Dunedin at this time as a lively new town of about 20,000 people, supporting three newspapers, all the trades in the world, all the professions, and all grades of society, from an earl's son to a chimney sweep.

'I pledge myself to both the earl's son and the chimney sweep, for both of them did I know; the chimney sweep once treated me to a bottle of champagne, and I, more than once, treated the earl's son to a glass of English beer. He didn't have enough money to pay for it himself.'

He went on to describe the Royal Princesses Theatre which was opened in the horse-sale yard of the Provincial Hotel. At night, after the horses had trotted away, 'a number of carpenters and builders made their appearance, with deal planks, and hammers, and nails and screws, and a stage, and scenery, and flies, and a box of props, and a green curtain, and every other necessary thing, and almost before you could cry "Jack Robinson" the theatre was enclosed, the stage was fixed, the dressing rooms were ready, the footlights were arranged, and the future Garricks, and Robsons, and Siddonses, were pulling on their tights and painting their cheeks.'

As soon as the curtain came down the carpenters re-appeared and

1. A Theatre in a Stable: *Otago Daily Times*, 1869.

by one o'clock not a trace of the theatre remained. The yard was ready for next day's auction. Such was the enterprise of the people of Dunedin in the 1860s.

Now Ben Farjeon's social status rose and he became a prosperous and respected citizen. He bought land, and went into partnership with Sir Julius Vogel, who owned the newspaper and later became premier of New Zealand. Five of Farjeon's plays were produced at the Royal Princesses by the Dunedin Stock Company, to which actors from England and America were often invited to play leading roles. He loved to entertain distinguished visitors, many of whom became friends, like Nicholas Chevalier, the Swiss artist who painted in New Zealand and Australia. Another visitor, in 1864, was Joseph Jefferson, the renowned American actor who made his fortune in the role of Rip van Winkle. A picture of the actor's eldest daughter was shown to Farjeon. Thirteen years later Farjeon married this daughter.

Notices of Ben's plays went to Jacob and Dinah Farjeon in New York, where they had followed their eldest son, Israel. His mother responded with unpunctuated joy: 'My beloved Benjamin, we have received your papers and they do indeed give a glowing description of your new play not more than it deserves I should like to see it performed.'

He was also sending money, of which old Mrs Farjeon wrote to the wild son, Morris, after Jacob's death: 'Your dear brother Benjamin made his last years very happy. We were not in want of anything and it must be very pleasing to him to know in his last moments I had someone to care for me now . . .'

It was in the 1860s that his novel writing began, novels which were to support Farjeon till he died. The first was short, printed in New Zealand, boldly dedicated to his idol, Dickens. And it was the great man's response which led the journalist to decide on returning to England in order to establish himself as an author. Although the Dickens letter was not produced, Farjeon led his friends to believe that it was most encouraging and suggested he might become a contributor to *All the Year Round* – the Dickens periodical – and that his dedication had been warmly received.

This unseen Dickens letter was a legend of Eleanor's childhood. Only after her father's death was it found. Eleanor, her brother Harry, and their mother read it together.

8

*Gad's Hill Place, Higham by Rochester, Kent*
*Tuesday Twenty-ninth May* 1866

Dear Sir,

I am concerned to find that I have by accident left your letter of last January's date unanswered.

Your dedication, as an interesting and acceptable mark of remembrance from the other side of the world, gave me great pleasure. And I read the little book with much satisfaction.

But I am bound to lay before you the consideration that I cannot on such evidence (especially when you describe yourself as having written "hurridly"), form any reasonably reliable opinion of your power of writing an acceptable colonial story for *All the Year Round*. As to my reproducing this story, such a proceeding is as wide of the design and course of this journal as anything can possibly be.

If you write and offer for *All the Year Round*, any original communication, I will read it myself, very heartily desiring to accept it, if I can deem it suitable to those pages. Do not, I beg, suppose that I intend to discourage you when I say no more. I simply mean to be honest with you and to discharge a duty I owe to you and myself.

Accept my thanks And believe me Dear Sir,

Faithfully yours

Charles Dickens

'"I don't call that so very encouraging," said Mother. And suddenly we all began to laugh. How like Father! To throw up everything impetuously, everything he had done and made and become, to rush away from where he was to somewhere else, and begin all over again in a heat of excitement, because Charles Dickens had written him – this letter!' [NN]

So, after thirteen years abroad, Ben Farjeon left his job, sold his property and impetuously returned to London.

# Margaret Jefferson

THE AMERICAN JEFFERSONS were very different from the London Farjeons. Four generations of actors and actresses went back to the 18th century, when Thomas Jefferson acted the King to Garrick's Hamlet. After this the family emigrated to America and became itinerant players, travelling from town to town, sometimes settling for a season, sometimes trudging on one-night stands with sledges or carts piled with props and children. It was a hard life and when, in 1842, the second and calamity-ridden Joseph Jefferson died, he left a third Joseph Jefferson, aged thirteen, as head of the family. This boy had been led on stage in crowds, played amid scenery and aped actors from the beginning. By the age of four he was performing with a comedian over six foot tall who tipped him out of a sack on to the stage. With blackened faces, dressed identically as Jim Crow, they stood side by side singing alternate verses and dancing, till the audience roared with delight, and showered the stage with dollars.

A Texan once suggested that they tour through Indian country, but Joe Jefferson declined this as being too dangerous. It was then recommended that they use their stage weapons for protection. Telling this story Jefferson said that he shivered to imagine himself facing a hostile Indian when armed only with a stage pistol whose tendency to misfire had several times compelled the heavy villain to commit suicide with a tablespoon. Jefferson was a natural comedian.

At the age of twenty, during a season in New York, the young man married an eighteen-year-old actress. Of this occasion Joseph Jefferson wrote in his autobiography: 'The important day arrived.

My new lavender suit fitted me to perfection : none of your ready-made affairs, but got up by a first-class Chatham Street tailor, and embodying in its value the savings of two months' salary. With a beating heart and, if I remember rightly, a pair of tight boots, I led my young bride to the altar.'

By the time the second child, Margaret, was born in 1853 it seemed that Jefferson's future was hopeful. He had done with buffeting about in barns, tents and taverns, he had acted with stars from England like Macready and Booth. He could paint scenery, fix engagements, stage-manage and direct, as well as act. Working his way up, he described his own ambitious nature : 'There is nothing a young actor enjoys more than itinerant theatricals. It is so grand to break loose from a big tyrant manager in the city and become a small tyrant manager in the country. I was one of those juvenile theatrical anarchists who, after having stirred up a rebellion in the greenroom, would shout to my comrades "Let's all be equal and I'll be King!" '[1]

However, by 1853 he was on his way to being a big tyrant manager himself and had played many leading roles. His children

1. *The Autobiography of Joseph Jefferson.*

*Joseph Jefferson*

*Margaret Jefferson*

were being brought up in a country farmhouse in Paradise Valley, Pennsylvania, no longer dragged from lodging to lodging and used as babes in arms on the stage, training for their future profession.

Maggie, whose miniature Jefferson had shown to Benjamin Farjeon in Dunedin, felt no desire to go on the boards. In 1870 she put up her hair with a 'gold-brown plait like a coronal, and mysteries of "switches" and "waterfalls" behind.' [NN] She had grown into a beautiful young lady, delicate and small. There was time on her hands in which to fill an autograph book with great names, read modern novels and be fitted for elaborately bustled and ruched ball gowns. With her father's success, luxuries increased: a new, more heavily furnished house in the unspoilt countryside, more servants, more social life.

The Jeffersons had always been a lively family, full of laughter and larks, picnics and charades. A community of aunts, uncles and cousins of all ages grew up in houses over the Jefferson estate in Buzzard's Bay, Massachusetts, where there were always friends, writers and actors staying.

Miss Jefferson would accompany herself on the guitar, singing in a sweet voice traditional Negro songs or the latest hits, which were remembered by her own children.

> *How now, my giddy cousin!*
> *I do not wish to hurt,*
> *But really, if you ask me, dear,*
> *I fear you are a flirt!*

Or the sentimental and lilting

> *Nita! Juanita!*
> *Ask thy soul if we should part.*
> *Nita! Juanita!*
> *Follow thou on thy heart.*

In modern literature Maggie had become an ardent admirer of the novelist B. L. Farjeon. (By this time Farjeon had inserted Leopold into his name in order to add dignity, so his youngest son maintained.) The novels were highly praised by reviewers: he was called 'a preacher of the brotherhood of rich and poor more powerful, graphic, and tender than any since Dickens'. *Blade o' Grass* was 'a great national social lesson' as well as 'satire as grim, suggestive and as applicable to the days we live in as those written by Swift were to his'.

Joe Jefferson wondered whether this writer, about whom his daughter was so enthusiastic, was the same Farjeon as the journalist he had known in Dunedin years ago. By 1875 he was sure and wrote the following letter to London:

*Orange Island, Feb 27th.* 1875

My dear Farjeon,

You will doubtless be surprised when you receive this.

I hope you will not have quite forgotten me for I have often thought of you since we parted and your increasing fame has not only given me great pleasure but I have always felt proud to think that I knew and admired you before you had made your great reputation.

My wife and daughters delight in all you have written and our fireside is often made happy by listening to your charming and useful work . . .

The letter was written to announce a visit to London in the summer. On arrival he wrote again:

*2y Hyde Park Place, Wednesday*

My dear Farjeon,

I am living at the above address. My family are with me and we will be delighted to see you. Won't you come and take family dinner with us on Sunday?

We are vulgar enough to dine at 3, and if you can bring yourself down to the level of that hour, and don't mind children (who don't mind anybody) do come. Or if you have time to drop in any time between this and Sunday I am nearly always at home.

Yours as of old,

J. Jefferson

So it was that Ben Farjeon met Maggie Jefferson. She turned out to be one of the prettiest girls he had ever seen. As for the young lady, she had a shock. Expecting a venerable white-haired author with a paternal manner, there appeared a lively black-haired man with a mercurial wit: he did not seem anything like fifteen years older than herself. He immediately made friends with her little brothers and sisters and became accepted in the family – not so long afterwards accepted as a lover.

The marriage between them was of a character which is not uncommon, but which makes for serious problems in the long run. She was full of female refinements, she liked things about her to be dainty, she was frightened of the dark and thunderstorms, she had genuine hysterics at the sight of a mouse and did not wish to take on responsibilities. Doubtless, as with Desdemona and Othello, the lover's stories of dangerous adventures in the wild were made doubly exciting in contrast to her own secure upbringing. His flamboyance and generosity, his coarse common touch, his emotional violence and physical energy were a thrilling, irresistible experience.

For Farjeon, who had buffeted his way in the world from the start, who had always bitten off more than he could chew, here was a challenge of a different kind, though one which his optimistic character hardly feared. A strong Jewish tradition and belief in family, his age of thirty-nine, his present success as a writer, were all pushing him towards settling down to domesticity.

They were married in May 1877 and set off for Switzerland, via Paris, with all the proper Victorian sentiments towards alpine scenery. In every town Farjeon bought his wife a cup and saucer in romantic remembrance of their stay: a silver cup painted with birds from Paris, a turquoise flowered cup from Montreux. His taste was more florid than hers, but their artistic feelings were equally set in the mid-nineteenth century mould, which revelled in luscious and stuffy luxury.

It was on the honeymoon the husband confessed that his mother had been one of twenty-six sisters, while his sister already had eighteen children. His wife responded in humorous alarm, "If you'd told me that before, I'd never have married you."

Their first child, Harry, was born on their visit to America in 1878, on the Jefferson estate in Hohokus, New Jersey. It was during the transit of Mercury that the frail, dark, monkey-like baby came. Greatly excited his father cried, "We'll call him Mercury!" But the mother got her way and called him Harry.

Before they left America to set up home in London, Farjeon went about New York on one of his buying sprees. 'Big furniture – a walnut suite – the bedstead six foot wide! Tallboy and dressing-table to match. An American rocker for Maggie. Then two more . . . Vast orders of fine silver plate from Israel [Farjeon's elder brother] – three or four dozen of every table implement, except, by some mercy, soup ladles – he must be spending hundreds of pounds, thousands of dollars!' [NN]

And so they returned to London, to the top two floors in Buckingham Street off the Strand, where Farjeon had had rooms previously. Here a second boy was born, even frailer than Harry. In the smoke and dank fogs that came down from the chimneys and up from the river, and with lungs that had to be drained, the child only survived eighteen months. During this time Maggie Farjeon became pregnant again and bore her third baby, Eleanor, on February 13th 1881. "I was disgusted with you for being so quick," she laughed years afterwards. "The only thing that saved your face was that you were a girl."

# 13 Adelaide Road

IT SEEMS THAT ELEANOR was noisy from the start. Her father invited a friend to the 'undress rehearsal of an entirely new and original uproar entitled *Our Daughter*'. This was a parody of Gilbert's sub-title to *Patience* which had lately been produced. He also wrote the following quatrain in her honour:

> *Imperious Babe! that yet can scarcely speak,*
> *Doth rival Chanticleer in piercing shriek,*
> *May not those lungs which now such yells emit*
> *One day enthrall a world with sense and wit.*

The children were not christened. Farjeon believed in no formal religion, although his novels express a conventional Christian morality. Mrs Farjeon taught her children prayers at night 'just in case', but this anxiety to keep on the right side of the Almighty did not attract her more sophisticated children as they grew up, and Eleanor was the only one who, late in life, took to God.

Their mother hated housekeeping and disliked food, but a servant girl was easy to come by and cheap, while the friends who visited were mostly theatrical or those of the Bohemian sort who did not require properly served Victorian meals. The Barrymores, the Blanchards, the Booths, Labouchère the editor and M.P., Nicholas Chevalier, were all easy going. It was always possible to send the maid out for a few extra chops. The couple were liked by so many lively and clever people that, in spite of confusion, ill babies, the vain attempts to keep things calm while Farjeon wrote, life was exciting.

In one of Farjeon's notebooks he wrote: 'Maggie in wonderful

16

form tonight, sang and played, was very gay and witty, enchanted everybody as usual.'

In 1883 Joe was born at 13 Adelaide Road, the Chalk Farm end, rent £16.5.0 per annum. A new nurse – 'dear, rosy, buxom little Fanny' – took the place of Julia, who had pinched Harry into chanting "I-do-love-Julia-I-do", and threatened him with a tiger under his bed at night. When this was discovered Eleanor wrote: 'Knowing Mama, I am certain she never touches him again; knowing Papa, I wonder she lives to be sent packing next day.' [NN]

The discoveries about temperament which marriage brings were, as always, full of the unexpected. Farjeon was nervy and erratic, especially when writing. He had a study, but seldom wrote in it, pursuing his family from room to room, so that meals had to be eaten on the space left over from pens, paper and inkpot. But his wife had a sweet temper and much good sense: she did not complain. He wrote prolifically, though never regularly, always smoking cigars. If the baby screamed, he slammed out of the house. If visitors called, he would give up writing and then work through the night, often going out at four in the morning to post his latest instalment. Having been a journalist and compositor he was most particular that his writing should be legible and the required number of words exact.

From Farjeon's diary of 1884 it is plain that there were many festivities around Christmas, besides the regular theatre-going.

'2nd January. The Children's Party a great success, though some of the little ones could not come. There were quite enough, little people and big . . . The Magic Lantern was a triumph, the most popular feature being the Story of Cock Robin. Then the Xmas tree was stripped, and the youngsters went home rejoicing. Mrs Huy stopped till the last – and when she went Maggie and I had another long chat. I stopped up till 3 in the morning, getting my Magic Lantern slides in order and finishing up the Xmas tree, carrying it out of the house, so Harry and Nellie should not see it when they came down in the morning. Our Xmas and New Year time has been very enjoyable.' [NN]

On January 7th he posted 7,000 words of *The Sacred Nugget* to his publisher, Tillotson. By the 14th he had sent off another 6,000 words.

During this week, besides his writing, Farjeon had spent three days clearing up the Buckingham Street rooms, gone to the theatre twice, and dined out once. He also devoted time to his children, playing a musical box and reading to them.

When Eleanor was about four, her mother, whose health after the Victorian fashion had always been delicate, became really ill. Her right lung collapsed. The specialist informed her husband, "She cannot live."

Mrs Farjeon suspected what was being said outside her bedroom door, but when Farjeon came in smiling she was deceived and lived another fifty years on one lung.

Despite the medical misjudgements of doctors and dentists, those patronised by the Farjeons had to be infallible. Every slightest instruction and pill was followed and swallowed without demur. So when, at the age of six, skinny little Harry was overcome with a nervous tic, screwing up his eyes and jerking, Maggie Farjeon took him to her queer faddy children's specialist in Queen Anne Street, Dr Eustace Smith. He pronounced, "Take him to Margate tomorrow, if you don't want him to have St Vitus's Dance."

His mother hastened home to set about packing and make arrangements for Fanny to care for Eleanor, Joe and her husband. Farjeon dashed out to make arrangements with a mysterious Mr Forbes who always fixed free first class train tickets in and out of Kent. Then he dashed home to find out how else he could help. Luckily an evening engagement interfered, so that the two women were left in peace to make everything ready for an early start.

At six o'clock on a fine summer morning Maggie Farjeon woke to discover her husband had not been home all night. She and Harry were about to leave for the station when a cab drove up to the gate. Its roof was heaped with bright red roses. The door swung wide and out tumbled Farjeon amid showers of more roses. He presented a bouquet to the grinning cabby. Roses spilled in the gutter and along the path, as he staggered up to the door and flung a bunch over his wife, crying, "I'm-coming-with-you-to-Margate!"

"You're not," she responded. "You're going to bed."

Apparently he had bought a barrow load of roses in Covent Garden with his poker winnings at the Green Room Club. Eleanor's mother told her that this was the only time she had ever seen Papa tipsy. It was most likely accurate, for although an exceptionally convivial man, he had a strong belief in the sacrosanct nature of the home.

Yet with all the sentiment, which came out pretty treacly in his novels, Farjeon was a determinedly honest man. He answered his daughter's questions directly, or else, with a kindly, friendly assurance, said that she was not yet old enough to understand: which reasoning she seemed willing to accept.

On the other hand his wife was devious, whether over sex or religion. Four years after Joe's birth, when Eleanor was seven, she was told that a new baby was coming. When Eleanor enquired where this baby was coming from, her mother answered, "Out of a flower." Harry, it seemed, had come from apple-blossom, Eleanor from a snowdrop and Joe from a geranium. The new baby was coming out of a lily-of-the-valley. After some insistence, the little girl was promised that she might see the baby before it was taken out of the flower.

Eleanor was puzzled to imagine how babies, so tiny inside a flower bud, must suddenly expand to their ordinary size when removed. However, she did not pursue the matter, only waiting eagerly for the moment when she would be allowed to see this mysterious process of aggrandisement. But Mama forgot. The crucial minute passed and suddenly there was a full-sized squalling infant in the house.

The new baby had a temper. His screams gave Eleanor headaches and made Farjeon angry so that he shouted, "Keep that child quiet!" and unable to work, banged out of the house as far as the club, once as far as Paris.

Because of her health Mrs Farjeon was unwilling to take on responsibility, but she soon discovered that there was little need for her to bother about the nursery: her eldest son, Harry, was a born organiser and managed the job excellently. Matters usually settled by parents or nurses were fixed by him: bedtime, rules for washing, punishments, the moral and social order. So he decided the new baby's name. He and Eleanor had just seen a pantomine, *The Babes*, in which the Captain of the Gay Volunteers was called Bertie. "He must be named Bertie," Harry said, and wept, while the baby howled next door.

The parents gave way, with the proviso that his full name should be Herbert. But Harry had *his* way: the youngest son was always called Bertie.

# 196 Adelaide Road

THE NEW HOUSE was larger. At the top were two big rooms for the children, a day nursery and a night nursery. From this a stair led up into the attics: 'Hot musty, fusty, dusty attics, crammed with trunks and things. You never knew what discoveries you might make there, and if anybody called up the stair, "What are you doing?" there was always the legitimate excuse of the Dressing-up Trunk to fall back on.' And in this attic 'squeezed in the darkest channel between trunks, in the thickest of the cobwebs and dust, you could crouch and cry, when you were most unhappy, till somebody came to find you.' [NN]

Weeping over the wrongs inflicted by the world is a special childhood indulgence which Eleanor well understood. The unfairness of life – grown-ups especially – is a burden which must be endured again and again before it can be accepted without resentment or despair. Eleanor was never one to resent, but her childish despair, though balanced by strong hope, went deep, and all her determined optimism was needed to counteract it. She described one of her 'bad days' in *A Nursery in the Nineties*.

'It hadn't been one of my "good" days. I knew it as I pulled off my things unhappily and went to bed. It wasn't that I had been bad myself; I knew quite well when I had been naughty, and I didn't make the mistake of calling my naughty days "bad" days. Naughtiness was my own affair, and not the fault of the day. No, the bad days were those on which all sorts of things had gone wrong, or fallen flat, or not been understood aright by other people. Not naughty things at all, but things which began in my mind by being delightful or important, and ended in other people's minds by being – well, somehow quite different.'

At the age of nine when I first read *A Bad Day for Martha*, the fictional account of this, the most moving of Eleanor's childhood stories, I was convinced it was written especially for me; so true to all my feelings were the humiliations of that awful day. Its final disaster was in disguising one brother as a fairy in order to delight the other, who would be woken by the wave of a tinsel wand. But the vision, dressed in a baggy muslin dress, with silver wings and a crown in his golden curls, set the child shrieking with terror.

Much later [1942] Joe wrote to Bertie of their sister's ardent visions: 'Nellie struggled hard to maintain my belief in fairies, and she used to send me notes from fairies, on small coloured papers with highly coloured borders which could not possibly be devised by mere human beings. I found these notes in various places, to which I suppose she subtly directed me. Do you remember any of this, or didn't you come into it? Although you were four years younger you may have given up fairies before I did.'

The sensibility recorded in *A Bad Day for Martha* was part of the resistance to reality which drove Eleanor to daydream. This shying away was also a means of escape from her own fears, her father's explosive temper, her mother's fine-drawn sarcasm.

That Maggie Farjeon did not like sex has always been said in the family. It may have come partly from her not unnatural dread of having to bring up twenty-six children, and Ben Farjeon's irritability may have been the result of this deprivation.

Whatever the emotional miseries brought on by parental strains, which are the lot of most children, Eleanor had other troubles which must have been wearing: she could not remember a time without a headache, or a night of restful sleep. Doubtless the headaches diminished somewhat when, at the age of seven, it was discovered that she and Harry were very short-sighted and must wear glasses. The specialist ordered, "Don't let them read too much." This was out of the question, but one book with extra small print was taken to the great man for judgement.

"May I read this?" the little girl asked. "It's smaller print than you let us."

The doctor took the book. It was Philip Sidney's *Arcadia*. He exchanged an odd look with Mrs Farjeon.

"And do you want to read it very much?" he asked.

Eleanor nodded, desperately anxious.

So the luxury was permitted for a limited period each day.

From a very early age she had been a voracious reader, with an insatiable appetite for words. Her progress must have been accelerated by the desire to keep up with Harry, for she was competitive. "I want a different same," she would say, when not quite able to enjoy equality. But literary guidance was given by Farjeon to all the children with a wisdom which would have been exceptional had he enjoyed the best formal education. If he was fortunate in having children whose tastes were compatible with his own, so were they in being allowed to enjoy the eight thousand books spread everywhere about their home.

'Of all the rooms in the house, the Little Bookroom was yielded up to books as an untended garden is left to its flowers and weeds. There was no selection here. In dining-room, study and nursery there was choice and arrangement; but the Little Bookroom gathered to itself a motley crew of strays and vagabonds, outcasts from the ordered shelves below, the overflow of parcels bought wholesale by my father in the sale-rooms. Much trash and more treasure. Riff-raff and gentlefolk and noblemen. A lottery, a lucky dip for a child who had never been forbidden to handle anything between covers.'

This was written in the preface of one of Eleanor's most successful collections of children's stories, *The Little Bookroom*[1], where she would forever be seen in the Ardizzone illustration: a small girl hunched short-sightedly over some fable, with musty volumes piled and tumbling about her. (Reproduced opposite.)

Like all true readers, as she grew older she did not relinquish those earlier much-loved books, but went on absorbing more and more, apparently at random. She read greedily with an undisciplined mind that never learnt how to know all of one thing while it gleaned smatterings of a thousand others. 'When I crept out of the Little Bookroom with smarting eyes, no wonder that its mottled gold-dust still danced in my brain, its silver cobwebs still clung to the corners of my mind. No wonder that many years later, when I came to write books myself, they were a muddle of fiction and fact and fantasy and

1. *The Little Bookroom.* Hereafter referred to as [LB]

truth. I have never quite succeeded in distinguishing one from the other . . .' [LB]

When Eleanor was about ten her father began the Sunday Books Game. Each child received from him a new book after Sunday dinner, Eleanor's first being a copy of Tennyson's *In Memoriam*, bound in morocco leather with gold edges and a red silk marker. Then came volumes of Keats and Shelley, soon to become ideals.

'Papa liked Shelley best,' she wrote. 'In spite of this I liked Keats best. I pounced on the *Ode to Psyche* and *Hyperion*. We agreed, however, that after Shakespeare these were the two best poets.' [NN]

In front of her secret journals Eleanor wrote: 'Fear is more pain than is the pain it fears,' and added a quotation from Milton which had also struck her:

> *Nor love thy life, nor hate, but what thou liv'st*
> *Live well; how long or short permit to heaven.*

23

So the words of Sidney and Milton affected her conception of fear and death.

Only very occasionally did Farjeon advise his daughter against a certain book, which advice she took meekly.

'He never told me that I *mustn't* read anything; only when he found me once in the dusty little bookroom reading *The Tragic Comedians*, he said, "I think you'll like that better, Nell, when you're a bit older." So I put it down, for there was plenty else to read.' [NN] But he must have been amused by some of her choices. Fénélon's *Telemacus*, even allowing that it now seems heavily old-world, is a dull book. Yet at nine Eleanor preferred it to a diamond necklace when offered the theoretical choice. Jewels were for the beautiful, and she knew that she was plain. She did not openly resent this fact, but resigned herself to her fate; in any case, books opened an infinitely more glamorous world than any experience in life.

Promiscuous reading complemented her writing and left her with a literary education of extraordinary richness and variety. Her wide knowledge was relied upon all her life by great numbers of people far more diligently taught.

'That dusty bookroom whose windows were never opened, through whose panes the summer sun struck a dingy shaft where gold specks danced and shimmered, opened magic casements for me, through which I looked out on other worlds and times than those I lived in.' [LB]

# Early Writing

ELEANOR could not recall a time when she was not writing, and Farjeon soon realised that his daughter had talent. To the small girl writing seemed the thing to do. Papa was always writing: it was important. Among all the wonderful books about the house some had been written by Papa, some by authors she had met. So soon as she could guide a pencil she began to write songs.

The Farjeon children were kept supplied with marbled exercise books, in which they were encouraged to put down stories, poems and plays. Such tasks were undertaken diligently and seriously. For their best efforts Farjeon kept a book of his own, and sometimes they were told to copy into it some special poem or story. This was a great honour. Inside was written:

> This book belongs to B. L. Farjeon,
> 196 Adelaide Road,
> South Hampstead,
> N.W.3.

so that it should not get lost. When Mama told the children that Papa would rather lose a pound than lose that book, Eleanor felt immense pride.

Always both sentimental and romantic, it seems right that her first complete poem should be a valentine. Her sweetheart was Button (Wyndham Albery), eldest of the three Albery boys whose father owned Wyndham's Theatre. Wyndham was called Button, having swallowed one in his infancy, and he came second to Harry in Eleanor's heart. They were decreed 'sweethearts' by the grown-ups, and at the annual Christmas party Button would always present Eleanor with a bouquet; only once, in the embarrassment of the moment, he gave the flowers to the little girl sitting next to her. This mistake may have prompted doubts of his fidelity in the valentine poem written when she was six.

## KEEP TRUE TO ME

*My heart has never beat before*
*As it did beat just now;*
*I want you but to keep to me,*
*And I'll give my hand to thou.*

*I'll never turn away from thee,*
*If always you keep true;*
*But if you always turn away,*
*I will not keep to you.*

*But I will go out far away,*
*And find a lover true to me;*
*But if you never turn away,*
*I'll never, never turn from thee.*

*You've turned away from me just once,*
*But if you won't again;*
*I'll give you all the love my heart,*
*Will ever and can contain.*

The 'true loves', 'beating hearts' and an abundance of 'thees' were a tendency which her father tried to curb. Because Eleanor so admired antique romances she adopted their language and there was a tussle over the following line in her version of *Alan-a-Dale*.

*O gentle is my own true-love,*
*And like a flower is she,*
*But they have riven her mefrom*
*A rich man's wife to be.*

Farjeon promptly placed the 'me' after 'from', in spite of his daughter's protests about wanting her words to sound 'old'.

'Then Papa was very emphatic about 'from me' being better than 'mefrom' because it was more natural, and he did not want me to write affectedly. He wasn't anywhere near a temper, but he was so much in earnest that I had to do what he said, though I still thought, in my heart of hearts, that I was right to say 'mefrom' in *that* poem, anyhow. I changed the word reluctantly, and minded very much. When Papa had gone out I changed it back, and never let him see it.' [NN]

Before these poems she had written less derivative stories in prose. *Kitty's Dream*, composed at the age of five, shows an understanding of form, a sense of continuity and remarkable perseverance. A strong feeling of dogged determination comes across from the story, written in capital letters and filling a small exercise book.

With the days of infant prettiness behind her, it became obvious that the straight-haired, bespectacled girl was not suitable for her mother to dress up and show off. She became very much her father's daughter. Her self-portrait in *A Nursery in the Nineties* is not flattering.

'When I try to make a picture of myself it seems to me that I was a dreamy, timid, sickly, lacrymose, painfully shy, sensitive, greedy, ill-regulated little girl; not selfish on the whole, very affectionate and desirous of affection, almost as unwilling to inflict pain as to suffer it (I was a coward in most respects), and intensely absorbed in my writing, my reading, my family, and my imaginative life.'

Everything she wrote must be shown to her father. 'I wanted him to see it, of course, but I could not bear showing it, or being there while he read it. When I had pushed it under his door and run away, I had a stomach-ache till he came and told me if he liked it. He never kept me waiting. Even if he was writing his own stories, he stopped at once to look at my last poem, and came straight to the Nursery to talk it over with me. He taught me how to correct proofs and to be particular in the clearness of my "copy" for the printers, long before I had any printers to consider.' [NN]

When Eleanor was seven Farjeon placed her at his Remington typewriter, explained some basic essentials and left her to work out the letters. This seemed a good chance to complete her novel, *The Adventures of Reggie*, begun a year or so previously. Unfortunately the system of shifting the carriage and paper proved mystifying and, when her father returned some half hour later, Reggie's adventures had been compressed into a solid block at the end of the first line.

By now, under the influence of the theatre, she moved on to

drama, and in another small exercise book wrote the opening scenes of *Snow White*. The young dramatist had mastered the technicalities of exits and entrances, the setting out of characters' names, stage directions and dramatic writing. Her dialogue often had the brutal pertinence that distinguishes children. Snow White's royal father responds to the messenger who comes to tell him of his wife's death, "She's dead. I must marry agayne."

When Eleanor rewrote the play in adult life she retained this line: it was her private joke.

Although the work remained incomplete she now moved on to a more ambitious drama in seven acts, *The Fairy Cave*. Act IV is notable for its 'mournful experience', followed by the inexplicable end of the butler, who 'gets mad and sawers' (swears?) after drinking 'brandy, whisky etc.' Mary, the heroine, meets her death at the hands of the 'Wicked little Gobling' who sticks a sword into her as she lies sleeping. With the exclamation "Oh" she dies.

In *A Nursery in the Nineties* Eleanor comments on Act VII: 'For simple pathos, this burial scene can only be compared with one in Shakespeare,' which shows that she was familiar with Hamlet by the age of eight.

## Act VII

A gorden it is night Enter gardner with spad, and with a gun Jack, and fanny, and mrs. green, and santa clause, and Alice, and gobling, and w. fairy, with a loaded gun, and fairy queen holding mary in white.

JACK: Poor mary.
SANTA: dig the grave gardener.
GAR.: Il dig the grave sir.
          [digs a grave and fairy q puts mary in
MRS GREEN: I could never bear such a seen.
FANNY: nor I tis very sad.

*Damon and Pythias*, written at the age of nine, shows development and sophistication. The plot thickens at the start of Act II (after 8 months elapsed).

```
                [enter MITTI disguised] [Enter HENRY, and
                MIRIDA]
MITTI:          My dear sit down. (Aside to HENRY) Get a knife.
                [HENRY goes to a draw and gets a knife
                [MITTI throughs off his disguise.
MITTI:          Now will you marry me.
MIRIDA:         No!!! You have dicived me.
MITTI:          Give me the knife Henry. I will kill you if you do
                not. Will you?
MIRIDA:         No!! I cannot.
                [MITTI raises the knife to her heart.
MIRIDA:         (screaming): Richard!!! Richard!!!
                [Enter KING, RICHARD, HARRY, DANYEL]
RICHARD:        (rushing forward): Stop!!! stop sir!!! let her be!
MITTI:          She is a lyair.
HARRY:          She is not.
DANYEL:         Don't you dare to hurt my daughter.
HENRY:          Take your daughter then. And go.
KING:           You go. Go yourself.
                [Exit all]
```

Eleanor's childhood friend, Nina, remembered her later as "a queer little thing, of most extraordinary intelligence". Adults were lavish in their praise of her writing. One languishing verse, *A Fading Flower*, written when she was ten, so pleased the theatre manager, Augustin Daly, that he took it to New York and had it printed in one of his pink satin theatre programmes. The impresario wrote from Daly's Theatre:

My dear Farjeon,
    Here is a programme of our opening night in the Home Theatre – with your little one's poem. I have heard it charmingly commented upon . . .

To have attained expertise, however derivative, by the age of ten shows ability. But the next recorded poem of sixty lines in blank verse is startling in its Miltonian grasp of an abstract idea, in its handling of language and wide, though poetically over-conscious, vocabulary. Eleanor tells of the poem's inception. 'When she was eleven, Miss Farjeon chanced on a reference to Chaos, in an abstruse mythology, as the deity who had created order out of disorder. This novel view gripped her imagination; she felt it was time that the name of Chaos should be vindicated, and determined to do it on the spot. It was evening, and she was about to dress for a performance of *Richelieu* at the Lyceum Theatre, but the heat of inspiration must not be allowed to cool. Placing pencil and paper on her marble-topped wash-stand, she wrote with her right hand, while performing her ablutions, and brushing her hair, with her left. For the first time in her life she essayed blank verse, a medium in which she was able to write without pause; the epic was finished as the brougham drew up at the door.' [NN]

The following extract shows the style:

> *Before the world was made what changes space*
> *Each day, nay ev'ry hour did undergo!*
> *The fire, the earth, the air, all reigned in turn,*
> *And water oft in sweeping torrents rushed.*
> *But Chaos leapt into unending space,*
> *And unto each and every element*
> *Assigned its place; with arms commanding waved*
> *Each cloud, each torrent, and each flame away.*
> *The wind was wild, and water loudly roared,*
> *The fire sprang upwards. In the midst of all,*
> *His work beginning, Chaos, a mighty god,*
> *Repels the darkness, and above his head*
> *Appears the Zodiac in shining stars.*

The process by which such a work may be written down in metre straight from the unconscious is as mysterious to those who experience it as to any outsider. But if anything may be called inspiration, this is it.

Farjeon spent the next day typing out copies and, in a ferment of enthusiasm, spreading them among his friends. Several members of the Green Room Club accused him of having had a hand in it, to which he replied, "I couldn't write lines like these to save my life." Hall Caine's response was most satisfactory:

Eleanor, aged 11

Dear Farjeon,

The poem is very remarkable. More so, perhaps, in the extraordinary range of ideas than in its literary quality, though quite astonishing in that respect for a child so young. I was not wrong in supposing that a granddaughter of Joseph Jefferson, and a daughter of your own, must have genius. It is a great privilege you enjoy and a heavy responsibility you live under. Good luck and great fortune to you and yours!

With hearty greetings,
Hall Caine


By the time Eleanor was twelve she was writing on a variety of subjects, unhampered by any school curriculum. Throughout her life she drew on the store of Greek myths, Norse legends, fairy tales, Dumas, the Arabian Nights, Shakespeare and the Bible. All her massive reading was assimilated and ready for use.

There was also a great deal of sharing of ideas between Eleanor and her brothers. Harry, Joe and Bertie all wrote stories, poems and plays: they were like the Brontë children in the intensity of their communal creativity. After a night at the theatre, the acting, script and décor would be discussed next day and often incorporated into their make-believe games. A favourite game was 'Thousand Word Tales'. In it Eleanor and Harry became Irene and Cola de Rienzi – characters in Bulwer Lytton's novel *Rienzi*. Two little girls also took part, but Joe and Bertie were found to be too young to join what was a most demanding collaboration. Each player had to write the first thousand words of a story, read it to the others and then pass it on. The next instalment would be added by the next child, who met his own story at every fourth instalment. The quartet came together once a week and in two months concluded four tales. By this time the children had written thirty-two thousand words.

# Harry and Eleanor

MEETING a childhood friend after thirty years, Eleanor asked what she remembered of the Farjeons.

"I remember you and Harry walking round and round the houses, he a little ahead of you, you trotting at his elbow, arguing and arguing with your heads together. I never knew what it was about but I *never* saw you two walking in the streets without arguing," came the reply.

What they were actually doing was playing a game they had invented called TAR. This had come into being after their second visit to the theatre, when Harry was eight, Eleanor five. The show was a pantomine called *The Babes* and it obviously made a great impression, for, besides the new game, their little brother was to be named after a favourite character, Bertie. Family friends like Uncle Willie [Edouin] acted the Boy Babe, Aunt Alice [Edouin] the Girl Babe and Uncle Lal Brough the Bad Villain. The Good Villain Ralph wore blue boots – his boots were most beautiful.

At home after the matinée brother and sister shared out the roles. Harry was Tessy and Captain Bertie, while Eleanor was Ralph (who married Tessy) and the Boy Babe. Harry said, "We are Tessy-and-Ralph" and they were. Later he said, "We are Harry and Nellie" and they were themselves again (Nellie was her family name). This diversion, which began quite simply as the usual children's make-believe, was to become more and more absorbing until it created a world of dreamlike complexity. The fascination of manipulating characters and situations stimulated Eleanor's imagination: she became adept. Any role, any drama could be taken over and developed; she was intoxicated by her own fancies, though they were always disciplined by Harry's rule. His power was absolute, his word law.

Soon other heroes and heroines were incorporated, those from *Grimms' Fairy Tales, Alice in Wonderland, Little Women, The Three Musketeers*, etc. The problem of sex was never a problem as far as casting went, the transformation from themselves into chosen individuals seeming to wipe out age, sex and type. Harry took the parts of Jo, Amy and Professor Bhaer. When Shakespearian characters joined the troupe Harry was Titania and Eleanor, Oberon.

As they wished to keep this very special, very exciting game secret, Harry had the idea of calling it by the initials of Tessy-and-Ralph – TAR.

Eleanor wrote: 'It was, I know, a comic little couple in spectacles, her hair never too tidy, his hair always too long, that set forth daily, sometimes twice a day, from Adelaide Road, on adventures nobody dreamed of. For ten years we faced the secret smiles and open jeers of the neighbourhood. Our absorption was almost complete, though sometimes the "Git yer 'air cut!" of the arabs annoyingly destroyed our self-hypnosis. Once when this happened Harry marched up to the offender. "There is an H in hair!" he said severely, and passed on.' [NN]

Harry would lie awake at night planning a plot or series of incidents for next day, when they would go walking along the fields of the Finchley Road playing TAR. During those sessions Eleanor explained that she was like a medium, flowing into or becoming possessed by other streams of being, for TAR was not something that replaced life, TAR was life itself, her chief experience until she was twenty-nine. For days on end she became hero or villain, committing crimes or heroisms, duelling, plotting against kings, winning or losing on cricket pitch or tennis court, dying many times in many ways. 'The creative imagination we had inherited from Papa's side, the sense of impersonation that must have come from Mama's – and that fluid element in our dual being, which made me alive, at its inception, to Harry's wish – enabled us to secrete ourselves in a world of illusion within which we became, not one, but fifty persons at once (by changes of thought and mood so swift the machinery of the drama never creaked). Harry had only to say, "We are This Person and That," and we instantly *were* those two, till

34

some movement of the drama necessitated an exit or another entrance; then "We are So-and-So and Such-and-Such" he murmured (like a stage direction in italics) – it was enough; once more we were those two. I could not be anybody till Harry said so; he could move freely about my one personality of the moment, because the course of the play, and its stage-management, lay somewhere in the recesses of his mind. I waited only to know who I was next; and guided by his unrevealed direction, I played my part, emotionally absorbed. Harry must have been in the position of the Creator watching his puppets, even allowing them to affect their own destinies when they did things he was not quite prepared for. So actual, so exciting, so fascinating was this twin gift of ours, so much more marvellous was the life we could make for ourselves than the one we had found made for us, and so fertilely did the game develop as we grew older, that the game of childhood had no excuse for dropping away with our growth. My own development took place far more within the boundaries of TAR than within those of life. At an age, and long past it, when life's horizons should have been widening, they kept their narrow circle, while those of TAR widened increasingly. I had no desire for new adventures, friends, or experience, outside this powerful game. When I should have been growing up, it was a harmful check on life itself, for its imaginative extension did not include natural knowledge. Because of it, I was never aware of my own sex until I was nearly thirty years old, and it took at least two years more for emotional crudeness to get abreast of mental ripeness.

'But if it checked me on the one hand, I acquired through it on the other the power to put in motion, almost at will, given persons within given scenes, and see what came of it, and I think I owe to TAR more than to any other element in my life, the flow of ease that makes writing a delight.' [NN]

The desire to be identical with Harry was so intense that Eleanor became able to follow his mental processes almost by instinct, merging her thoughts with his to an extraordinary degree. Once when the Alberys gave a party where, alone, she would have suffered agonies, Eleanor sang a song with her brother. Harry said afterwards that they had made it up as they went along. In fact he had invented the words and tune instantaneously while his sister blended herself into his lead.

Certainly Harry was the nearest thing to du Maurier's Svengali I ever met, and he made that almost incredible character seem real. There can be no doubt that when playing TAR he could in some way hypnotise his sister for, until the magic words of release were spoken she could not free herself, nor did she wish to be free.

Joe and Bertie were admitted to TAR later as they grew capable, and were very useful in making up Dumas' Four Musketeers, when Harry took the part of D'Artagnan and Eleanor the part of Porthos, that handsome, bumptious, vainglorious soldier who was the very opposite of the gawky girl, so fearful of being seen in public. Then, when the allotted time was up, Harry would say, "We're Harry-Nellie-Joe-and-Bertie" and it was over. But Joe and Bertie's position was subservient and after a while they branched off into their own kinds of amusement.

Another form of fictional exercise was practised by Eleanor alone. Sleepless nights were the start of the story-telling habit which never stopped. The Awake-at-Night Game began with epics in which her own favourite characters, whether from drama, books, or reality, could all take part together, Apollo and Diana being chief among them. That a brother and sister should have been chosen for the leading roles seems natural. This imaginative agility was put to use later, for as an adult those tales and rhymes composed in wakeful hours would be written down next day.

At the age of seven the revelation brought about by spectacles – patterns on the wallpaper, subtleties of facial expression, colour and outline – also had a startling effect on Eleanor's imagination. This sudden light on the world was an awakening over which she would exclaim with delight for the rest of her life. The lace of a spider's web, the reflection in a drop of water, small fine objects became infinitely dear, and filled her poetry. Having up to this time lacked such experience she had developed acute senses of touch, hearing, smell and taste, which were not lost now she was no longer half blind. But the mystery of things remained all important. She did not care for dolls, though soap bubbles blown from a clay pipe out of doors, snow scenes in glass globes and kaleidoscopes which shifted magically thrilled her, as did musical boxes with far-away tunes. It was the thing out of reach and which could not be quite apprehended that attracted her always, creating a state in which her mind spun into freedom.

# Education

HARRY'S AUTHORITY in the nursery seemed absolute. His moral code of Fair and Unfair, Good and Bad, Truth and Lies, Taking Turns, was insisted on with Spartan strictness, supported by a complex system of rules and taboos, and if ever rules were relaxed only Harry might relax them. When he played his 'Nursery Call' on the piano, Eleanor, Joe and Bertie hurried from wherever they were and whatever they were doing, back to the nursery. They knew that they had not been summoned for any frivolous reason: Harry had had an idea, made up a new game, or needed their co-operation in his system of government.

Since Mama had discovered that she was no good at keeping the children quiet while Papa worked, she allowed Harry to take over. And now the parents seldom interfered, for they knew the children were safe under the eye of their despot.

For formal learning there were governesses. Eleanor wrote of a ladylike spinster: 'One never knew how Miss Milton felt, only how she behaved.' [NN] But there came a time when a new governess arrived who understood how to manage: she had a firm character for all her kindness. Miss Newman, whose life was only a little romanticised in Eleanor's novel, *Brave Old Woman*, described how in her first interview she and Mrs Farjeon were getting along comfortably when the door burst open, an impetuous gentleman with curly black hair and sparkling brown eyes darted into the room and looked her rapidly up and down.

"I like the look of you! You're not to teach them anything they don't want to learn! The girl has headaches. Leave her alone."

So a new regime began. Harry, by this time thirteen, was working downstairs with a tutor. Suspecting laxity, he came up to keep an eye on his people and was deeply shocked by what he saw.

"Bertie! Get off the table."

"Why shouldn't he be on the table, bless him?" asked Miss Newman.

"Don't tip your chair, Joe."

"Let the child tip his chair if he wants to!"

"Nellie, have you sponged?"

Sponging was the routine which had to be gone through before anybody was allowed to touch the piano, for Harry had found this the answer to sticky keys.

With this final attack Miss Newman, impregnably good-humoured, shook her fist at the boy. "Go away, Harry, you're a Disturbing Element."

The younger children stared aghast at their champion's daring. Harry turned to go with his parting shot: "And you're a Demon."

The name Demon stuck to the governess, for whom the whole family soon felt an affection and gratitude that was lifelong. In *Brave Old Woman* Eleanor described the schooling of the Farrar (Farjeon) children just as she had known it.

'She fulfilled Mr Farrar's requirements of "a person", and stayed because he had respect for her character and a liking for her nature. As for his children's brains, he had decided long ago that if you are born with a good mind, life and your inclinations will do the rest. He underestimated the value of education, because he had never had or apparently suffered from lack of it. His children had every opportunity to read, see and hear the best things for themselves; they absorbed intensively what they liked, and left what they didn't. Allie (Eleanor) and Jeff (Joe) had not "examination minds"; Gillie (Bertie) was obviously developing scholastic qualities, but Tudsy (Miss Newman) was not erudite enough to foster them. She gave the children tuition rather than education; she brought into their days what was much more valuable, her good humour, her common sense, her unruffled serenity in conditions that were always flying off at a tangent. Regular hours of study were constantly broken up by anything that, in the Farrar world, seemed more important than lessons or discipline. If Allie had "one of her headaches", if she felt like writing a poem instead of learning her dates, if Mr Farrar thought he would like to take a child with him to Cheapside or Fleet Street, or the Army and Navy Stores, or if a visitor called – the demands of the schoolroom melted into thin air.'

So when Eleanor explained that she did not like sums but wished to learn German – she wanted to read Schiller – there was no objection. To sweeten the grammar Miss Newman copied out Schiller's *Semele* in Roman script, which they translated every day. After lessons Eleanor would rework it into blank verse. 'Apart from this, I dawdled,' she wrote. 'I was allowed to sit at the piano as long as I liked, muddling out Schubert and Mendelssohn accompaniments.' [NN] She was offered piano lessons but refused, knowing that music was Harry's province and abashed by her inferiority before him. Later in life she very much regretted that her considerable musical talent had been left to chance. Certainly the songs she composed for *Nursery Rhymes of London Town* and *Kings and Queens* are seldom forgotten by any child who has had the luck to learn them.

Bertie, too, soon gave up music. He put a note on his mother's dressing table: 'Can I stop learning the violin? I make my ears ache when I practice. Bertie.' It is doubtful whether Bertie ever regretted his violin.

Otherwise Eleanor's education seems to have been limited to a skirt dance in the dancing class.

She was taken to the theatre continually. Shakespeare, Oscar Wilde's plays, *The Prisoner of Zenda*, the Irving-Ellen Terry productions, Daly's productions, Sarah Bernhardt, Dan Leno in pantomime and Beerbohm Tree who, in his production of *As You Like It*, had real rabbits hopping about the stage in the Forest of Arden. Leading actors generally gave the Farjeons a box, sometimes chocolates and ices were laid on for the children, and afterwards there was always the backstage visit and being kissed by actors' greasy faces.

On one occasion they saw Henry Irving in *Charles the First*. When in the last act the King took his children on his knee, Eleanor could hardly hear his words for the sobbing in the auditorium, and by the time it came to "Remember!" she was lying against her mother's shoulder on one side with Joe leaning on the other, and both of them sobbing their hearts out and soaking Mama's sleeves. The curtain went down and up and down, while the children continued to sob. The theatre began to empty and still they sobbed.

'And then the door of the box opened, and there was a rustle behind us, and a lovely voice said, "Oh, those poor *dear* children!" and Queen Henrietta Maria's arms went round us and she kissed and comforted us till we did stop crying. But talking was out of the question for Joe and me; if you tried to say a word it wobbled into lots of syllables, and our noses were stuffy and shiny, and our eyes bulged with crying and our heads ached. And of course it was heavenly to be comforted by Ellen Terry.' [NN]

Farjeon himself had three plays produced, although not in a West End theatre, and not much was said about them.

As her father filled the house with books from shops and sale rooms there was little likelihood of Eleanor remaining unlearned, her memory was so retentive, her imagination so easily fired. By the age of nine she could reel off the names and occupations of the Nine Muses, with a reasoned explanation of why, in her opinion, Orpheus should have been the son of Euterpe and not Calliope. And she was not shy at home where, in concerts devised for the grown-ups by Harry, she would sing and recite with confidence. He stage-managed and played from his piano stool. For these occasions Mrs Farjeon would arrive stylishly dressed in long white kid gloves, while Farjeon wore his opera hat.

Yet if asked to perform outside the family circle disaster followed. Eleanor had grown self-conscious about her appearance. Those thick, steel-rimmed spectacles, her dark hair that would not keep in place, though crimped with curling-tongs for parties; the pallid thick-fleshed texture of her cheeks and her awkward movements made her shrink from notice: they were not the attributes of a fairy princess or even a heroine.

One afternoon, at Mrs Charles Wyndham's annual party, Eleanor wore a Swiss costume which her father had brought back as a present from Interlaken. It was beautiful, the skirt of scarlet satin, thick and soft, the black velvet bodice laced together in front and decorated with a big chain of silver filigree roses that clinked as she moved. But this was a fancy dress and it was not a fancy dress party, so hers was the most conspicuous costume in the room. To feel conspicuous was agony and she shrank into herself, trying to become as obscure as possible. There was her friend Olive, even prettier than usual, happily performing a skirt dance, holding up her lace flounces and floating like a snowflake over the shiny floor on which Eleanor could hardly keep her footing.

Then, as she described in *A Nursery in the Nineties*, she was asked to recite. 'It was no good. I would have to. I knew Mama knew that I had got "A Pound of Tea" by heart at last, and was now learning "It was the Schooner Hesperus". I couldn't do anything but get up and walk uncertainly along the treacherous floor to the end of the room, which seemed very big and full of people as I stood there trying to feel like a little girl going shopping. I wetted my lips and began in a monotonous little voice:

"A pound of tea at One-and-Three,
A pot of Strawberry Ham,
A . . ."

Oh, horror, I had said it wrong! The jumble didn't begin till the third verse.'

So the child started again, got through the first and second verses and stuck.

Somebody said, "She's forgotten it, poor little thing."

At which Eleanor burst into tears, slithered along the polished parquet with clanking chains, and sobbed into her mother's lap.

The afternoon's long humiliation continued for, through all the following games, wherever she stood the black and scarlet dress proclaimed her, and whenever she moved her silver ornaments clinked mercilessly, announcing to the world, "This is the little girl who forgot her piece and cried."

# Joe and Bertie

I T  S E E M S  C L E A R that Ben and Maggie Farjeon wished their children to become artists of some sort. The home tutor, Mr Lindford, soon discovered that Harry had a remarkable aptitude for figures – like his father – and suggested the boy should study for a mathematical scholarship. But Farjeon discouraged this, as also the study of dead languages. His son was going in for music.

For the rest of the children, it seemed obvious that Eleanor was to be a writer, while Joe, it seemed likely, would become an actor. He was given extra dancing lessons, performing hornpipes and jester's dances as well as singing for visitors. At such times Harry would play his latest composition on the piano, while Eleanor recited or sang. Little Bertie showed less obvious artistic talent, but he was delighted to Bend for any audience. This consisted of lying on the floor with his feet in his mouth and arms hooked under his knees. Then he would roll round and round the room.

Bertie's competitive nature soon drove him to higher ambitions: he taught himself to juggle. In 1944 Joe wrote to his younger brother: 'I think you rather stole my thunder over the juggling. By all the rules of family publicity I should have been best at it, and I believe I was rather surprised when I was not. This may have been the first occasion on which you overtook me – a process which has been repeated many times since.'

As Harry and Eleanor were paired, so were Joe and Bertie. Joe was the good boy, who would certainly go to heaven when he died. Eleanor would be saved because she tried so hard. Harry was practically God and always knew best, so there was no problem there. But over Bertie there were serious doubts, and strong signs that he might land up in Hell. He had a furious temper, he bit, he rebelled against Harry's authority and struggled to be on a par with Joe, who was four years older. But Joe had such a modest nature that he was not jealous of this ambitious youngster and, despite troubles, they remained chums. Once Bertie threw a knife. Joe just shut his eyes and quickly forgave Bertie, in case the knife killed him. The knife cut his temple. On this occasion Harry was really stern and Bertie was sent to Coventry.

Whatever the after-life held in store (and nurses had seen to it that Eleanor was afraid of Hell and the Devil), she had more faith in fairies and Santa Claus than in God. All four children assumed they would not, at any rate, be doomed to insignificance in this life. The ambition to excel in some form of artistic expression had been firmly implanted and, with the exception of Joe, confidence was not lacking.

In his incomplete memoir Bertie makes the following ironic comment on the belief Farjeons held of their innate superiority.

'Of all the gardens in the Adelaide Road, ours is by far the best, which is as it should be, for is not everything of ours better than anything of anybody else's? Papa is the best Papa in the world, and Harry is going to be the greatest composer in the world, and Mama is the best Mama in the world, and Nellie is going to be the greatest poet, there is no doubt of these things; and Joe is going to be the greatest actor, and I – what am I going to be? Once I wanted to be a cab-horse, a very humble ambition at which I can now smile. Later I wanted to be a man who could fall downstairs without hurting himself, I would just tumble right from the top to the bottom and get up smiling, and everybody would be amazed. Now I don't quite know what I want to be, my ideas are rather indefinite, but once I have made up my mind I can hardly help being extraordinarily good at it, our family is so remarkable in every way. Our friends are the nicest friends in the world, Joe is in love with the prettiest little girl in the world, our hens lay more eggs, and larger eggs, and smaller eggs, and more peculiar eggs than anybody else's have ever been known to lay.'

On reading this, the honest Joe wrote back to his brother: 'I never really felt clever, though I know I was supposed to be, and acted hard up to it.'

Harry, of course, had no need to act up to his cleverness, but Eleanor was only in part self-assured. Her social shyness was misery. Ball games were difficult for her and Harry owing to poor eyesight, but she took on her younger brothers' sporting enthusiasms readily, and complex cricket matches were devised with pen and paper, cards and dice, for indoor sport. On holiday in Norfolk, the four children would play cricket on the Trimmingham sands in the roles of their favourite players. Bertie later wrote to Joe: 'You were Abel, I was Richardson, Harry was Ranjitsinjhi, and wasn't Nellie, *when* she at rare intervals wasn't neurotically vomiting, Grace, speaking for him in a voice very like that of Porthos?'

During these happy holidays, on rainy days, the two younger boys also played chamber-pot cricket in their bedroom with the back of a hairbrush and a soft ball. If the ball went in the chamber-pot and stayed there, the batsman was out.

Cricket was a passion with Bertie. In South Hampstead he bribed two unwilling little girl neighbours with a penny each, to bowl underarm to him till he had made his first century. His father sometimes waxed angry about the obsession.

Joe and Bertie would go to watch the matches at Lords when quite young. As they wore curls to their shoulders in Lord Fauntleroy style until Joe was twelve and Bertie eight, they would avoid going down the Winchester Road where rough Board School boys jeered and hurled insults. For besides the long curls, they wore sailor suits and caps with 'HMS Terrible' on them. They also carried lorgnettes, since the oculist had decreed that they wear glasses as seldom as possible. So, sitting in the sixpenny seats at Lords, the two small sailor-suited ringletted brothers would raise their lorgnettes and gaze with dignity at Ranjitsinjhi's cuts and leg-glances, to the astonishment of surrounding adults.

When the indignity of long hair finally forced Mama to sheer off the curls, she suffered in proportion to the boys' relief. Bertie wrote, 'Growing up was not encouraged in this home.'[1]

Each child backed his own cricket team and there was high excitement over the county matches. Bertie included the whole of the Surrey team in his prayers, which ran: "God bless Abel, God

1. Herbert Farjeon's unpublished memoir, from which other extracts in this chapter are also taken.

bless Brockwell, God bless Hayward, God bless Hayes," and so on, right down to the final, "God bless Extras, Amen."

Yet for all the prayers, Farjeon and his wife left eternal matters for individual solution, though one time, when Eleanor showed some curiosity about God, her mother took her to church. However, she found the service excessively boring. On the subject of nightly prayers Bertie wrote: 'I imagine we were taught to pray in bed instead of on our knees, because it was thought best to be on the safe side again. True, by going down on your knees you might stand a slightly better chance of saving your soul – but you also stood a much better, or much worse chance of catching a cold – and not to catch a cold was held up to us as one of the main objects of juvenile existence.'

Ever since the second child had died and, later on his wife's lung collapsed, Farjeon had been terrified of illness in the family. Open windows, tops of buses, fog, east wind, rain and, worst of all, night air, were dangers which, if they must be faced, would not go unchallenged. Mrs Farjeon and her four children were armed with hats, shawls, mufflers, galoshes and umbrellas on every possible occasion. When venturing out in the dreaded night air they wore respirators over nose and mouth.

Yet despite all the coddling and all the efforts to stop them growing up, Joe and Bertie were far more worldly-wise than Harry or Eleanor. They adventured over garden walls for lost balls, cut their knees, got dirty and revelled in heroic stories from *The Boy's Own Paper*. Bertie, the tougher of this not very tough pair, described a local society which would have horrified the elder couple, who were still absorbed in the world of TAR.

'There are bad boys at the bottom of the garden. Joe turns up from who-knew-where one tea-time to tell me that he has been playing cricket in the empty garden at the back of ours. The house has been empty for a long time, so there can't really be any harm playing in the garden, though it is a bit lawless and we wouldn't have done it on our own. But the boys are bigger than we are, and the bigger you are the safer it is. They asked Joe to go over when he was watching them through the trellis, so he went, and they play with a hard ball and a bat with a real splice. Papa and Mama will not let us play with a hard ball, because it is much too dangerous and we might get hurt, but we needn't say anything, though we don't *say* we needn't say anything,

45

and Joe is practically positive that it would be quite all right if I went with him tomorrow afternoon.'

Apart from the hard ball, Joe and Bertie had the feeling that their parents would not understand about these boys who discussed sex in the most ungenteel manner, so their visits to the empty garden were kept secret, until it was discovered that the boys were related to Bram Stoker, Henry Irving's business manager. Bram Stoker was also the author of *Dracula* and well known to the family. Then it was possible to own that they had found new friends.

The brothers shared an air gun of which Joe wrote: 'The only time I remember vividly using the air gun was out of the bedroom window at 196, at a cat. I never dreamt that I should hit the cat, and to my alarm I did, but the cat merely scratched itself and looked annoyed. However, it cured me, and I've never done any big game hunting since.'

Joe was the one who made friends with neighbours: on one side the German Franks, who shouted, and on the other the Italian Lutgens, who gabbled – so Bertie said.

The annual Christmas party was another source of friends, when fifty or more children were invited. For this occasion Farjeon would go to the Army and Navy Stores and buy a giant fir tree that reached the ceiling. Sometimes three or four feet had to be cut off the bottom. And then for several days the drawing room door was locked against all children.

At the party, from a marvellously decorated tree, each guest would carry away six or seven presents, which Farjeon had collected on his travels throughout the year. There were strings and strings of Venetian glass beads, exquisitely coloured and patterned; there were French scent bottles, compasses, purses, glass birds, soldiers, dolls from Paris, sweetmeats, Noah's Arks, and pencil cases.

Eleanor wrote of her father: 'How jolly he was! How sudden! How like a skyrocket followed by coloured stars! How like the thunderstorms he loved to watch.' [NN]

When he took the children into his study it meant a treat. He would give each a selection of beautiful pieces of coloured paper with which to make pictures or enhance objects back in the nursery. There were glazed and coloured Indian boxes, box within box within box, till the last one was too tiny to open. There was a set of Chinese carved ivory tubes strung with bright silk threads, which diminished or multiplied magically as the tubes were drawn back and forth. Best of all there was a box with a glass top which never came off, in which lay midget men, yellow butterflies, three balls, a white winged crane and beetles. When a red leather 'rubber' was passed over the glass, the creatures gradually came to life, flying up against the glass, bumping, skittering and twitching their limbs. Such was the enchanted world with which their father, with an enthusiasm that equalled their own, fed his children's imaginations.

Certainly his moods were the most dominant in the household: small as he was, any room he entered was pervaded by his energy. Rages over badly cooked meals, breakages, or when noise in the Adelaide Road disturbed his writing, harrowed the family. Bertie described in his memoir a summer afternoon when he was dreamily listening to the tune of *The Man who Broke the Bank at Monte Carlo*, clapped out by the rattling teeth of a barrel-organ:

'My father's door has opened. He is clearing his throat. He always clears his throat when he is angry.

'"Papa, Papa! Don't stop the barrel organ! I don't believe I knew the barrel organ was there until you cleared your throat, but now I know, and if you stop the barrel organ it will spoil everything. The man is doing no harm. Please, please, Papa! He didn't know that you were working. It is not the man who always comes on Tuesdays, it is quite a different man, so how could he know? Why be so angry with him?" I am terrified. There will be blows one day, there will be blood. Through the window pane I see my father hastening, with quick steps across the road. The organ-grinder has not seen him yet. He has no idea. "*The Man who Bro . . .*"'

In this family Victorian modesty regulated or suppressed discussion of bodily functions, and Eleanor was the only one who, as an adult, entirely got over her prudish upbringing. However, Bertie wrote with relish of a liberated brother and sister with whom he and Joe played.

'Honey did not inhabit quite the same world as we did, there being a streak of something disturbingly daredevil in his composition, and even more than daredevil, as we astonishingly discovered when he and his sister Muriel were in our garden. Muriel was a rather pretty, rather cheeky girl, as daredevil as her brother, for she once referred to her drawers in our presence, which was a tremendous moment . . . it was she who egged Honey on that morning to tell us what he had once said, and the more he demurred, the more she pressed him and the more apprehensive we grew.

"Go on," she said. "Tell them."

"Shut up, Muriel!"

"Oh, do tell them, you might!"

"What for?"

"They won't mind."

"Well, *you* tell them."

"I will if you won't. I swear I will."

"All right, go on then."

And it was there, on the gravel path by the vine, that Muriel rather lowered her voice and announced, with sisterly pride, "He once said Damn Jesus!"

There was an awed silence. Muriel examined our faces to see the effect, so I smirked a little, but Joe, I'm sure, didn't like it and wished it hadn't happened, because Honey was one of our friends, and it upset things to think of our friends having said that, besides which, he was in love with Muriel.'

It appears that Joe was far more susceptible to love than the others, for he is the only one whose early passions for the opposite sex are mentioned. Certainly Harry and Eleanor's emotions were so fully employed with idyllic fantasies that they had none to spare for everyday amours.

# Insubordination

ALTHOUGH SOCIALLY Eleanor developed at a snail's pace, her literary talent raced ahead. She picked up styles and mimicked them with precocious expertise, still showing her father everything she wrote. But now she had a story which seemed to her better than any previous effort and she planned, with his approval, to enter it for a competition. The story was of 20,000 words and was completed in bed during an illness. Called *The Tricks of Pepita*, it was laid in Spain, for she had just been reading *The Corregidor's Hat*. 'I sent it down to Papa and lay back on my pillows, awaiting the awful moment when we must face each other about it. He came in rapidly, and walked round and round the room. "I have hopes of you, Nell! I have hopes of you!" he exclaimed.

"Do you like it, Papa?"

"It is the best thing you have written," said Papa. He stopped by my bed. "I think you are going to make a writer." Then he took my hand and looked at me, smiling anxiously. "I don't think it will win the prize, dear. Will you be very disappointed if it doesn't?" ' [NN]

Eleanor cared more for her father's good opinion than for any prize. On learning this, tears rushed into his eyes as he beamed and kissed her.

Joe wrote to Bertie much later: 'Nellie knew Father better than any of the rest of us.' Certainly Ben Farjeon had more affinity with his daughter than with any of the boys.

It was always a lively household, full of activities, artistic and emotional. There was the family newspaper, *Farjeon's Fortnightly*, there were Harry's concerts; the younger boys took their athletics

49

seriously and bicycles, cricket bats and tennis racquets littered cupboards and halls in proper middle class fashion. Unlike her mother, Eleanor did not sew, but she could make beautiful paper flowers and draw with considerable skill. Her illustrations show no great individuality: Richard Doyle, *Art Nouveau* and Kate Greenaway being her types of model. An elegantly furnished doll's house was the secret envy of Bertie, who would not openly admit to such preference, *The Boy's Own Paper* motivating him to appear manly at all costs.

During Eleanor's early teens the family bonds seemed as strong as ever, and it was not until the eve of her sixteenth birthday that, for the first time, the idea of defying Harry entered her head.

This evening, sitting with her parents, she remembered that tomorrow her bedtime would be advanced by five minutes, according to Harry's nursery law. For every year five more minutes staying-up-time was allowed to each child, Harry being as strict with himself as anybody else. Alone with her parents, Eleanor turned and asked why her brother sent her to bed.

"Because you let him," her mother replied, exchanging an amused glance with her husband.

"All right, I won't."

On the birthday night the two younger boys went to bed on time as usual, while the elder pair remained up reading at the table. Their mother and father sat on either side of the fire. 'I felt horribly nervous and glued my eyes to a page I could not read. Presently out came the silver watch, and was laid on the tapestry cloth at Harry's side, where he could keep an eye on it, till the exact second. All too soon:

"Bedtime, Nellie!" The watch went back into his pocket.

"Oh," I said casually, "I'm not going."

"What?"

"I'm not going to bed yet," I repeated.

Harry got up, came round the table, said "Goodnight, Nellie," kissed me and went back to his place. Nothing had happened. Could it really be all right after all? A few moments later I addressed some remark to him. He did not answer. I spoke again. He took not the least notice.' [NN]

This ritual of bidding his sister goodnight and then pretending she was no longer present was kept up for about a fortnight. During the rest of the day Harry behaved normally.

So bound was Eleanor that she found it difficult not to believe, with her brother, that she was in the wrong. Yet she held on to her vestige of independence and from this time slowly, slowly began to free herself from his authority. She wrote that, although the hurt to her feelings went deep, the rift made no difference to the regular game of TAR which continued unabated with a kind of suppressed hypnotic hysteria.

*10*

# 11 Lancaster Road

YET AGAIN the Farjeons moved to a more opulent home, still in South Hampstead: 11 Lancaster Road. Eleanor, now 17, was given the huge front bedroom, furnished with solid mid-nineteenth century American furniture of enormous size. She had the 6 × 8 foot matrimonial bed which her father had bought in New York, a great chest of drawers with gabled looking-glass above, and a desk that filled the wide bay window. Even so there was plenty of room to pace up and down, up and down, trying and failing to write the Great Work that would satisfy the expectant authoress and shake the literary world.

The only tutor now, for Miss Newman had left, was M. Lambert, an impoverished French gentleman who walked twelve miles from his home in Dulwich to give Eleanor and the younger boys French lessons. The whole household felt embarrassment at his extreme poverty, his emaciated figure, his long walk, especially as he was painfully proud and such matters must not be mentioned. But when Maggie Farjeon was able she would persuade him to stay to lunch, serving the meal in a separate room where a display of lavish helpings could not offend his sensibilities.

With the move, Farjeon became possessed by a new mania. It was not buying books at auctions, or boxes of sole at Billingsgate, or gloves by the six dozen for his wife's tiny hands, or roses in Covent Garden, but gold paint. Bowls, candlesticks, vases, ivory chessmen and plates were coated with gold, picture frames were dotted. His new study was swathed in newspaper on which stood pots of gold paint with brushes, and all the objects waiting for sacrifice. The room reeked of turpentine. The author's fingers and clothes gleamed, while his wife hurried round hiding her most precious articles. With the excuse that his study was now unusable, Farjeon was back with the family, writing his latest novel, *Miriam Rozella*, all over the dining-room table.

But the house was expensive. It had been an unwise move at a time when B. L. Farjeon's popularity as a novelist was on the wane. His stories seemed dated to public and publishers, and he grew extremely worried as to how to support the family. Joe and Bertie had gone to school, but he took Joe away, in order to make him act as his secretary. His temper, always uncertain, became more and more unreasonable. Eleanor wrote: 'Why, if he loved us so, why if he was so proud of us, must he make us and himself unhappy?' [NN]

The sight of their mother's white strained face after a scene was terrible to the children, and these paternal rages made them fearful of outward expressions of wrath for the rest of their lives. Joe and Eleanor were always anxiously amiable, while Bertie, who could be

*Benjamin Farjeon*

irritable or sharply sarcastic as an adult, hardly ever dared genuine
fury. Harry's aggressive nature was restrained by such a powerful
will that there was little danger of it ever going out of control: with
him hard quiet disapproval was sufficient to quell almost all defiance,
and it was impossible to imagine him raising his voice in anger. But
between Harry and his father there must have been tensions, for
both were devoted to Maggie, and neither could brook opposition.

Eleanor enlarged on her father's worsening temper: 'I suffered
almost as much for Papa as for myself, and more for Mama. Each
subsiding storm left us throbbing, him most of all. His love for us
came back on him like a boomerang; his pride in us, his generosity,
his wish for us to be happy, was never changed.' [NN]

In 1898 Harry and Eleanor completed a light opera *Floretta*. It was
shown to Battison Haynes at the Royal Academy of Music, where
Harry was now a student. To their surprise and delight the
Academy did what it had never done before and decided to give a
public performance at St George's Hall.

'An exciting crowded time lay ahead of us. Harry rose at six in the
morning to copy the parts, and I rose to read aloud to him while he
worked. Composition and orchestration he had to achieve in solitude, but he had an astounding faculty for listening to Charles
Kingsley and copying – and even transposing – music at the same
time. If I went too fast, he did not pause, but flung a crumpled paper
at me and I slowed down. Occasionally he held up the small dictator-
ial fingers that could barely stretch an octave.' [NN]

During rehearsals Eleanor was puzzled, for the producer pulled
her pigtails when the Comtesse D'Ayelle sang:

> *False butterfly!*
> *Oh, if thou for my beauty art athirst,*
>    *That wish will soon be past;*
> *Thou hast kissed many. I am not the first,*
>    *Nor will I be the last –*

"Where did you get your knowledge from, young lady?" he
demanded.

As Eleanor explains, in the nineties, when one was eighteen, one
didn't know what sort of knowledge was meant. She wrote from a
kind of sophisticated innocence which never quite left her, despite all
the enlightenment brought by time and circumstance.

Friends were enthusiastic about the opera, the press was kind. Henry Irving wrote:

My dear Nellie,
   I wish I could have been present at the performance of the Opera. Your father is so old and dear a friend of mine that the success of his children is very near my heart. With every good wish and my love to all at home.
   Affectionately yours, Henry Irving
      What night or morning are you coming to us?

Important among musical friends were the Corders, who also lived in South Hampstead. Frederick Corder became Director of the Royal Academy of Music and taught Harry. His children, Paul and Dolly, became friends of Bertie and Eleanor. Because of these musical connections Eleanor and her parents were included in the end of term Academy picnics, when a launch was hired to take professors and students up the Thames for an outing. 'We steamed past lock after lock to the dark green velvet reach of Cliveden. While the long tables were being set by the water, we scattered over the lawns, and afterwards wandered up through the rich background of trees, till, from a little unsuspected church, sounds issued more moving and beautiful than those of the world's greatest organs. The music drew us inside – it was Battison Haynes, who had strolled away by himself, and finding the small church open sat playing the simple organ like an angel.' [NN]

On festive occasions such as the Academy picnic, Farjeon was at his best, presenting baskets of flowers and fruit to all the ladies, from the prettiest girl to the elderly chaperone. He was, like his daughter when years later she overcame her shyness, the life and soul of the party.

Returning home in the hot summer night, while the launch waited at Boulter's Lock, Whitworth Mitton sang *Songs of Araby* as the ecstatic Eleanor had never heard it sung before. This was the party from which much of the riverside picnic in *The Two Bouquets* was derived when Eleanor and Bertie wrote their operetta almost forty years later.

At this time Bertie, aged twelve, had begun to edit *Farjeon's Fortnightly* – its motto: *Non bonus, non melior, sed optimus* (Not good, not better, but best). There were serial stories, poems, interviews, and competitions with prizes of one halfpenny, a penwiper or a goldfish. The chief contributor was the editor himself, but many others helped to fill the typed pages: Eleanor and Joe, Paul and Dolly Corder, Wyndham Albery, the author Tom-Gallon and Farjeon himself. In the first number, October 11th 1899, the youthful editor interviewed Miss Eleanor Farjeon.

Of course, everyone has heard of Miss Eleanor Farjeon, the great authoress and librettist, who has so captivated the public by her charming tales, that she could almost go about the streets singing "Follow me", only she would not think of doing such a thing, as she is so modest and charmingly simple.

At 6.00 pm I entered her apartment and found her reading.

"Take a seat," she said on seeing me, and when I was seated said, "Now, what have I got to do? I hope you don't think me silly, but this is my first visit from one of you interviewers."

I informed her that she had to answer the questions I put to her. So I started with,

"What do you consider your best work?"

"It is difficult to say," she answered, "as my works are all so different, but I think my libretto of *Floretta* is the most important. Of my stories I consider *Fairy Dust*, which is as yet an unpublished work, the best."

"Is it true that you had *Floretta* produced at St George's Hall?"

"Yes, it was done in the middle of July last."

"Do you find your brother, Harry Farjeon, very difficult to get along with?"

"No. I give him my libretto, and anything he wants altered, I alter as we always have to give in to the composer, of course, but he is very easy to get along with."

Miss Nellie, or Eleanor, Farjeon, has been writing for ten years, her first poem being a valentine.

Competitions in the magazine were often set by Miss E. Farjeon, and when set by others often won by her. In one December issue a silver pig was won by W. Albery for the best comic Christmas Dinner menu.

The comments Eleanor makes on her role as librettist show how strictly she had been trained by Harry. There is, though, confidence in the way she speaks of her 'best work'. Bertie's question about getting along with Harry most likely stemmed from his own difficulties, for he was the only one who rebelled from the beginning, disputing or side-stepping authority in a manner that was galling to the self-righteous master of the nursery.

Five months after the first interview there was another short article on the young author: 'Nellie Farjeon. What she wants to be, and why. By her, herself.' This has a more worldly and self-conscious ring.

Although by no means desirous, from many points of view, of being otherwise than what *I am*, I elect to write upon the question of what I *want to be*, as, of the two subjects offered me, this opens up a far wider field for discussion.

What do you want to be? This, though the shorter query of the two, demands a longer reply.

In the first place, being ambitious of gaining fame, I turn to the fields of literature, because I believe whatever talents I possess lie in that direction; and I not unnaturally look to those talents to assist me in my endeavour to make a name for myself.

In the second place, it seems to me that an author has great power for good over the minds of his readers – and, alas, for evil also. For it is unfortunately true that the tastes of the public are being gradually corrupted by the trash which is now-a-days put into their hand by the men and women who live by the pen; since, such matter not only utterly utterly fails in conveying any good and healthy lesson to the reader, but most surely saps the mind with its unnatural plot, its feeble construction and its illiterate style. But this is the dark side of literature; and I, for one, am not so entirely selfish as to desire to gain celebrity by using my pen as a disgraceful tool to serve my ends. And while I am fully conscious that I can never approach the eminence attained by our great writers, who shine as far above me as the stars in heaven; yet by constantly striving towards the high standard of perfection which they represent, I can at least keep my style both wholesome and pure; and thus, however little my works may be read, however little merit they may contain, I shall at least be satisfied that I am not demeaning the noble profession to which I belong.

57

This prosy homily from an eighteen-year-old girl who is clever and well-read seems remarkably simple-minded. What the dreadful novels of unnatural plot, feeble construction and illiterate style were is not revealed, but Ouida's *Moths* might qualify. Chambers 1903 Literary Dictionary announces that Ouida's ideals were tawdry and unwholesome, and damns her style.

From another piece in *The Fortnightly* of 1900 there is a telling little sketch which uncovers Eleanor's agonizing shyness and the bitterness of social ineptitude. This is her entry for the Compliment Competition:

SHE:   (Archly) Isn't it too bad that you poor gentlemen are obliged to ask a dance of every girl you are introduced to?

HE:   Charmed, I'm sure!

SHE:   (After a few turns) How hot it is! What do you say to sitting out in the conservatory?

HE:   Awfully delighted!

SHE:   (After a long pause) Oh, I'm *so* sorry to trouble you – but would you mind bringing me an ice?

HE:   Most happy!
      (He does so and at the conclusion of the dance, goes off in search of fresh worlds to conquer).

In the two years succeeding *Floretta* Eleanor wrote two more libretti for Harry, both of which comic operettas were produced by the Royal Academy of Music. The first was *The Registry Office* in the Gilbert and Sullivan style, the second *A Gentleman of the Road*, an updated kind of *Beggar's Opera*. The lyrics show considerable ability to turn out neat and singable words.

### THE GALLANT HIGHWAYMAN

*In case you aspire some repute to acquire,*
  *In the highwayman's risky profession.*
*A detail or two I will mention to you*
  *Which I happen to have in possession.*
*You must not forget that all's fish to your net,*
  *From a prince of the realm to a drayman –*
*There's no profit too small that is profit at all*
  *In the eye of the gallant highwayman.*

*If a lady you meet from the circles élite*
  *In her coach, do your utmost to spare her;*
*It is proper and right to be very polite,*
  *For it wouldn't be courteous to scare her.*
*There's a tear on your lash as you collar her cash,*
  *Then you bow, lift your hat, and – away, man!*
*Her coachman and sich you may leave in the ditch –*
  *That's the rule of the gallant highwayman!*

At thirteen the more cynical brother, Bertie, wrote satirical verse nor, as an editor, was he afraid to dispraise. After including a letter of fulsome approbation from his sister, there came another definitely critical from his friend Paul Corder. The editorial comment was: 'We only wish that our other readers would send us suchlike letters, pointing out the chief deficiencies of our paper, which, we fear is far from perfect.'

This objective attitude was one which Eleanor admired, although she found disparagement of her own work almost impossible to take. Bertie was the only critic to whom she deferred in her adult writing and, during their collaborations, when she would scorn the suggestion to alter a comma by anybody else, Bertie could discard whole pages of her work as too whimsy or sentimental, at which she would sit down and try again.

# Death

DESPITE THE SUCCESS of the three operettas, Eleanor could not get down to what she felt to be serious work at the big desk in the bow window. The operettas had been written to Harry's order and were therefore, in a way, the same as playing TAR. During the writing Harry was able, as always, to transpose his thoughts: the work was not absolutely her own.

For Harry, though, life had changed. In 1901 he began to teach at the Royal Academy and the interest he found in his pupils was matched by their affection for him. The trouble he took, whether they were bright or dull, to make every detail absolutely clear, with his amazing patience, persistence and invention, amounted to genius.

In appearance Harry was quite different from his untidy, blowsy, dreamy, soft-hugging sister. In neat black clothes he moved with a quick skipping step, his small hand held objects fiercely and his dark deep-lined face, however shaded it might be by a brown eye-shade and small thick spectacles, was openly alert and watchful. His monkey-like figure never weighed over seven stone.

Both Eleanor and Harry adored and were adored by any child willing to submit to their influence, and for each child they would invent stories and games with the ease and ingenuity learnt from years of experience with TAR. In Harry's judgement certain subjects, mostly artistic, chiefly musical, were never to be spoken of in a normal voice. On the morning after a visit to *The Ring* its performance would be discussed and criticised in great detail, but with tones of reverent hush, as though one was in church and Wagner

God. And one night, most memorable to Joe and Bertie, when they had turned out the gas light and lay half asleep, the door opened and Harry stepped into the room.

"Rubinstein's[1] dead!" he announced in an awed whisper and left.

One of the high moments for Eleanor was the occasion when she first heard *Die Meistersinger*. With her remarkable sexual immaturity, those emotional ecstasies over love which afflict most young women well before their twenties did not trouble her. But in this opera she was swept away by the triumph of youth. And her father, always so quick and eager to feed her transports, saw to it that she visited *Die Meistersinger* three times in the season. Her enthusiasms, like his in their unbalanced ebullience, were a driving force which went racing along all sorts of unexpected paths all her life. The path might finish in a dead end, but hardly ever in disenchantment. They enlivened Eleanor's physically uneventful youth with a passion that rose to glorious heights.

Theatre-going was a family custom, and on the evening of January 22nd 1901, Eleanor was sitting with her parents in a horse-drawn light green Atlas bus, on the way to the Alhambra Theatre. They were to see a music hall performance which included the Romantic Nautical Ballet, Sharp and Flat, the Kaufmann Family, and, best of all, Houdini, 'King of Handcuffs'. They arrived at Leicester Square to find people standing about in groups, the air buzzing with the news of Queen Victoria's death. There was a sense of shock: the Queen had reigned for sixty-four years. 'Her powerful little presence possessed the English throne with a sort of immortality that made it hard to believe queens ever died,' Eleanor wrote years later.[2]

Farjeon turned to his wife. "We must go home. There'll be no performance to-night."

So they crossed the road and took the Atlas bus back to Swiss Cottage. On the joggling seat inside, Eleanor sat thinking, 'Now something big has happened. After this I can't fritter any more.'

Yet the longed for inspiration would not come. She had grown so adept at imitation that her imagination was swamped with second-hand images, through which her own originality could hardly be glimpsed. In the introduction to *Silver-Sand and Snow*, aged seventy,

1. Anton Rubinstein: pianist.
2. *A Company of Queens.*

Eleanor explained: 'In my youth I dreamed of being a "real" poet, but half way through my life the dream died, and whatever figments of it remained went into writing songs and verses for children.' At the age of twenty Eleanor was certainly not a real poet; she was to wait nine more years before it became a possibility.

Inspiration, that spur to ambition and self-indulgence, which so excites the young writer at the start of a career, seemed elusive. Eleanor waited with infinite optimism for the flood that was to send words spinning down her own poetic river. Yet, although it did not come, she believed in herself; this was the great strength implanted by her father, which gave her the courage to battle on despite every set-back. On the other hand it created a kind of conceit which helped to inhibit the self-criticism that would have made her work less prolific and more incisive. At this stage, when she was twenty, Eleanor wrote poetry quite lacking individuality, although technically most adept.

In 1902 she was working hard at a collection of fifty-nine poems, illustrated by her own pen-drawings and water colours, elegantly heightened by her father's favourite gold paint. Amid the verses shepherds recline with professional languor, maidens greet the dawn with an *Art Nouveau* flourish of uplifted arms, while naked cupids abound, although bereft of sexual parts; only one or two lucky ones sport a navel. The pictures match the writing: both are clever and arch.

It is an amusing game to seek out the varied sources of these poems. Their plagiarisms are not intentional, I feel sure, for it would have been considered disgraceful to filch knowingly from another artist. With Elizabeth Barrett Browning, Eleanor demands, 'How do I love you?' instead of 'How do I love thee?' Her *Eastern Love Elegy* has a clear *Omar Khayyam* ring, only it is more highly sugared: 'Thou art the flower of the harem, O my beloved, my fairest!' *To a Coquette* is her seventeenth century style, very like George Withers. *Ode to the Old Year and the New* has a similar pattern to Tennyson's *Death of the Old Year*, while Wordsworth, Browning, Herrick, Shelley, Scott and Keats hover above the pages in meek attendance.

From the coy lilt of an eternally smiling china shepherdess whose heart broke when her shepherd at the opposite end of the mantelpiece was broken, *The Japanese Fan* stands out as more genuine and amusing. It is in the style of her future light verse for children.

> *Oh, I wish that the world were arranged on the plan*
> *That was used in constructing the Japanese Fan!*
>
> *There the houses are built on the tops of the trees*
> *With every appearance of comfort and ease,*
> *While the rivers, (which usual methods ignore)*
> *Flow in at the chimney and out at the door.*
>
> *The fishermen fancy it rather a lark*
> *From the shores of the moon in their junks to embark,*
> *And the many-hued birds think it excellent fun*
> *To prop up their nests on the rays of the sun.*
>
> *And ladies in gowns of artistic design*
> *On the summit of stately pagodas recline,*
> *While the flowers of the almond tree fly through the air*
> *From no-one knows whither to no-one knows where.*

The poems were typed and, with the illustrations, sent to be professionally bound between stiff blue linen boards, with gilt lettering on the spine and on the page edges. It was entitled *Poems* by Eleanor Farjeon. Inside on a loose page between the marbled end papers :

63

TO MY DEAR FATHER, B. L. FARJEON,
HIS LOVING DAUGHTER GIVES THIS
BOOK AS A CHRISTMAS GIFT.
IT WAS COMMENCED FOR HIM IN JANUARY
AND FINISHED IN DECEMBER, 1902.

On July 4th 1903, Farjeon took his daughter up the road to the jeweller, Zahringer, in College Crescent, and there bought his wife yet another birthday present. 'She had a table full of presents already, but Papa was not content. Something more. Nothing was ever enough.' [NN]

Before nightfall the novelist had gone to bed unwell, and then from day to day his wife's face became more and more anxious. There was the coming and going of specialists, consultations, a night nurse was hired, and there was whispered talk which included the dread words 'catheter' and 'operation'.

'Every day I went to see Papa in bed, and relieve Mama for a little while. Every day I sat with him and saw him more and more frequently contracted with spasms of pain. He groaned through his teeth, but afterwards smiled at me. One day, after stifling a sound he said, "Give me your hand, Nell, I think if I hold it, it will help me through the next one." He did not moan through that next one; but I could have done so, he gripped my hand so hard.

'Then he said abruptly, "You'd better go now, Nell." It was my last memory of him.' [NN]

Maggie Farjeon, in her dressing gown, carrying a candle, wakened Eleanor in the middle of the night. She spoke softly, "Papa is very ill. We've sent for the doctor. Tell Harry. Don't wake the boys."

What Farjeon died of is not known. In *A Nursery in the Nineties* Victorian reticence clouds his illness.

64

# 12

# Crow's Nest

THE DEATH OF FARJEON was a blow to the family, not only
because he was so loved but because he left no money. They had
lived precariously on his contracts and three hundred pounds a year
from Joseph Jefferson.

There had been good reason for the novelist's anxiety over his
diminishing popularity, with the increased expense of a bigger house
and grown children. The battle up the social scale from ignorance
and poverty to that of a respected and seemingly prosperous author
had been a hard-won triumph. Yet at the end of his life his finances
were little better than at the beginning.

Among his papers an unsigned will was found, earlier than the
valid one which left everything to his wife. In the former will he had
bequeathed to his children and friends certain personal mementos,
concluding:

'I bid all my friends an affectionate farewell.

'God bless my darling wife and children. It has been my strenuous
endeavour to do work to the best of my ability and to make a happy
home. My dear wife and children have given me much happiness. I
trust they have drawn happiness from me. Children, be good to your
mother and to each other. Do your duty in life, and use your talents
worthily.'

Eleanor described her father's death in *A Nursery in the Nineties*
without a touch of that sentimentality or romanticism which so often
coloured her writing rosy pink. Her sharpness is almost bitter.

The funeral was coming; I wasn't going; but I suppose Aunty

Fan thought it would not do for me to be in my flowered crêpe summer frock. I went to John Barnes in Finchley Road to buy something. I'd seldom had a ready-made before, and never a black dress. My skin was muddy, not good for black at all. I said to the assistant, "I want a black dress."

"What sort of dress?"

"I don't mind."

She glanced at me and brought something in delaine. It went on me, an indifferent fit.

"Will that do?" she asked, standing me before a looking-glass. I scarcely looked, and answered "Yes." Then I bought some sort of hat. When I got back Christie [a friend] met me in the hall. She kissed me and said gently, "How sweet you look, Nellie." But I knew I looked horrid. It didn't matter anyhow.

The flowers began to come, the flowers and flowers. The drawing-room was full of them, wonderful wreaths from the Clubs, and the rich friends. Humble wreaths and bunches from the poor ones. We liked them; they seemed to comfort Mother. Then suddenly they became to me intolerable. The scent was overpowering. I could hardly bear to go into the drawing-room, where the wreaths had to lie on top of one another and the first were beginning to wilt. Yet they were comforting – there seemed so many people who loved him. And oh, the letters!

"Answer these." Mama gave me them in handfuls. I thanked them for her, as well as I could. I wrote to Mr Barrie, 'I'd like you to know that after he read *Sentimental Tommy*, Father always said, "I take my hat off to J. M. Barrie."' Henry Irving wrote again in reply to my letter, beginning not 'My dear Nellie' but 'My dear Friend', and I wrote to him, 'Thank you for calling me your friend.' I'd suddenly realised I was no longer a child. Everything was about to change, for all of us.

The day of the funeral came. The blinds were drawn down. I stayed in my room with Mama and Aunty Fan was there too. Mama was prostrate. The carriages stretched up the road, out of sight. The quiet bustle died away. The house was deadly still. Papa had gone; the three boys had gone with him.

Another bell. The maid said, "Mr Willard." Uncle Ted! Why, he was to have been at the funeral! I ran downstairs. There he stood, immaculate as always, but his strong, dominant, intellectual face was twisted with pain. "Nellie, my dear! I have mistaken the time." "Yes, Uncle Ted, they've gone. Not long. You could – " He shook his head, kissed me, and turned to go. He appeared shocked with himself. Suddenly down the stairs ran Mama, her hair untidy, her eyes swollen. She threw herself into his arms. "Oh Ted! Oh Ted! the children are so good." "How can they help it, dear? They're your children." He kissed her, the tears streaming down his face, E. S. Willard, who was almost a great actor. Papa said he would have been a great one, if he had had a touch of heart.

The destitution this respectable middle class family now faced was something unimaginable in England today, for there was no Social Security. But Benjamin Farjeon had imbued his children with a sense of the struggle for survival; to him hunger had been real enough. The children were not helpless, like their mother.

It was at once apparent that a cheaper house must be rented. So 137 Fellows Road was taken: a hotly red brick, narrow terraced five-storey house of the early 1880s. Both sides of the road were walled with these houses, which exuded an air of stuffy gentility. Above the dark basement a few steps led to the front door, over which there was an arch with a rose cast in brick on either side.

Harry was made professor, the youngest ever, at the Royal Academy of Music, earning 5 shillings an hour for lessons he gave there. Joe was given the job of assistant in the box office at Wyndham's Theatre by Charles Wyndham. Sixteen-year-old Bertie's promising academic career at University College School must obviously end soon: the fees could not be afforded. As for Eleanor, it was accepted that as the plain unmarried daughter she would remain at home to companion her mother and, like Christina Rosetti, write poetry. The prospect was not pleasant for any but Harry.

Then, in 1904, came an invitation to visit Joseph Jefferson in his American home, Crow's Nest, overlooking Buzzard's Bay. It was just what was needed to cheer the family. Now all those Jefferson uncles, aunts and cousins, so familiar by name, would become known, in company with the 'adored' Joseph Jefferson.

'Adored,' Eleanor wrote in her unfinished memoir, 'is not too strong a word, for it was not stage genius only that gave him his unique place in his country's affections. It was an irresistible quality in the man himself, a sunlight, an over-running lovableness, a contagious humour which, while his audience was his, made Joe theirs. Wherever he acted he had to be enshrined in the memories of each new generation. On his long annual tours, in small 'one-night-stand' towns where he might never appear again, business came to a halt, shops were closed, children kept away from school, streets decorated, and a 'Jefferson holiday' was proclaimed, so that young and old could afterwards say they had seen Joe Jefferson play Rip Van Winkle.'

Maggie Farjeon, Eleanor and Joe left England in May, while Harry and Bertie were to follow, for Harry must finish his work at the R.A.M. and Bertie his last term at University College School. Bertie hoped that his grandfather might pay for further university education: his talent and enthusiasm for classical literature seemed to lead that way.

Of these brothers Eleanor commented: 'Bertie's brain, keen and brilliant, was a scholar's. Harry's mentality was of larger scope; turned in almost any direction, its powerful impersonal grasp might have qualified him to be a great philosopher or mathematician.'[1] But of course Harry had had even less formal education than his brothers and was destined, by his own absolute decree, to be a great composer.

So Eleanor sailed across the Atlantic on the first of her heart-stirring adventures in the New World. Of this passage she exclaimed: 'Oh, the emotional daze of that journey from Swiss Cottage to Buzzard's Bay.'

Uncle Boll met them on the Boston quayside, from whence a train took them to a country station. There the Jefferson coachman was waiting with the carriage, in which they rode towards Buzzard's Bay, at last turning off the road and driving through the maples of Grandfather's estate, to approach the big house where 'the piazza was thronged with Jeffersons gathered there in dozens, but it seemed to me in hundreds. When I climbed down from the carriage I could not move. I saw Mother go running up the steps away from me, running back to the girlhood when I was no part of her life. I saw a figure rise from a cane chair and come to meet her, I heard her cry "Father!" while on the piazza above me all the gay Jeffersons

1. Unpublished memoir by Eleanor Farjeon. [Memoir] hereafter.

Eleanor's brothers: Harry, Joe and Bertie

crowded about the first embrace for twenty-six years, little Meenie in old Rip's arms again – and I stood down below them sobbing my heart out; till some of the laughing cousins, Charlie's Sal and Tom's Connie flew down to comfort me – "Nellie! Don't cry, don't cry!" They pulled me up the steps, and I too found myself in Joe Jeffersons's arms.' [Memoir]

*The family on board a steamer*

In that idyllic summer of picnics, charades, jaunts on steamers, and youthfully romantic love affairs, Eleanor's passion for family expanded to her American relatives. Together the new cousins visited fortune-tellers, swam by moonlight, and went to each other's heads. Mama, back among her own people, was full of sweetness and laughter. 'Was there ever so radiant a colony as the American Jeffersons, so full of charm and merriment and beauty?' the enthusiastic kinswoman demanded.

Joe Jefferson had had ten children by his two wives, and most of the children still lived on and around the old man. The main house, which he built for a second time after fire destroyed the first with his collection of paintings, was large and full of modern conveniences. There was a telephone and electric light furnished from a power house on the premises. N. H. Dole wrote in his book *Joseph Jefferson at Home* that the electricity 'typical of its owner, keeps the whole establishment in a glow of brilliancy.'

A huge ornate mantelpiece for the dining-room had been specially imported from India, while on the sideboard stood a massive silver loving cup with three carved figures of Jefferson in his most famous roles: Bob Acres, Dr Pangloss and Rip Van Winkle. The walls were covered with paintings, the actor himself being a skilled artist in something of the Corot style. Among his present collection were a Gainsborough portrait of Sheridan, a Goya bullfight, a Rembrandt portrait, two landscapes by Daubigny, with whom he had made friends on his European travels, a Corot, Morland and Hoppner. There were also pictures by modern Dutch and French artists whose studios he had visited.

Each of his children kept a summer residence on the wooded estate, and each home was filled with a constant overflow of friends and family. But Eleanor and her mother stayed in the big house, with the luxury of a private bathroom.

So from every side came comfort, informality and friendliness, with food unimaginably beyond their British nursery standards, and memories of the day when Papa had raged down to the kitchen in the middle of Sunday lunch and rowed the cook for overdoing the beef. That time the cook had shouted back, "You're no gentleman!" To which he had retorted, "And you're no cook!" Which repartee entirely restored the author's temper, if not the nerves of the rest of the household.

But in Buzzard's Bay there were soft-shell crabs, clams, succotash, chowder, chicken Maryland, Boston brown bread and baked beans and sweet corn, all perfectly prepared. On Sundays Eleanor and Uncle Boll would plan their ice cream campaign with considerable care. They ate only two platefuls of vanilla ice at the Big House, then hurried off to Maddy's mountains of strawberry ice, and then on to Duddy's home, where they gorged on hot chocolate fudge and angel cake. An afternoon siesta allowed time to recover, after which they were completely restored by an evening swim in the bay.

Jefferson, now seventy-five, was energetic, planning his next season's tour and at the centre of all activities and amusements. One day Eleanor was watching him prune the roses in his whiskery old straw hat and admired the size and colour of the flowers.

"Ah, but they haven't the scent of your English roses," he responded. "I've tried importing them; your gooseberries and strawberries too. They lose their flavour in our bright dry climate, they don't like it. There's something in your grey English weather they thrive on. It's the moisture."

As soon as the eldest and youngest Farjeon brothers arrived there were fresh diversions. Harry invented new games, organised concerts in which he astonished his audience with improvised ragtime. He composed the 'Buzzard's Bay Suite', each piece being dedicated to one of his American girl cousins. He also directed and rehearsed two theatrical performances in the blazing August summer. This was bold, seeing that most of the older generation and some of the younger were professional actors. Harry would summon his cast to a secret spot in the woods, Skunk Hollow, and read the plot which he had devised, with a rough outline of each part, leaving his cast to fill out the dialogue and character. In the first play Eleanor was a witch, whose discourse she composed in rhymed curses and incantations. For the performance Harry, as in the past, stage-managed from the piano, where he provided incidental music.

For the second play he cast his sister as the heroine, at which she was considerably alarmed, protesting to everybody, "But I'm not pretty enough for a heroine."

"You will be when we've made you up," said her cousin.

"But Dot! A Juliet in spectacles!"

Cousin Dot firmly countered, "You must take them off."

On the night Eleanor's glasses were confiscated and Dot set to work on her appearance so successfully that Harry did not immediately recognise his sister when urgently calling the cast together. Then he exlaimed, "Nellie? I say!" and quickly brushed aside his surprise to disclose the ordeal before them. "Listen, everybody! None of you is to look at the audience. They have come on purpose to break you up." [Memoir]

When the show began the make-up behind the curtain was nothing to the make-up in front. Maggie Farjeon appeared as a geisha girl, in a flamboyant kimono, with almond eyes and a mountainous headdress of birds and flowers. Uncle Tom was a dandy Frenchman, with waxed moustaches, an imperial beard, cane and glossy top hat. Fat Uncle Fluff (the nickname must have come because he fluffed his lines on the stage) was hung with curtains, padded with cushions and nursed a potted palm. In her description of the scene Eleanor fans her own excitement: 'Imagination and some old theatrical costumes – yes, that was all the Jefferson rogues and vagabonds had ever needed for their fun. That was the evanescent brand of humour which the Farjeons too had inherited from the strolling players who had acted with David Garrick and steamed their showboat up the Mississippi.' [Memoir]

Her grandfather, she wrote, was the pivot on which the summer wheel spun round. 'In spirit he was the youngest old man I have ever known, and young or old the most fascinating. Whatever he did expressed his full-hearted enjoyment in life, whether he was fishing or painting or weeding his garden, writing light verse or summing up his experiences as an actor and a man in prose that has outlived him.' [Memoir]

Before the end of their holiday the Farjeons were being urged to settle in America. Joe could act, Eleanor write, and Bertie study Greek just as well in the States as in England. But Harry's career at the R.A.M. was against it, and his plans were, as always, inflexible. Music for him lay in London, and only for a short time was the temptation to emigrate enjoyed in anticipation.

To their lasting disappointment the Farjeon children never saw their grandfather act Rip Van Winkle, Abel Drugger or any other of the roles which had contributed to his great fortune. But in the bits of memoir Eleanor left, she described an evening when the actor in him came to the fore. Two or three players from New York were staying on the estate and after supper everybody sat on round the dining-table. The men drank whisky and told anecdotes, but when Jefferson capped one story with a better, the actors nudged each other, egged him on and soon became silent. 'I cannot remember a single tale he told, but I know that for an hour he kept us in a state of pure delight, while every dialect danced on his tongue, and each joke's point was timed with perfect art. Better than any humour was the delicious chuckle of the teller, a contagious chuckle that kept the room rippling with laughter. This was the only time I saw my grandfather act, the only time I made one of his charmed audience. For he had played his last upon the stage.'

Back in London, six months later, the Farjeons received a cable to say that Joe Jefferson had died.

In his will the actor forbade family litigation: whoever went to law would never benefit. And his properties, the Louisiana plantation, Orange Island with its salt mine and ice plant, the Buzzard's Bay estate with the house full of pictures were worthy loot. However, the lawyers were not forbidden to go to law among themselves, and this they did with zest, taking the main part of the estate. The youngest of the ten children, Uncle Frank, was left with enough income to spend the rest of his life travelling round and round the world on luxury cruises. The eldest daughter's share was not so considerable: ultimately it came to something between five and six thousand pounds, which Harry carefully invested. But this sum was only settled after years of litigation.

Among other things, Maggie Farjeon was left the paintings, which were auctioned by the American Art Galleries, New York, on April 27th 1906. A huge subscribers' catalogue limited to one hundred and fifty copies was printed, gold lettering on the stiff white cover, with full page illustrations of almost all the seventy-four pictures for sale. The net result of these 'valuable paintings collected by the late Joseph Jefferson' was, so family gossip says, £1,900. Even in 1906 this auction was admitted to have been a farce and there were strong suggestions of collusion among dealers, all the more likely because not one of the Jeffersons had been there to see to their poverty-stricken relative's interest.

# 137 Fellows Road

'As my eyesight is as myopic as my insight, I have spent most of my life in vague landscapes, within and without, and found both full of wonder.

'I see myself now, at the age of twenty-four, still loitering in this internal dream under the wing of my family; passive until reality should act on me, not going forward to grasp life – a failure for which D. H. Lawrence took me to task. I was nearly thirty before I gave life a chance to grasp me. I ran away and hid when I might have been falling in love, and could have been bearing children. I was ignorant of my human longings, and among people was unconscious of having any individuality beyond my acutely painful shyness.' [Memoir]

So, while her two younger brothers began the struggle to earn a living, first on the stage and then, far more happily, in journalism, Eleanor day-dreamed, spending her dress allowance of £24 a year on theatre tickets. When she went to Wagner's *Ring* at Covent Garden four nights running there was never a dull moment, for Harry had so primed her with every motif in the music that each note spoke of crucial events out of the past, or foreshadowed them in the future. She forgot her terror of heights in the gallery 'as Wotan took his disobedient child into his arms and dissolved her immortality with a kiss.' [Memoir]

She went to the first night of *Peter Pan* and did not like it; she saw Duse play Marguerite Gautier, having seen Bernhardt play the part fourteen years earlier. With her mother and brothers she was at Henry Irving's final performance at Drury Lane, when he played Beckett in Tennyson's play. This is the theatrical night which she would have chosen from all others to see again. She wrote:

I think Irving's most wonderful moment that night was in the very quiet scene before the last, when (as in a parallel scene in *Hamlet*) the man who is soon to die muses as if he were already in eternity. The play came to an end, and the storm broke. Harry glanced at his watch.

One couldn't count the curtains either before or after the farewell speech, spoken with that mingling of gentle dignity, proud humility, and infinite courtesy which no other actor equalled when addressing his public. The tall frail figure, with eyes that seemed red-rimmed with weariness, bowed to us again and again, until it was decided behind the curtain that this *must* be the last call.

On our side of the curtain it had not been so decided. However often we had seen our Irving, we must see him yet once more, and then once more. The lights went up, some of the boxes emptied, a few people left the stalls, the attendants came about – but you might as well have tried to stop an unspent thunderstorm as the tumult in the house. Mother tried vainly to get us to our feet. The gallery, I don't know how, surged down to the stalls and into the orchestra pit. They got hold of drum-sticks and beat the drums; they roared out the cry of the knights in the play – "King's men! King's men!" – but what they roared was "Irving's men! Irving's men!" Bram Stoker, half smiling, half worried, came to where Mother was sitting and whispered, "What's to be done? There's a private ceremony about to take place on the stage, and we can't get on until these people go." Mother laughed helplessly, "Look at *my* little lot!" Her little lot were clapping and stamping madly, with the stalls and dress circle, amphitheatre and gallery.

Then some stir on the stage told us that we had won. The curtains parted, and our Irving was standing there in evening dress, with his company and a group of guests behind him. Dead silence fell. With a smile full of charm and affection Irving let us into the secret of the little ceremony, and invited us to join the party on our side of the curtain. The farewell presentation to him was made in the presence of his audience, and when all was done he turned to us again, saying gently and finally, "And now, *good night*." No attempt was made to get the curtain up again. The theatre filled with the shuffling of hundreds of feet towards the exit doors.

Harry took out his watch. "Exactly three-quarters-of-an-hour," he said. [Memoir]

In Fellows Road in the retreat of her little top room Eleanor continued to try and sublimate in pen and ink the unripe emotions of her fantasy life, but she owned that for most of the time the pen was idle in her hand. She dreamed fantasies by day and lived them by night, 'sleeping so badly that I often did not close my eyes till dawn. If I had not slept by one or two in the morning I gave up trying to, and summoned my world out of the vasty deep; then my mélange of Greeks and Elizabethans sprang into life of their own. I wasn't even conscious of keeping them in motion. To them was now added the vast scene of the Nibelung Saga, in which were united my passions for music and myth. I swam with the Rhine maidens, flamed with Loge, rode the storm with Brünhilde, and forged his sword with Siegfried. Nothing in life approached the scale of my world in the dark.' [Memoir]

The actual quantity of writing achieved, despite daydreams, was considerable: a novel, *The Romance of Christina*, long, immature and imaginative, was written in a state of fervid self-indulgence, enjoyed, Eleanor explained, as another would enjoy secret drinking – 'I would slip away for another nip of secret writing.' The novel was offered to Smith Elder, but rejected on an encouraging note.

In the autumn of 1908 Eleanor decided to bring out a book of poems, after some haggling, at her own expense with the publisher Elkin Mathews. Her letters to him are models of charm and clear thinking.

> 137 *Fellows Road, South Hampstead, N.W.*
> *October 1st,* 1908

Dear Mr Mathews –
   Or rather:
Oh dear! Mr Mathews!

I *did* hope that if I were to contribute £10.0.0. towards a Vigo Cabinet volume, a volume less than double the length could not exceed £20.0.0. The estimates you have sent me, however, seem not to be on the original basis of my *contributing towards* a volume, but cover the entire cost of production. Does the fact that the book is too long to appear in the Vigo Cabinet Series preclude the possibility of our making some similar arrangement as to its production in a 'non-Series' form?

If so, I shall have to try to modify the length of the volume or the size of the edition, as either of your estimates would incur an outlay of over £30.0.0. which is, I fear, quite impossible for me. I do not feel justified in entering on any arrangement without clearly understanding my liabilities, and am in some doubt as to whether there might not be further charges for advertising, distribution to the Press, etc., if the book were produced on this basis, or whether you would undertake these yourself.

I would also like to know the exact relation in which you, I, and the book would stand towards one another. I suppose the entire edition would be mine if I paid the entire cost, and that I should receive money on every copy sold – a problematical contingency, I know, but it is as well to have this definite. At what price would you suggest that the book should be offered to a reluctant public (in wrappers), and what would be our proportions of the plunder?

The Copyright would, of course, be exclusively mine, and I could reproduce the poems in any way and at any time I wished.

I note that you say : 'Corrections and alterations extra.' This does not, I suppose, mean the corrections of ordinary printers' errors, for which no charge is usual?

Of the two specimen sheets submitted I prefer (probably because it is the more expensive!) the Crown 8vo long primer, the composition, machining and paper for 500 copies of which would be £26.10.0. What would be the cost of smaller editions of 250, 300, and 350 copies?

I hope you will not succumb beneath this volley of questions, but I think they are necessary in case you do not feel able to revert to the first idea of my contributing some specified sum towards the production and leaving the rest of the responsibility with you.

I shall be glad to hear from you soon, as I would like to settle the matter with as little delay as possible.

Faithfully yours,
Eleanor Farjeon

The next letter of 30th October begins:

Dear Mr Mathews,

I cannot sign, in its present form, the agreement you have drafted with respect to "Pan-Worship". It seems to me curiously one-sided; and the privilege of publishing my poems at my own expense appears to include the ceding, in some degree or other, of various sorts of "rights" which I think, under such an arrangement, should remain exclusively my own. I had better take the clauses of the agreement in order . . .

*Pan-Worship and Other Poems* was published in December for two shillings and sixpence. Eleanor, or rather her mother, paid £37.17.6 for the edition of five hundred copies. Fifty copies were distributed to the press and one hundred sent directly to the author. The rest were for sale, two thirds of the price going to the author and one third to the publisher, who had given up his demand for translation rights, musical rights, and the world copyright.

The poems were among those which Eleanor later classed as derivative, and not worth very much. But the title poem, *Pan-Worship*, gives a picture of the ideals and sentiments which were now engrossing the poet and which, curiously recycled, appeared in her first truly original story book, *Martin Pippin in the Apple Orchard*. This is an example taken from the middle of *Pan-Worship*.

> *O virgin Greece, standing with naked feet*
> *In the morning dews of the world against the light*
> *Of an infant dawn! Old Greece, ever-young Greece,*
> *The pagan in my blood, the instinct in me*
> *That yearns back, back to nature-worship, cries*
> *Aloud to thee! I would stoop to kiss those feet,*
> *Sweet white wet feet washed with the earth's first dews:–*
> *And leaning ear to grass I would re-catch*
> *Echoes of footsteps sounding down dim ages*
> *For ever the music once they made on thee:*
> *The flaming step of young Apollo when*
> *With limbs like light and golden locks toss'd back*
> *On a smooth ivory shoulder, he avenged*
> *His mother's wrongs on Python. The dreaming step*
> *Of Hylas in the woods of Mysia.*

And then, one sleepless night, the spoof Elizabethan poet, Nathaniel Downes, was invented. Before morning Eleanor had composed seven lyrics, repeating them again and again in the dark until they were fixed in her mind. With daylight the poems were written out in good Spenserian spelling, after which the poet's love story was put together, set in Sussex for no better reason than that the Sussex cricket team was captained by the family hero, Ranjitsinjhi. On completion the manuscript was sent off to Blackwood's Magazine. Old William Blackwood wrote back to say that he liked the piece, and were the poems genuine? Eleanor replied that she never expected her fake to be taken seriously. To this the editor wrote: 'We'll print it without explanation and see what happens.' There was also a cheque for twenty-five guineas.

Scholars were deceived, literary reviewers took the work for genuine, but Edward Thomas commented later that no Elizabethan poet would have written in the metre used for the final poem.

The poems pertain to have come from Nathaniel Downes's only preserved work, *The Shepheard's Gyrlond*, printed in 1594, and are introduced satirically, with the kind of stolid serious discussion commonplace to scholarship: 'The song to Sleep, too, is little more than an exercise in the graceful imagery of the period, with an experimental use of the Alexandrine on the Spenserian stanza in a verse which otherwise departs from the Spenserian style.'

The following sonnet is given as one of the flowers from the *Gyrlond* 'worth preservation before Nat's tragi-comedy developed its culminating situation.'

*My deare, my onely loue, my bosomes floure,*
*With laughing misicke dayly mocks my sighs,*
*And I beneathe her hardly wielded powre,*
*Grow faint with longings that she doth misprize.*
*The lyttel god wych dwells within her eyes,*
*Still drawes my teares – O drawe them into her*
*Whose natural sun her natural fountein dries,*
*That sluggishly her streames of pitie stir.*
*Wilt thou not teach thy laughter how to weepe?*
*Then I could teach my sorrowe how to smyle.*
*The fayrest rose is shee whose bosome deepe*
*Admits the heav'nlie deawes a litil whyle.*

*Vouchsafe this mem'ry for my barren yeares,*
*Once to have seene thy laughter grac'd with teares.*

Despite the Farjeons' comparative poverty, there were servants to cook and do housework. Eleanor took no interest in domestic labour until later it was forced on her, and then she cooked with skill and gusto. Sweeping and polishing were not important to her myopic sight and were in themselves boring occupations. But she was practical and a great support to her mother and brothers, especially in any lively concern such as Harry's 'Element Teas', which he gave for his pupils every year before the summer examinations.

> Mother and I spent the morning bringing every chair in the house into the drawing-room, setting up Harry's blackboard and easel near the piano, and preparing in the dining-room trays of cups and jugs and sugar bowls, with plates of bread-and-butter and fancy cakes. The bevy of boys and girls arrived at two o'clock, last year's smiling, this year's a little shy. The first hour was rather quiet, towards the end of the second a breeze of laughter came from the drawing-room. At ten minutes to four Harry darted out – "Tea in ten minutes, please!" – and darted back. We put on kettles, filled the teapots, and carried in the trays. Young Olive Groves and little Vivian Langrish jumped up to hand round the plates.
>
> The cups were filled and refilled while Mother and I talked to the old pupils and made friends with the new ones. At half-past four Harry called "Time", and we left him and them to what became a riotous end of the party. We never quite knew what was happening to produce such gales of mirth, as he chalked up problems and shot rapid questions, allotting marks to the swiftest answers. The prize for the highest score was a box of Fuller's peppermint creams. [Memoir]

Harry's fame as a teacher so increased, and with it his private pupils, that with great gratification to himself he had to arrange a timetable of the most meticulous economy. There were so many teaching periods, so many pauses for rests, so many half hours for composition, for reading, for the household accounts, so many hours off for the theatre and concerts, or for seeing friends and playing with their children. His obsessive nature was satisfied by slotting in

81

occupation for every second of the day. The rigidity of Harry's mind even towards pleasure was illustrated by an example Eleanor gave. One evening after a concert it had been decided that he would go home, while Eleanor went on to a party. Suddenly she said:

"I don't think I'll go after all. I shall come back with you."

"But you had decided to go!" Harry responded in amazement.

"Yes, but I've changed my mind."

"I don't think I *could* do that, after I had decided on a thing," was the brother's comment.

Yet despite all his strictness and formalism, most children were drawn to him as to the Pied Piper of Hamelin. At one children's party they all streamed upstairs after him and down again when he went to fetch a special shoe for Hunt the Slipper. Edward Thomas's daughter, Myfanwy, said that she looked on him as a prince. When they went for walks and he retailed marvellous stories she would long desperately to take his hand, but never dared.

The Dickensian Christmasses were still celebrated, as in Ben Farjeon's time, with a huge children's party. Economies were cast off in December when everybody lavished presents on everybody else.

One Christmas morning, in company with two old theatrical friends, Aunty Lou and Grandma, young Bertie unexpectedly announced, "Now we will play Fido!"

He ranged the company on chairs at the far end of the drawing-room in order of age and handing Joe, the youngest, a string and pair of scissors, ordered him to pull and call for Fido. He then vanished through the door.

Joe called coaxingly and pulled. Yards of string crept through from the passage, till at last, on the end, came a little pork sausage. The prompter's voice told him to cut the string when he had his Fido and pass the end to Eleanor. She took her end and pulled and called, till presently in slid another Fido, a glossy saveloy.

At this period Appenrodt's delicatessen had just opened and varieties of sausage were a novelty. The family had never seen such a mortadella as followed the saveloy to Harry's feet. Like the dogs in the fairy tale, Fido's size increased with each new arrival. Next the longest liver sausage ever seen crawled over the carpet, and finally Grandma hauled in a bumping scarlet wurst of mountainous girth, which Bertie propelled from behind into her lap.

Eleanor said that this joke offered a glimpse of Bertie's art in stage production: 'In suspense-sense, timing, and accumulative effect it foretold his skill in arranging the running order of a show; but no sketch in his Little Theatre revues was more hilariously received than FIDO in Fellows Road that Christmas morning.' [Memoir]

At this period Bertie was working on Lord Northcliffe's weekly, *Answers*. He had begun as a reporter on the *Manchester Daily Mail* because Northcliffe, out of respect for his old friend Ben Farjeon, had offered his youngest son an opening in journalism. However when, one day in Manchester, Bertie was told to go and get the 'grief story' from a woman whose husband had just been killed in an accident, he revolted. Without producing a word of copy, Bertie took the train back to London. Instead of being dismissed, as everybody expected, Northcliffe gave him another job on *Answers*, where Joe, after an unsatisfactory period on the stage, followed him.

Joe's acting career as a light comedian had been hampered by his distaste for dressing room life: bad language, drinking and, worst of all, an unchivalrous attitude to women, disgusted him. His health was never strong, so that when he was offered the part of an elderly libertine he left the stage for good, with his weak chest for excuse.

Of this brother Eleanor wrote: 'What does one do about a chap who has all his wits yet seems to *prefer* the worst of a bargain among friends? Who won't laugh at a dirty story, but keeps laughter bubbling with his own infectious fun, in which there isn't a coarse word or doubtful innuendo? What could one do but be fond of this chap, who, crying, "I feel *such a devil*!" helps himself recklessly to a dry biscuit? Joe might have been uneasy in Swift's company, but how he and Lamb would have loved each other!' [Memoir]

The brothers took bicycling holidays in France together. On two occasions Eleanor accompanied Harry to Wiesbaden, where he consulted Dr Pagenstrecher about his eyesight. Eleanor loved Germany: the beer gardens, the journey down the Rhine, Wagner. Then she and her brother could indulge in TAR to their hearts' content – she was a clever virgin in her late twenties, he a clever and equally virgin professor over thirty. They walked together through the Black Forest he, doubtless, a little ahead and she at his elbow, with their heads together, just as they had done as children in the streets of South Hampstead, talking, talking.

And then, suddenly, in 1910 came a shock: Harry made his sister aware that TAR was over.

'The magic life of Make-Belief I had shared with Harry for twenty-five years ceased to be, and when I knew for certain that this was so, my own life seemed to cease. Harry's decision was not harsh, it was necessary. I did not know, in my bewilderment, that my life was about to begin when, pushed off the bright cloud of illusion, I fell through a vacuum and at last touched earth.

'It was almost too late. Not a word was said between us, not a question asked by me or a reason offered by him. The end had come like this, as unarguable as death.' [Memoir]

So Eleanor, who felt she knew and was known to her elder brother to the deepest level of their natures, was set free. Her misery and dismay were for a time overwhelming, but youthful resilience and her vitality, which could not be suppressed, burst out again, and with this release the shyness that had dogged her social life somehow disappeared. Then friendship and love emerged in the real world.

# Friends

B Y 1910 B E R T I E, aged twenty-three, had found his own circle of intimates, partly centred round the Bax household, where they played cricket, partly centred round the Corder household, where they played tennis.

The Bax brothers, Arnold and Clifford, were grandsons of a wealthy men's hatter who had a shop in the Strand; their father, Ridley Bax, had made more money by building houses. He owned a large welcoming residence in Hampstead off Haverstock Hill, Ivy Bank, in whose extensive grounds lay a cricket pitch. Like Bertie, the Bax boys were cricket fanatics and, like him, neither had had a university education: in their case from choice, not necessity. Arnold went to the Royal Academy of Music and Clifford went travelling round the world, where he picked up a taste for Eastern mysticism.

So there was art and philosophy as well as sport to attract young people to Ivy Bank. Arnold was now a composer, Clifford a poet-philosopher-aesthete. To the house came the pianists Myra Hess and Harriet Cohen, the socialist medical student Maitland Radford and his poet sister Margaret, the actor and writer Stacey Aumonier, the beautiful sisters Joan and Rosalind Thornycroft, both artists and daughters of the sculptor Hamo Thornycroft, and a doctor lately down from Cambridge, Godwin Baynes. He had been more or less adopted by Mrs Bax when his father could not afford to send him to a university.

Eleanor was introduced to this group, and the stimulation of fresh ideas and friends started all kinds of changes within her. She was not slow to make up for time lost in the mists of TAR. But, as she realised later, it was almost too late: she was twenty-nine.

The Corder household in Albion Road was headed by Frederick Corder, Harry's last professor. His son Paul, also a musician, became for a while Bertie's close friend. In Paul's garden studio, beyond the tennis court, the young people collected to discuss art and life. Here came Arnold Bax, the violinist Aldo Antonietti and his handsome sisters, Eleanor, Joe, Bertie, with Dodds Corder, who was an amusing gossip and great theatre-goer. On the tennis court Bertie was the best, Eleanor the worst player. The studio had been built by Paul, for he was a craftsman, an excellent joiner, weaver and engineer. It was furnished with folk handicrafts and artistic decorations. There were handwoven rugs, Kelmscott books, Burne-Jones sketches. To the world of drama, opera and concert-going was now added the influence of Diaghilev's Russian ballets, with their riotous russo-eastern design and colour, the supreme dancers, choreographers and musicians. Bakst's designs were displayed, Russian garments worn.

It was for studio entertainments that the collaboration between Eleanor and Bertie began. Together they wrote words for patriotic parodies, Eleanor composing the music. Myra Hess would beg Bertie to sing her favourite comic song *Bill Bloggs* again and again, while Eleanor's proudest moment was when Arnold Bax gravely announced, "You know, Nellie writes better tunes than any of us." Two parodies have survived: *Thank God that I'm an Englishman* and *The Coastguard's Song*, both of which were later utilised in Bertie's revues.

### THE COASTGUARD

*There's a man we daily meet with*
*Who is England's pride and boast,*
*He is one of the silent heroes*
*Who guards and patrols our coast;*
*When the ships go down at midnight*
*He's the first to sound the alarm,*
*And he buttons his coat*
*As they man the boat*
*And he takes his dear wife in his arm —*

*"Oh mother!*
*We can't let the ships go down, mother!*
*We can't let the ships go down!*
*There's a wick to light*
*In the lamp tonight,*
*We can't let the sailors drown, dear mother!*
*So it's up with the flag on the flagstaff –*
*I'm the servant of King and Crown!*
*There's a better word than beauty*
*And the word I mean is duty –*
*So, we can't let the ships go down!"*

*What is that? 'Tis a cry in the darkness!*
*'Tis the cry of his little son*
*Who has fallen into the foaming deep –*
*Yet his life may still be won.*
*What is that? 'Tis a flare in the blackness*
*And a rocket falls like rain!*
*Can it be? Yes! Yes!*
*It's a ship in distress,*
*And the coastguard's course is plain –*

*"Oh mother!*
*We can't let the ships go down, mother!*
*We can't let the ships go down!*
*There's a wick to light*
*In the lamp tonight –*
*We must let our little one drown, dear mother!*
*And it's up with the flag on the flagstaff –*
*I'm the servant of King and Crown!*
*There's a better word than beauty,*
*And the word I mean is duty!*
*So, we can't let the ships go down!"*

From the Bax brothers Eleanor received literary encouragement at this time. Clifford, who did not live with his parents but had a house in Chelsea, invited her to visit him. He was twenty-three and publishing *Orpheus*, subtitled 'A Magazine of Mystical Art'.

In her memoir Eleanor wrote: 'I went uneasily to Jubilee Place. I knew that Clifford was charming and gentle, but also choice and exclusive. He knew positively where he was going; what would he make of my flounderings in a mass of uncertainties? Longing to run away, I rang the bell. Clifford opened the door, and we struck up a lasting friendship on the step. We spoke the same language – I in ignorance, he in experience – in our love of poetry, of Greek and Elizabethan classics, and of our intimations of immortality.' She was soon as easy with him as with her own brothers.

From Arnold she received help with her latest fanciful novel, written under the influence of the modern mystical Irish writers; for after his recommendation to friends in Dublin, it was serialised in *The Irish Review*. James Stephens spoke of *The Soul of Kol Nikon* as 'a work of Janius'. There is a select band who find this work delightful, but I find it as unreadable as did Edward Thomas when he gently but firmly told Eleanor that he could not read more of The Little Grey Man who 'sank his hand in the moon-ray and drew forth a silver horn and offered it to Kol'. Another remarkable scene was on Mild Bertha's lap when 'Kol Nikon climbed intoxicated into the sweetness and dabbled among the flowers with his hands and lips . . . then lifting his head saw the swell of her green-clad bosom heave softly above him, and such a longing for it was on him he knew not how to satisfy . . .'

Clifford Bax appealed to Eleanor's immortal longings. He kept a book of his friends' horoscopes and as a Theosophist was interested in the occult. Eleanor told him how her mother had been terrified by seances in her youth, though now the family sometimes played at table-turning. Of course Mrs Farjeon, Harry, Joe and Eleanor played strictly fair, but when Bertie joined them remarkable messages came through from the other side.

Such larks did not deter Eleanor from her belief in powers on the Other Side. She took seriously a character analysis made by an unknown sewing woman in Wiltshire, who only had to handle letters to understand a disposition. Both Eleanor and Bertie were Platonists at this time and shared spiritual searchings which he later abandoned and she, much later, confirmed. She was attracted to the idea of re-incarnation as a possible answer to imperfect man striving towards perfection.

Out of many smatterings I was slowly discovering my spiritual convictions, just as, in a different way, I was slowly discovering myself as a writer. Plotinus's doctrine of emanation from a Supreme Deity satisfied me of the flow of spirit throughout the universe, and its existence in all human beings. For a while it was enough. I thought of the spiritual flow as Love, and the Supreme Being as God. It seems strange to me now that in my search for immortal love, nothing had led me yet to read the Gospels.

"Do you ever feel," Bertie asked me, "that the world was made especially for You?"

"No, not more than for everybody else."

"I feel it was made for me." [Memoir]

Bertie was obviously the more arrogant and sure of himself at this period. But his sister was already following his advanced ideas on socialism, art, women's rights and sex, till both were emancipated from the stolid Victorian principles upheld by their mother and Harry.

And now Eleanor fell in love for the first time and wrote sonnets to the loved one. Who he was is not known, and those few who could have told are dead. Godwin Baynes is one of my many discarded candidates, who in any case was now a most important influence. In *Edward Thomas: The Last Four Years* Eleanor wrote of him as 'the sun-god of our brilliant circle. This giant rowing-blue from Cambridge (six-foot-four in his socks), with a heart and brain to match his physical prowess, was the most popular man I have ever known. When he was talking to you he compelled you to feel that you were more interesting to him than any other person in the room, and I still think that at the given moment this was almost true.' 'Almost' is an important word here, for Baynes was a man who aroused strong emotions and, quite often, disillusionment. In 1912, in a Galway church, he married Rosalind Thornycroft on a whirlwind of romance and Celtic Twilight, she wrapped in an Irish peasant shawl.

Among Eleanor's papers there is a menu dated March 25th 1913, which was almost certainly composed and typed by her. What the special occasion for this dinner was cannot be surmised, but the jollification was plainly in honour of Godwin Baynes, the sun-god doctor who, because of his height, was known as 'Tiny'. All the songs and speeches would have been comic or satirical:

| MENU | TOASTS |
|---|---|
|  |  |

| | |
|---|---|
| *Hors d'oeuvres Anastatique* | "THE KING" |
| | Mr Paul Corder |
| *Petit Marmit Empyema* | "THE QUEEN" |
| *Crème Mal de Mer* | Mr Herbert Farjeon |
| | "THE ARMY AND NAVY" |
| *Filet Sole Pagani* | Mr Arnold Bax |
| | "OUR COLONIAL |
| *Noisette de Cholera Germ* | POSSESSIONS" |
| *Haricot Gangrene* | Mr Maitland Radford |
| *Pommes "Tiny"* | "THE GUEST OF THE |
| | EVENING" |
| *Poulet passé aux Enfers* | Mr Stacey Aumonier |
| *Salade* | DR GODWIN BAYNES |
| | will Retort |
| *Pêche Melba* | "THE COSMIC EQUATION" |
| *Croûte Notary* | Mr Lynn Hartley |
| | "THE COMMERCIAL |
| *Scruts* | PROSPERITY OF THE |
| | BRITISH PEOPLE" |
| *Desserts: Hluss, Badajos, Hunkh,* | Mr Clifford Bax |
| *Oids, Djemli (with or without* | "TURKISH WOMEN" |
| *Djeli), Djeli (with or without* | Mr Francis Colmer |
| *Djam), Djam (with or without* | "LADY W." |
| *Djemli).* | Major Ford |

| WINES | |
|---|---|
| *Lymph, extra sec, 1863* | During the evening the Russian |
| *Sparkling quinine* | Ballet (engagements |
| | permitting) will dance |
| | "Scheherazade", "Prince Igor", |
| | etc., etc. |

Baynes, who loved and was much loved by women, went in for romantic paganism. One woman in love with him for years was a painter, Olive Hockin, with whom Eleanor now and then shared a lonely life in the Berkshire woods. Seeing how she lacked physical courage, Olive Hockin determined to get her friend over some of these fears. Producing rugs and sleeping bags, she informed Eleanor that they were sleeping out. 'It was my first night in the open. I did not sleep much, and did not want to. Every sleeping moment was a waste of the difference from all I had been used to. In the early morning Olive stripped and plunged into the lake; I did too, but slipped more timorously into the water's brink, and when I found it shelving out of reach took my bath under the trees. In the middle of the lake, quite far away, a flat stone rose from a hidden base, like a little altar. "There's something on it!" called Olive; "Someone has been there." She swam out, and presently came back smiling. "It's a crown of wild parsley. Godwin has been sacrificing to the deity. Swim out and see." But I could only manage a few strokes in salt water, and in fresh none. Olive tried to persuade me to let her carry me on her back, assuring me that she was strong enough to bear me, but I feared my own fear if I lost confidence and clutched her. These were the days when I dreamed of becoming a poet, but not of playing Arion to Olive's dolphin. She laughed and swam out again to the crowned altar, and I was alone among the reeds.'[1]

This sacrifice to Pan accorded with Eleanor's burst of paganism in the earlier poem, *Pan-Worship*. But whoever it was roused her first adult love, one result was thirteen sonnets of far more worth than anything yet composed. Number IV expresses the daze in which this emotion wrapped her.

> *Be patient with me. This is still too new.*
> *Oh, if I fail to wear when you are near*
> *The early comradeship, to find the clue*
> *To laughter, to change clouded eyes for clear,*
> *Remember I am going in such a dream*
> *As puts bewilderment upon my days,*
> *And the old habits, an uncaptured stream,*
> *Flow in some outer region seen through haze.*

1. *Edward Thomas: The Last Four Years.* Referred to hereafter as [ET].

*I will resolve this presently; will learn*
*Not to outwear you in this instant mood,*
*And loving you, with all my strength will turn*
*The loving of you only into good;*
*Will hear you laugh, and laugh with you as well,*
*And make the time that was, still possible.*

In 1911 Clifford Bax published a book of Eleanor's poetry, *Dream-Songs of the Beloved*, in which none of her sonnets were included. These poems seem to me immature, for she still takes over the male lover's role, as she had done ever since in TAR Harry played Titania to her Oberon. The poem *Silence* is the one which expresses a new sensibility.

*Words and the body always have been much pain to me,*
*Little fetters and drags on immensities*
*Never to be defined. I am done with these.*
*Meanings of silence suddenly all grow plain to me.*

*Something still may sing like a joyous flute in me*
*Out of the life that dares to be voiced aloud,*
*But speech no more shall swathe like a burial-shroud.*
*Things unencompassable now are eloquent-mute in me.*

# Edward Thomas

RUMOUR GOT ABOUT that Godwin Baynes was analysing a new patient who suffered from depression. When missed from parties and meetings he was treating this patient. The man turned out to be a writer, Edward Thomas.

Thomas had married when he was nineteen and now, aged thirty-five, lived with his wife and three children in a Hampshire cottage earning a meagre income from reviewing books, writing essays, or commissions from publishers such as *The Life of Marlborough* or *The Feminine Influence on the Poets*. He complained of this work, yet wrote beautiful prose.

At times bad moods and melancholy took on the magnitude of a serious psychiatric disturbance and cures were mooted: holidays, pills, analysis, a vegetarian diet. Often, to escape from his family and guilt at the suffering he caused, Thomas would stay with friends. In London he would meet Belloc, Masefield, D. H. Lawrence, W. H. Davies, Walter de la Mare and Edward Garnett; writers who liked to talk together. He himself was a splendid talker, but he was bitter about his failure as an author. Once, when asked for advice on becoming a journalist, he replied, "You need three things: facility, servility and money." He had none of these.

It was through Bertie that Eleanor met him. The men struck up a friendship, cemented by their mutual love of Shakespeare and fishing: while staying in the country they would sneak away before breakfast to catch trout. In London they met for meals, and on one occasion Eleanor accompanied her brother. In *The Last Four Years*, Eleanor's published memoir about Thomas, she wrote of this meeting: 'My first impressions were of his tall easy figure, his tawny colour, the grave pleasant tones of his voice, and a swift sidelong glance from his keen eyes when Bertie introduced us. Talk was rather diffident till we reached the tea-rooms, where Godwin's presence glowed on and put us at our ease. I don't remember anything he said, but to look at and listen to Edward was enough; he had a higher degree of beauty of person, voice and mind than I had ever known combined in anybody, or have known since.'

It was 1912 and Joe had married a Boston girl, Fan Woods, whose relatives had long been friends of the Jeffersons. When Joe left Fellows Road the balance of the family altered: it became less cohesive with the appeasing brother gone. For Eleanor some sort of escape was overdue. Aged thirty-one she described herself as emotionally immature as a girl of eighteen, although her shyness was past. Joan Thornycroft knew her at this period as full of talk and bounce when in company.

Eleanor was attracted to Edward Thomas. They met at Fellows Road and Ivy Bank. From the paper games that were played at Bax gatherings there remain two sheets on which each member of the party had been allotted scores for certain chosen characteristics. Eleanor kept these score sheets, the first of which gave the following results.

|  | Pride | Vanity | Ostentation | Joie de vivre | Christianity | Paganism | Will | Fire | Grit | Adaptability |
|---|---|---|---|---|---|---|---|---|---|---|
| Eleanor | 3 | 0 | 0 | $8\frac{1}{2}$ | 8 | 2 | 7 | 8 | 9 | 6 |
| Godwin | 4 | 0 | 2 | 10 | 5 | 5 | 9 | 7 | 8 | 8 |
| Arnold | 5 | 5 | 3 | $6\frac{1}{2}$ | 3 | 7 | 4 | 9 | 5 | 4 |
| Peter (Bertie) | 8 | 0 | 0 | 6 | 6 | 4 | 6 | 5 | 8 | 4 |
| Rosalind | 6 | 1 | 2 | 7 | 3 | 7 | 6 | 5 | 8 | 5 |
| Clifford | 8 | 5 | 2 | 6 | 8 | 2 | 8 | $1\frac{1}{2}$ | 7 | 6 |

On the second chart Thomas comes in and receives low marks for everything.

| Edward | 5 | 0 | 0 | 2 | 3 | 5 | 4 | 0 | 4 | 3 |
|---|---|---|---|---|---|---|---|---|---|---|

Edward Thomas

Soon Thomas and Eleanor were corresponding in between meetings for lunch or tea. He ceased to address her as Miss Farjeon and began to talk about his work, his children and his wife's unfortunate passion for pregnancy. "During the nine months before her baby is born, her face is one perpetual smile. My wife could be the happiest woman on earth – and I won't let her."

Such confidences did not come easily to Thomas, but it is a noticeable fact that reserved bookish Englishmen of sensibility are often attracted to a very different kind of woman, whose vitality or even crudity can in some way comfort or release them from their deadening unease or refinement. Thomas did not feel a reciprocal sexual attraction to Eleanor, it was her enthusiasm and admiration, her good humour, intelligence, wit and openly loving spirit that won him. By these qualities he was soothed, warmed and encouraged.

In *The Last Four Years* Eleanor wrote: 'I wonder now how the sort of person I was could have become a companion to the sort of man Edward was. No one was quicker than he to distinguish what was genuine from what was sham; and to a quarter-century spent in unreal dreams I added a lamentable ignorance of the realities he loved best. I couldn't tell a sycamore from an ash, and was apt to write of trees as temples of Pan. But I could walk and carry a knapsack, and thanks to my father had been brought up on nothing second-rate in poetry.'

They both stayed at Clifford Bax's country house in Wiltshire for a cricket week in August 1912. The matches were arranged by Clifford, whose literary team was not chosen entirely for its sporting skill. Part of his plan was to get to know the lovely English villages more or less within reach of London and, when these had been carefully picked, to write a letter to the local cricket club offering an engagement with the Manor House eleven. So Bertie, Thomas, the Baxes, Radford and others met to enjoy the people, the pubs, each other's company and sport in a variety of beautiful surroundings. Thomas was not a joyful cricketer and his scores for the Wiltshire week were even lower than his scores for the personality game. But on this occasion he taught Eleanor to map read and they trudged contentedly about the open country.

Hoping to help, Eleanor risked discussing some of Thomas's emotional problems and commented on the fact that he was seeing less of Godwin Baynes.

"Godwin can't help me," Thomas said. "When he first came to see me he made me feel that I was the most important person in the world to him. As I came to know his world I found he gave the same impression to everybody – and I don't like being one of a crowd."

In Thomas's marriage there were tensions very much increased by poverty. Luckily Helen Thomas was a skilful manager and took pleasure in domesticity, making her home charming and creating excellent meals out of little. Eleanor wrote that Helen's deeply wise humanity came from life not literature: 'The wisdom was in her hands when they were making bread, or sewing, or digging, and in her voice when she was comforting her baby.' [ET]

It was a year before the women met for the first time. A letter from Helen was 'short, and warm and touchingly humble. She hoped I would not be disappointed in her, she wasn't intellectual, but "very primitive". I wondered, with a slight pang, what sort of woman she imagined me to be. I soon came to know how little at ease her simple nature felt itself among Edward's more sophisticated friends.' [ET]

The meeting between the two women was to be on Petersfield station, but when Eleanor got out of the railway carriage there was no one who could be mistaken for Thomas's wife.

'Helen had always too much to do to be punctual; for her a coming guest meant breathless preparations, a bedroom full of flowers, an oven full of cakes, everything shining that could be made to shine. I hitched on my knapsack, and as I crossed the line saw a quick energetic figure scurrying towards me on the Bell Hill road. I waved my stick, called "Helen!" – and she called back "Eleanor!" – we met laughing, and embraced, and after that looked at each other.' [ET]

Helen Thomas's description of this encounter in *Time and Again* gives her view.

I knew her as soon as I saw her walking with quick steps and an eager expression on her face. Her skin and hair and eyes were dark. The hair was black and done in a careless bun from which strands escaped. She looked very gipsyish in her bright cotton dress and thick walking shoes with a large rucksack on her back.

"You are Eleanor," I said and "You are Helen," she replied and from that moment all shyness and diffidence fell from me and I felt utterly at ease with this girl – for though thirty years old she had the complete unselfconsciousness and eager inquiring manner of a much younger woman. She talked of Edward and I of the children and soon we were at the cottage. She loved the tiny house and flung her arms around my neck in her impulsive way, to show how happy she was to be there.

Soon the children came in and Bronwen and Myfanwy found that she was the perfect companion for a child. She could draw and cut out all sorts of things in paper, she could sing and play all sorts of games and best of all she could tell enchanting stories. No wonder they adored her. She loved them and never grew impatient of their constant demands. For Edward and me she was just as perfect a guest. Her witty, vivacious talk and eager appreciation of our simple ways made her the easiest person to entertain. Indeed the entertaining came rather from her than from her hosts. For her abounding vitality and quick intelligence made her a match for Edward's talk, and I could see how they stimulated each other and how her wit delighted Edward and banished for a time his deep seated melancholy.[1]

Thomas showed the first sign of irritability that night at supper. 'Some nothing Helen said or did, or hadn't done, caused it. It took me by surprise. She speaks in her book of the flash of astonishment on my face when it occurred; but it passed without spoiling the evening. At other times it did not. As my visits became more intimate, I saw how he was the greatest sufferer when he could not help "inflicting five persons at once". Bronwen, a child of eleven, who adored her father and was adored by him, seemed to know by instinct that the way to help irritability is not to be hurt by it.' [ET]

Of these continuing Hampshire visits Helen Thomas wrote that at the sound of Edward calling as he came down from his hilltop study, Eleanor's 'whole being would come alert, her eyes shining and her expression assuming an expectancy most tender and deeply moving. I could not feel any jealousy of the girl's love for Edward. For one thing jealousy is not part of my nature and for another I realised the innocence of this inexperienced girl's emotion.

'She gave no thought to anything but the present and the rapture of being near the first man she met whose mind kindled her and

1. *Time and Again* by Helen Thomas. Carcanet Press, 1978.

whose affectionate manner fed her own unsatisfied heart, and who was moreover a man of great physical beauty with an elusive charm which made him beloved among a large circle of friends. Edward was aware of Eleanor's devotion, but with the most sensitive tact kept it at a lighthearted level which she happily accepted.' [*Time and Again*]

This passion absorbed Eleanor and a steady stream of letters passed back and forth. In her memoir she quotes almost two hundred from Thomas which cover the four year period of their friendship. Unfortunately only his half of the correspondence exists, but this shows how extremely attached he became, how often arrangements were being made for their next rendezvous. Eleanor needed to love and Thomas needed devotion. But they guarded their relationship carefully and interest was often channelled into literature and the practical difficulties of a writer's life. Eleanor was well primed as to editors and publishers and could help with her ideas and knowledge, encouraging persistence with a book of stories for children based on proverbs, *Four and Twenty Blackbirds*, which Heinemann published.

Thomas suggested that, on one of her lonely cross-country walks, she visit his friend, James Guthrie, at The White House in Flansham, West Sussex. So one day she knocked at the door unexpectedly, to be welcomed into a world of seething artistic activity: painting, printing, writing and music. Here was another family to be embraced by her affections and boys to be taken on as sons. The following picture was written by the eldest boy after a visit.

'. . . And then the other day Miss Farjeon turned up and spent the night and the gist of a day, so we have been quite flooded with people. Miss Farjeon is great fun. She stumps along with her knapsack and her chalala (shillelagh?) in her hand, looking for all the world like a pilgrim. And in she comes, straightway, and goes into the pantry and eats a pancake and a little pastry off a tart and lights a cigarette – she lights a pipe sometimes – and talks and shouts and laughs and turns the place into a very haunt of merriment. She is one of the most marvellous personalities I know.'

Although now deeply in love, living through the whole Thomas family as an extension of her desire, although bubbling with enthusiasm for the new experiences which were crowding her life, Eleanor was not as blind in her raptures as she appeared, for although on every emotional wave words came in a theatrical gush, her intelligence seldom ceased to function and a sound instinct for self-preservation always worked against her impulsive nature.

In the summer of 1913 there was also a first visit to Wilfrid and Alice Meynell's Sussex estate at Greatham, on which homes had been built for their now grown-up children. On this occasion Viola, the daughter who was Eleanor's especial friend, took her guest to see a five-year-old niece whose knee had been cut by a rusty scythe. The little girl lay very ill in bed, for the wound had gone septic. The two visitors sang a song with the white, big-eyed invalid. As they walked away from the cottage both were weeping.

Next day the medical student, Maitland Radford, arrived, ready to accompany Eleanor on a ramble to Lewes where they intended to join Edward Thomas. But when he was taken to see the sick child the walk was at once abandoned. There were urgent telephone calls and that afternoon a surgeon arrived from London. Immediate arrangements were made to take Sylvia into hospital.

This was the incident D. H. Lawrence used in his story *England my England*, spoiling his intimacy with the Meynells who had so befriended him. That such tactlessness was half-consciously motivated is likely for, as Bertie wrote, 'Lawrence never forgot or forgave a good turn.'[1]

Eleanor was always strongly affected when the young suffered, whether physically or mentally. The next time she met Thomas everything his son did seemed to irk. Later she questioned, "Don't you think you are unnecessarily hard on Mervyn?" to which he wearily replied, "Perhaps I am – but I dare say it gives him something to kick against."

However, her words took effect, for in Thomas's next letter there is mention of what a good walk he and his son had just had and how they didn't annoy each other.

A poem written around this time suggests that Eleanor had come to know one aspect of herself well.

> *She had no life except to be what men*
> *Required of her to be,*
> *They came for sympathy, and came again*
> *For sympathy.*

1. *The Twisted Genius*, an article by Herbert Farjeon.

*She never knew the way her heart to spare*
*When they were hurt or worn,*
*Whatever one may for another bear*
*By her was borne.*

Young Bronwen, sharing her father's love of wild flowers, was shocked to discover her favourite visitor's botanical ignorance. She decided to set the matter right and, gathering a hundred specimens, gave her an intensive lesson. Next day a ruled examination paper was produced. Eleanor wrote that with a memory for names like wax she topped 90, and Bronwen was proud of her pupil. An appreciation of Bronwen was expressed in the poem *Bronwen of the Flowers*: it is pretty and soppy and veers off into those stock characters – virgins and merry dames. A poem of this date dedicated to Myfanwy, the baby of the family, is more original.

### MYFANWY AMONG THE LEAVES

*Dying leaf and dead leaf,*
*Yellow leaf and red leaf*
*And white-backed beam,*
*Lay along the woodland road*
*As quiet as a dream.*

*Summer was over,*
*The year had lost her lover,*
*Spent with her grief*
*All along the woodland road*
*Leaf fell on leaf.*

*Then came a shuffling,*
*Such a happy ruffling*
*Of the dried sweet*
*Surf of leaves upon the road*
*Round a baby's feet.*

*Year-old leaf ran after*
*Three-year-old laughter,*
*Danced through the air*
*As she caught them from the road*
*And flung them anywhere.*

*Old leaf and cold leaf*
*Brown leaf and gold leaf*
*And white-backed beam,*
*Followed down the woodland road*
*Myfanwy in a dream.*

In the introduction to her selection of Edward Thomas's poems there is a recollection of being educated by him in country ways. 'Just as certain friends who share their thoughts with you will sharpen your thinking, he had the effect, when you took the road together, of quickening your seeing and hearing through his own keen eyes and ears. You would not walk that road again as you did before. You would know it in a new way.'[1]

It was on being presented with his book *Light and Twilight* that Eleanor asked, "Haven't you ever written poetry, Edward?"

"Me? I couldn't write a poem to save my life."

But she had realised his book was full of poetry.

A year later the American poet, Robert Frost, saw this too and said to his friend, "You've been writing as good poetry as any man living, and didn't know it."

So between them Eleanor and Frost set Thomas off on the finest of all his literary forms.

1. *The Green Roads*: Poems by Edward Thomas. Bodley Head, 1965.

*16*

# Poets

ROBERT FROST AND EDWARD THOMAS met late in 1913. Both were poor and neglected writers, both had a wife and three children to support. They became immediate friends, and as they walked, ate and sat up late they pursued poetry indefatigably. It was with the understanding of how Frost used language for his own poetic ends that Thomas began to use words in a new way.

In *The Last Four Years* Eleanor recorded that in September 1914 Thomas wrote his first poem. 'Now he hastened every day to his study on the hill, to review other men's poetry because he had to, and pour out his own because he couldn't help it. He could hardly wait, he wrote, to light his fire before he began. "It has perhaps become a really bad habit." From March 1915 it was almost as though he was writing against time.

'The dark moods that had tormented him lightened with this release into self-expression.'

Frost has been given credit for the discovery of Thomas as a poet, while Eleanor's earlier discernment, her help and encouragement have been lightly dismissed. But Thomas was one of the lucky first in a long list of men and women to benefit from the perspicacity of the now confident Eleanor.

When the Thomases joined the Frosts for a holiday on the Gloucestershire border in August 1914 there were other poets living nearby, and Eleanor rented rooms with Mrs Farmer in Ledington. In one of her long letters, 29th August, 1914, to Maitland Radford, now a doctor with the British army in France, she described the two families:

Five minutes away across the meadows and near no road at all, are the Thomases on another farm, where the cider is inferior to the cider I drink here twice a day by the jugful; and one minute up the road in a small cottage are the Frosts, a dear family and worth coming a long way to know. Americans of his type reconcile me to America – or go a long way towards it; and he is better even than his work. I am sure the people who do really fine work always are, or they couldn't have done the fine work – people can't produce above themselves. But that lets in the bad workers too, so this generality leads nowhere. I do sincerely hope that the bad workers are better than themselves; if they aren't, all the "poets" in England who have been writing war "poetry" are damned for ever and ever; especially Harold Begbie. I like Mrs Frost too, but how fragile and worn she is. Yet their habit of life is a very easy one, though it has all the hallmarks of real poverty; and he must be a very easy man to live with. Is it the children or what? It does baffle me to see women worn and worn by life, while men still keep their sap. They're good children too; the eldest girl is strong and sweet, and the boy a fine little resourceful fellow. He hoes potatoes and gathers plums for hours as though he loved hoeing potatoes through; it's like digging for nuggets and getting three every time. I am very much at home with the Frosts. I leave here on Tuesday, and they do, too, but they only go a few miles off to winter with the Abercrombies. This is a district of poets, but I have seen no one but Frosts since I came; they have threatened to take me to call on the Gibsons, but I did not bring my white kid gloves so it wouldn't do. I'd like to meet Abercrombie. Gibson is at present in mourning because Rupert Brooke has enlisted. Edward considers enlisting, I believe, if work is so slack that he becomes useless as a supporter of his family. Things there are very bad, in every way – worse than I have ever known them. I do not see why he and Helen don't both break down utterly. Yet such good walks and talks and occasions are possible for him and with him when he's cut off from his family.

With so many poets around, Mrs Farmer the landlady asked Eleanor whether they might not be invited to a Sunday supper party, which she would give. In fact, would Miss Farjeon invite the poets and their wives for her? The Gibsons, the Abercrombies, the Thomases and Frosts.

On Sunday Eleanor was with the Frost and Thomas children as usual. She returned to the farm to change into her best cotton frock and came downstairs to find Mrs Farmer in her apron barring the dining-room door.

"The guests will be sitting in the parlour before supper, Miss Farjeon, and as I shall be busy in the kitchen, would you be so kind as to entertain them for me?"

So saying she opened the door to the front room. It had been refurbished and dusted, a mid-Victorian parlour crowded with little tables and mahogany furniture, plush-covered chairs and sofa, over which oil lamps diffused yellow pools of light. Mrs Farmer indicated the books laid out.

"The guests may like to look at the photograph albums."

Eleanor kept a straight face as the visitors arrived and settled down to admire old photographs and converse politely in hushed voices. Then Mr Farmer was sent in by his wife. He was a countryman with bad teeth and a chuckling manner, but now he too was subdued, dressed in a thick suit and collar. He sat and perspired, and said the missus would soon have supper ready.

At last the double doors were flung wide and their powerful hostess stood in her best black bombazine, welcoming them to a table loaded with huge joints of ham and beef, pies and birds, salads, pickles and home-made bread. On the sideboard waited tarts and trifles, cheesecakes and quarts of cream. There were flagons of Eleanor's favourite rough cider.

'To pick at the food would have been to insult Mrs Farmer,' she wrote. To begin with the clatter of knives and forks took the place of conversation. But as the tankards of cider were emptied and refilled talk began to flow. To his wife's shame Mr Farmer took off his coat and collar. "Can't help it, Mother; I'm sweaty!" he beamed and, at ease now, joined in.

Finally Mrs Farmer lifted a gigantic Stilton cheese from the sideboard, which was passed from poet to poet down the table till it came to Mr Farmer. Chuckling, he too dug in his knife, gave Eleanor a wink and pronounced, "I likes it when they looks out o' their little winders and wag their tails, but I don't like it when they squeals between my teeth."

The meal ended in jubilant mirth and then the ladies rose to thank their hostess and depart. But the male poets' attempts to rise ended in collapse. They regarded one another with comical consternation. At length Frost and Thomas tottered to their feet, clutching each other for support, and set forth followed by Gibson and Abercrombie, also clinging together to keep upright.

'Two brace of poets staggered out into the moonlight and went hilariously homeward like two sets of Siamese Twins. I have boasted ever since of the night when I drank all the poets of Gloucestershire under the table.' [ET]

By the end of this holiday Eleanor's thoughts were taken up with the war. Bertie had just joined the army, and she wrote of this to Radford.[1]

'I was rather surprised at his passing the physical tests, especially as he hasn't had those varicose veins cut out; and he only just squeaked through on the eyesight. At one place he tried they took nobody with glasses, but he tried another where they were less particular. There was talk of several of the other boys joining with him – Lynn [Hartley], Major [Ford], possibly [Stanley] North, and especially Bunny [David Garnett]. Bunny and Bertie had spent the week-end at Wisbech . . . Well, while there, Bertie announced his intention of enlisting and Bunny was Bunnyesquely enthusiastic and arranged to go with Bertie on Tuesday morning; but he didn't appear, and in a letter that followed was Bunnyesquely apologetic, pommelling himself as a "rotter" and so on, bidding Bertie "chuck me up, my dear", and giving a list of reasons why he'd cooled off. But the fact that he had cooled off seems to me the sanest of all reasons, and no other matters much. Amongst them he mentioned that he'd just got a post – a salaried post – as a fungus-discoverer, and this may be vital to his family, whose income is liable to be guillotined like that of all other pen-folk.'

David Garnett, known as Bunny, was the son of the Russian translator Constance, and the bookseller Edward Garnett. He popped in and out of the Farjeons' lives, always looked on as something of a trifler, though when his first novel was published in 1922 Bertie was impressed, despite some gentle ridicule. "I see," he said, "*Lady into Fox* – Bunny into Author!"

1. Letter from E.F. to Maitland Radford, 4.9.14.

After a short period of drilling, Bertie was invalided out of the army on account of varicose veins, for which he was admitted to St Bartholomew's Hospital. Both his brothers would have been too short-sighted to be considered for war service, even by the most enthusiastic enlisting officer. Harry continued to teach at the R.A.M. and Joe continued as a journalist and author of crime fiction.

Eleanor's own war effort was short-lived owing to head and back aches. She joined The Women's Emergency Corps and in a letter described her scene of work to Radford who, being in love with Viola Meynell, would have taken a special interest.

'Then to-day I sat at my typewriter at the Little Theatre where for some hours a day I do office work for The Women's Emergency Corps – it's the only way in which I can be ever so faintly useful; and in a pause of work I looked across at another typist, and found I was getting a sort of cool restfulness from watching the lines of her as she sat; and knowing the person who most gives me that particular pleasure I said, "Hallo, Prue"[1] and she made a suitable rejoinder, and soon after your address materialised. It is very jolly to have found her there, and the days have become something to look forward to. But anyhow I'm glad to be there; it's a relief to be driven through endless routine work at a pace that doesn't let you sit and wonder what on earth you should do next and why; though it's *very* stodgy routine work.'[2]

Viola Meynell also wrote to Radford of this encounter, recording that everyone took Eleanor the most difficult work 'because she takes it so smilingly and is at the same time the most competent of all.'

Maitland Radford was important to many of his friends, having an eye, so John Wheeler later wrote, for relating the small everyday things to the larger principles of life. In *The Last Four Years* there is a description of how disconcertingly illuminating Radford could be about people. 'His swift tongue cut clean through sentimentality to the heart of whatever was under discussion, social or psychological.' In one letter he warned Eleanor against the tendency to sentimentalise herself. 'Whatever you do, Nellie, as you grow older – don't go *cosy*.' But he never succeeded in reforming that, for the anxiety to placate went too deep. Another caution came against destroying

1. Viola Meynell, daughter of Alice and Wilfrid Meynell.
2. Letter from E.F. to Maitland Radford, 4.9.14.

herself through too much sympathy. 'One day when I was going to visit Sylvia Lucas in the hospital I saw your face as you were leaving her room,' he wrote. Radford was a man of great charm and quickness. The following undated wartime letter came from his Hampstead home in Well Walk, where he and his two sisters lived with their parents. The letter seems to have been written after he returned to England in 1916, thoroughly disgusted with war.


Dear Nellie,

Thank you very much for the two books.

I said a great deal that was quite unjust on Thursday and that is not part of my everyday thoughts at all. I should like to tell you that. The world is so horrible, devilish. This numb brutality going on and on till it is a sort of nightmare that there is nothing sweet left to believe in. And then I suddenly see this unreality in my personal life and I feel quite frantic. I get it out of proportion. I should like you to know that I recognise that. It doesn't last.

I think I am really writing to you because you said Prue was your best friend. That is something to believe in. Make it real, Nellie, *make* it stand for fine things. Shall I tell you the worst thought I have ever had of you? It is that your love for people is not exacting enough – that it helps them to be self-satisfied and cosy. If you are Prue's friend I want to think that you are seeking good together.

Don't write about this – I don't think so. Unless you are angry with me. If you are not write and say that it is a fine day.

Maitland

Maitland's younger sister Margaret also had a strong hold on Eleanor's affection. She was a wild and fascinating character, who later went so mad that she was shut up in lunatic asylums, from which she would escape to sleep on Hampstead Heath, haunting old friends at meal times. Dressed in rags, her eyes gleaming from a face dark with grime, she was an alarming figure of my childhood. Eleanor was one of the few who never refused to answer the door when she knocked and stayed for hours, unable to stop talking. Eleanor's letters to France in 1914 chiefly concern Margaret, for she knew how anxious Radford was for his frail sister.

My dear Maitland,

I'm out with myself for not having written to you last week. It was not one of my best weeks and you must forgive me. Saying even that seems odd, though, for when I write to you I have a sense of groping after a sort of disembodied spirit passing through an existence of which I know nothing in a world which I cannot conceive. My letters go out at random like shooting-stars. They seem as likely to hit Mars or Uranus as your quarter of the earth . . .

A day or two ago I walked to No. 32 to arrange about trains, and found Margaret in a very clear gay mood making a suit for a Belgian boy out of a green curtain. Your mother seemed to doubt whether Belgian boys had legs that shape but Margaret insisted that they must have because she had cut them out by a pattern – "Nature may err but Buttericks cannot lie" was the spirit of her argument. She is very eager about Coldharbour, and is going to pack a pair of knickerbockers because she suddenly remembered a pony, brown, fat and glossy like a chestnut, who lives there. There is also a white pony, she says, but I have no knickerbockers. After we had tea and Margaret had read me her new book of very lovely poems – (she does make the heavenliest pictures out of her vivid delicate thought, and if her ear were as good as her eyes I believe I'd never have a word of criticism to offer) – we went to her dressmakers where I saw the last fitting of the dress which Prue and Lobbie [Olivia Meynell] and I helped, or didn't help her choose. At least I can't be sure whether the beautiful deep blue was my choice, or Prue's, or neither's. It's made very plain and graceful – do you care about this, though? You would if you saw her in it. She looks like a stained glass saint by Burne Jones.

*Shed Hall Greatham, Pulboro, Sussex*
*Monday, October 12th 1914*

My dear Mait,

I think this letter will be written in scraps, but it is better to begin it. You will see where I am, but first I'll write of where I was. A week with Margaret in Coldharbour, and instantly after a week with Prue in Greatham, is like being left Carnegie's fortune on top of Rothschild's. But that's the lovely luck I'm having now. Shall I tell you what your little sister Margaret is like? She is half an angel and half a changeling, and altogether a child. She's a flame in a sheath of spun glass. She has a more delicate fancy and a more nipping wit than will ever come into combination again. She talks more than is good for her, oh Lord much more! The loveliest sight in the world is to see her laughing, curled up in a deep armchair like a squirrel, in her blue gown, her chin almost on her knees, her head bent sideways, her hair loose, a very transparent flush on her face, her eyes half screwed up and glancing their merriment. – Dear me, it is like having a butterfly in one's care, a very delicate responsibility, Maitland, and a magical experience. Her spirits are too vivid for her fragile body, but at the end of the week I began to feel that with a string of such weeks on those high hills in that dry sparkling weather her body would get abreast of her spirits. On the journey down I was a little anxious, because to go in a taxi, to go in a train, to leave home at all, seemed to have become such an unaccustomed thing to her; but she was more happy than fearful, so that when she went through the ticket-gate a soldier on the platform said to her, "What will you do when you're old, darling?" She never will be, any more than your Mother will be. There's something about you Radfords. – The first evening she was very tired, and there were of course other times when she was tired too, but they lessened during the week. Every day was perfect for sunshine, and every night for moonlight. We would walk a few minutes and find, one morning a meadow full of lovely slopes and cows and calves; another a deep lane full of acorns and burning beech; another a common very brilliant with bracken and blackberries looking across all England lying below in mist and sunlight, till the downs lounged up like a blue wall and stopped one from seeing to the end of the world; or else a very still pinewood, where we played our flutes in a hollow until the buzzing air called us out in search of aeroplanes – six of them from Aldershot. One we saw as plainly as I see you (as they say); and one we thought we saw; and several more we heard. And an ancient cottager strained vaguely after her daughter's finger pointing to the clouds, muttering: "I've never seen one yet, and I never shall – and you two young ladies might do each other a kindness and brush one another's backs."

These tiny rambles, with flutes and a book of poetry, and a paint box, and a pencil and pad, might happen once or twice a day, with a trip to the post-office as an extra, and perhaps five minutes on the road before bed to look at the moon. And we drove a good deal, once to Ockley by day, and once to Dorking by dusk (Herbert Watson came down on the Saturday for three or four hours, and stayed twenty-eight, and had to go back from Dorking on the Sunday evening, so drove us over); and once round Leith Hill by moonlight; and once we drove all day all over Surrey, through places called Abinger Hatch and Holmbury St Mary; at which last we had tea at the Holly Bush and looked at a "Cottage" for Margaret which she could rent at £100 a year instead of £10. "But that's all nonsense, Eleanor, and in a few years prices will fall." And home under one of the really rare sunsets of a lifetime, Margaret breaking into a wild foam of nonsense verse, I flinging back the spray at her every other line. It was cold when we reached home, and dark, but there was a lamp in the window and hot supper on the table and such a fire in the grate. We said to each other: "Early to bed to-night, Margaret." "Yes, early to bed to-night, Eleanor", and at nine I turned out the lamp, and we were almost gone when that fire leapt up and suddenly Margaret ran back to it and said "I'll tell you a story" – and she told me one, and another, and then in her voice as innocent of tune, but as strange and sweet to hear as the wind, she began to sing – such songs, pure improvised fancy, lovely tales of towns by the sea where the cobbles are like fish-scales and maids with flowers and ribbons in their hair run down and put their hands in the foam and wish their true-loves home; and of a princess on a green grass-plot with a glass bell in her hand, with which she rang a hundred miracles out of elf-land; and odd snatches like nursery-rhymes, as brief and aimless –

> "A tailor sat a' stitching with his thimble
> And a bear came in at door,
> So he popped up very quick and nimble,
> And never was seen any more" –

this coming and vanishing very swiftly in the middle of longer ballads. She concluded with an amazing song which she commenced by thumping my knee hard, declaiming resolutely –

111

*"One day there was a man*
*Who said I will be God"* –

I wish I could tell you the whole of that one. But that evening, Mait, was like a rout of folk-lore. They were songs and scraps and fancies that never could be written down, though they came almost without a halt: but they might be sung again, slightly varied, and so descend from generation to generation of Radfords and become part of the delight of one corner of England. And in centuries to come some young sprout of Cecil Sharp [folk song collector] might collect them from some old sprout of a Radford, and preserve them for ever under "Folk-Songs of Hampstead, Vol IV". She improvised for an hour and a half.

Another night she gave me the most brilliantly amusing description of her schooldays, her school, her school mistresses (each a vivid and unmistakeable flash – her gym-mistress, for instance – "a woman, you know, Eleanor, who was constantly being arrested for masquerading as a woman"); and herself as a schoolgirl. She was irresistible about herself, and wound up with a picture of herself arriving late, jumping up from her chair, seizing books and coats and mufflers from anywhere, flinging them on anyhow, and slogging up to the school door with distraught vague eyes – she looked no more than fourteen, I promise you. – Another night she demanded of me the commonest popular songs I knew, and I sang her Bertie's and my self-made repertoire complete. I believe I was in form that night, for certainly neither of us ever had such an audience.

And when last Tuesday we'd done with all the tremors of trains and taxis again, she skipped gaily up Well Walk, and so differently from the way she'd arrived at Coldharbour, that it warmed the cockles of one's heart. I left her in the hands of a lovely person called Harriet. It is insufficient to have seen Harriet for two mere half-hours in one's life.

I see plainly this letter must end here. It is Margaret's letter. But Prue, who is in the room (*her* room in *her* homestead, such a perfect room) says, "You must write him a little of Greatham next." I will soon.

Here are our greetings. I found yours on my return from Coldharbour, and was glad of them.

With love, Nellie

The next letter written on October 25th 1914 from Fellows Road was euphoric.

My dear Maitland,

Get ready for a bombshell – yes? Well then, yesterday morning at 11 o'clock Bertie and Joan [Thornycroft] were married at the Hampstead Registrar's. Please don't be acute and wisely superior and say it's no bombshell. It is quite true that many of our friends weren't surprised, because this last summer must have made certain things very evident to them; but *their* knowledge went no further than that it was quite possible, while ours extended to the point that it was highly improbable. They only made the decision two weeks ago – or rather, Joan did; and very rightly, I think, refused to wait a day longer than necessary. It does not seem possible to tell you more than bare facts. You must guess at the joy that is in us all. It is past speaking of. As for beloved Joan, I never saw such radiant beauty as hers these seven days. She came every day to be with Bertie, who only returned from Bart's yesterday week, and is still too feeble to walk much (he was three weeks in hospital); and if ever being in Joan's presence was like coming into a cowslip meadow with a fresh spring sparkling in sunlight, this week it was ten meadows with ten springs and ten suns in the sky . . .

The letter continues with a description of walks with Viola Meynell and then considers her parents, Alice and Wilfrid Meynell:

Last year I was rather timid in the midst of the Meynells, but I felt very much at ease this year, and was immensely interested and privately amused and sometimes made very sorry by my study of Meynellism. You can't help studying it if you live amongst it. Here's a secret for you to keep. I don't like Mr Meynell one tiny scrap, and I think he's a soft-voiced Tartar and a sweet-mannered humbug. Perhaps I am one too, because we contrived to get on very well together, on a sort of gently teasing basis. Water had run very low, and had to be preserved preciously, and one day when he heard me washing in three thimblefuls in the bathroom (because, hang it all there were moments when washing was an absolute necessity) he had a sort of fit in the garden below in the bosom of his family, and demanded in real agitation and wrath (wrath in a velvet gown) who was "up there turning on the hot water tap?" So I had to poke my head out of the window and defy him, and between us we worked it round into one of those jokes which alas will never be allowed to die. It is quite true that after that I used my nightly hot water bottle to wash in the mornings.

Mrs Meynell I find an extraordinary pathetic figure. The family never forgets it is her name that creates the family distinction, yet actually she is a mere figurehead in the establishment. Prue told me her Mother was never consulted about anything or her wishes considered (by her Father, I'm sure she meant). She is one of those who are affected by the war to a pitiable and quite useless state of grieving, and we played games a good deal to keep her mind off it. I played chess with her during the day, and we all played cards in the evening. I would not trust Mr M. at cards, or at croquet. Or indeed, Maitland, at most things. I like Mrs Meynell very much. I find I like all the lady Meynells . . .

Margaret Radford, who must also have stayed at Greatham in 1914, wrote to her brother: 'Mrs Meynell is making a muffler but there are said to be a great many dropped stitches and even large run-away holes in it. But Eleanor tells me that the soldier who wears it – the muffler made by England's greatest woman poet – will have round his neck a sort of worsted cat's cradle.'

In December 1915, before Christmas, Eleanor described a long weekend in Steep spent with the Thomases.

The Saturday was good, and we had a long walk, and the Traveller's Joy was like bloomy smoke all up and down the bare bushes and trees; standing on a steep slope and looking down into a valleyful of white puffs was most lovely. And at one heavenly corner was a circle of bushes where it lay thick like a bridal wreath. Edward says that corner is always beautiful, most of all when the may is out. – Sunday and Monday were very very wet and Helen was ill and low-spirited, and Edward upset and irritable, trying not to be sometimes because I was there perhaps, but not very successfully. I cannot make very much difference in that household now, they are too accustomed to me, and they are quite certain of my love – and very often after that certainty people do not bòther any more. Somehow, though, after the heavy and rather miserable days the evenings turned out peacefully and happily. Baba was at her sweetest most of the time, and Mervyn better than I've known him yet. It *is* a tragic household, Mait. I love them past speaking of, but it's heart-aching.

. . . Would you like to see some poetry and some not-poetry? When I get my copies back from Margaret or Bertie I'll send one or two on to you; and as make-weight I'll add my six versions of "Tipperary" à la Whitman, Burns, Rossetti, Herrick, Swinburne, and Tom Moore. Bertie is running a series of them in the *Globe* – the other Johnny is doing Tennyson and Coleridge; I still meditate

Longfellow, Chaucer, Browning and Omar, and possibly Keats and Shakespeare.

Well Goodnight.

I wish you a happy Christmas.

Always with love,

Nellie.

Eleanor still aimed to be a great poet herself and worked seriously, but with Bertie editing a comic column on *The Globe*, she provided little larky verses of a topical kind which, she told Radford, could be turned out 'in my bath, or while knitting mittens, or on the tops of buses – with an ease that makes me suspect them up to the hilt; and I now earn anything from 7/- to 14/- a week, which seems to me astonishing wealth.'[1]

The sonnets she was writing were doubtless some of those to Edward Thomas. Her description to Radford explains the outward process: 'I've been writing poetry hard, which has been a great joy to me – writing in the way I like best, too; not with Morrisian fluency, (I'm inclined to suspect it when it comes lightly and with prolific ease); and not with niggling difficulty, (I suspect it much more when it's beset with continual troublesome effort); but with a kind of "possessed" concentration so that I spend three hours perhaps on fourteen lines, without a sense of time or labour, and emerge at the end with my sonnet almost as I want it, not very conscious of the change it went through during its birth, though as I never stopped and never plodded it must have gone through a good many. I do enjoy that sense of timeless absorption in work better than any other direct personal experience I get out of life. It is almost the only – dear me, I was about to write something startlingly untrue.'[2]

---

1 & 2. Letter from E.F. to Maitland Radford, 13.12.15.

# Sacrifice

AT THE SAME TIME as typing out Thomas's poems, sending them to editors and receiving the rejections, Eleanor was helping Viola Meynell type D. H. Lawrence's *Rainbow* manuscript. She and Lawrence had met when he was staying at Shed Hall, Viola's cottage, which had been adapted from a long low range of cowsheds on one side of the Meynell courtyard. Eleanor was staying at the cottage called Rackham with Margaret Radford, enjoying 'the heavenliest spring of all her 34', she wrote to Radford. 'I cannot begin to collect the memories of that time for you; but a heron used to fly over us every evening, and we saw swans in flight too, and nightingales sang round us in a ring, and there was a day when the beech arrived, and another when the oak arrived, and the first day of cowslips, and the first day of bluebells, and the fruit-blossom and primroses were thick as thieves, and the Downs were never the same and always the same; and Margaret lay under the apple-trees and played shepherd-tunes on your white pipe. I will never forget the loveliest spring in this terrible year . . . People came in on us for week-ends. One evening we had a great party – Margaret and I and Bertie and Joan and Miss Paget were entertaining Mr and Mrs Lawrence, and suddenly Francis [Meynell] and Lobby [Olivia Meynell] and young [Francis] Birrell arrived from nowhere, and there was singing and charades, and rather a fearful Strindbergian duologue between Bunny and me – it was a nice spontaneous evening. – I wonder what Bunny will become. I had two walks with him that week-end, and I do like his warm heart and his ready generous nature. But he must find himself somehow . . .'

In *The Last Four Years* she described supping at Shed Hall. 'It was Lawrence, not Frieda [his wife], who dished up the meal in Viola's little kitchen, where he had painted all the common pots and jars with bright designs in stripes and spots. He made the simplicities of the cottage life delightful, basting the mutton and stirring the onion sauce with the happy concentration of a child who is doing something it likes. Boiled onions did not contradict him, or baked lamb let fall remarks which excited his nerves to the pitch that sent Frieda weeping, but unsubdued, out of the room. His uncontrolled irritabilities astonished me at first but I soon realised that one must know Lawrence all-of-a-piece or not at all. Nobody held back so little of himself, no matter in what company, or cared so little for the embarrassments he caused. I did not like this side of him, but I accepted it equally with the things in him which stimulated and fascinated me, and for which I felt both liking and sympathy. He could be vividly entertaining when describing persons and places; and although his nature and Edward's were quite dissimilar (one as self-expressing as the other was self-suppressing), they had in common a scorn of sham and hypocrisy . . .'

During a weekend gathering at the Meynells in May 1915 cricket and croquet were played during the day, with charades and songs at night. Bertie and his sister performed some of their repertoire, and Lawrence sang the first Negro spirituals they had ever heard and taught them the jingling ballad about the murder of President McKinley.

On Tuesday Lawrence told Eleanor that he would accompany her part of the way when she set out on her planned walk to Yew Tree Cottage. It was twenty miles across the downs to Petersfield and they started early in a white mist that lay breast high over the meadows, Eleanor going with the long lope by which she was accustomed to match Thomas's negligent stride. But it was too fast for Lawrence. "I must teach you to walk like a tramp," he said. So they padded up the downs, sang scraps of songs and lolled on the grass every two miles.

A letter[1] to Radford describes Lawrence, revealing Eleanor's apprehension of the man far more openly than in *The Last Four Years*. 'He is a man who colours existence very strongly when you're with

1. Letter from E.F. to Maitland Radford, 15.6.15.

him, loveable, hateable too for some things, fierce, simple, keenly perceptive and very swift to drive at the truth (or one of the truths) of a person so long as it is a truth that lies within his own range of experience, and as it is a wide range he is more often right than not as far as he goes; but some elements are quite outside his range, and when he comes up against them he goes agley. Of course he sees everything through a tinge of sex – or almost everything. Not religion I think. But I mistrust his analysis when I am apart from him because it is too much destructive analysis. He tells you anything, with a most winning gentleness and sincerity; but afterwards he would relate anything you had told him to anybody else, I believe, and in that sense might be a little dangerous. But I am ashamed of being watchful and suspicious with anyone as friendly as he appeared. Yet I hated to hear him rend other people – *hated* it. And quite likely he rends me too. He's an odd and interesting man, and probably erratic in his moods of likes and dislikes, very impatient today of the person he felt kindly to yesterday. He is brilliant and entertaining, and talks a lot and very well, but without the *dry* literary cleverness that seems to possess every second writer one meets now.'

A little later she comments, 'So many people don't dare to be, or don't know how to be, *ordinary* in matters of simple feelings.'

The description of her day with Lawrence in *The Last Four Years* gives the atmosphere in which Eleanor was now so happy. To walk over the country with one's own walking stick, to look on socialism and crafts as honourable, to sing as one tramped, to find old pubs and sample their beer or cider, but beyond everything to have faith in nature and friendship and art, these were the highest satisfactions.

Lawrence had asked her to let him see some poems, and she sent a selection. His letter in response is a contrast to Thomas's letter concerning her writing, for Lawrence took it seriously, whereas Thomas never showed any real interest. Lawrence's criticism is potent because he picks on weaknesses that were always to limit her poetry.

*Greatham–Pulborough–Sussex, Monday*

My dear Eleanor;

Thank you very much for the poems. I think there is *real* poetry in them. It is strange, in you, that you never seem to fight things out to their last issue; and things which seem to me so amazingly potentially good. You have a far finer and more beautiful poetry in you than Margaret [Radford] has, even as such men as [Walter] de la Mare and [W.H.] Davies. But they get theirs verily smelted out, and you never burn yours to the last fire. I wonder why. It is the same here as in *Kol Nikon*. But these are better than *Kol Nikon*. How beautiful *Revolt* is, very beautiful, but for the faint tinge of sentimentality, a dross of smallness, almost cowardice, or disbelief, that should have been burnt out.

> *– but still in the cities of men*
> *Thou shalt spin thy thread of existence in a pattern not thine own*

That is very fine. But if you gave your real passion to it you would save your poems from their clichés of desolate waters and 'scale the steeps of the air'. *Underworld* also has something very beautiful about it.

> *I could believe the only voice that sings*
> *Is of the leafage sparkling into song*

But never to the last drops of bitterness will you drink, never face the last embrace of the fire in your poems.

I think I like the sonnets best. But there is a tendency for anybody in writing the Shakespearean sonnet to become facile. It is a form that lends itself to facility. But there is dignity and beauty and worth in these sonnets. I wish you had never read a line of Elizabethan poetry in your life, and then we might have had pure utterance from you. But I like them, I do: "Certain Among us Walk in Loneliness," and "When All is Said" expresses you perfectly. It is very good. But it is not quite true. We *can* by the strength of our desires compel our destinies. (Eleanor had written: 'We cannot by the strength of our desires compel our destinies'.) Indeed our destiny lies in the strength of our desires. Why are you a little cynical, or perhaps even a little conceited? 'Destiny is the strength of our desires.' Let that be your line.

I have decided to try to type my Ms myself. When I break down, I shall come to you for help.

It is sad, we have not got the Hampstead rooms; applied too late. But they were too small. We must try again.

Why don't you come down to Rackham Cottage for Whitsun,

you and your brother or somebody you can choose? I wish you
would.
    Love from Frieda and me
      D. H. Lawrence

So far Eleanor had failed, by the strength of her desires, to enjoy
reciprocal love. Sonnet XIX, which Lawrence mentioned, takes a
resigned tone.

> *Certain among us walk in loneliness*
> *Along the pale unprofitable days,*
> *Hazarding many an unanswered guess*
> *At what vague purpose wastes us on our ways.*
> *We know that we are potent to create,*
> *We say, I could be such or such or such,*
> *And lo, indifferent death swings back the gate,*
> *And life has never put us to the touch.*
>
> *So women with the aching will to bear*
> *Still to the barren grave must barren go,*
> *And men that might again like Titans dare*
> *Angelic secrets, die and nothing know.*
> *Alas! why were we born to woe and bliss*
> *If life had no more need of us than this?*

Lawrence was a great one for putting fire into the soul, or sticking
a pin into the mind, and his turning the phrase 'our destiny lies in the
strength of our desires', his questioning whether she were not a little
cynical or conceited shows great insight. However he admired the
young writer as a woman, and wrote in a letter to David Garnett,
referring to his homosexuality as 'a blasphemy against love', 'Go
away, David, and try to love a woman. My God. I could kiss Eleanor
Farjeon with my body and soul, when I think how good she is, in
comparison.'
This year Eleanor had a terrible scene with her mother over
Edward Thomas. Maggie Farjeon now feared that her daughter was
having an affair with him and suddenly objected to an imminent
visit, although of course Helen Thomas and the children were in the
cottage whenever Eleanor stayed. Doubtless gossip had spread, and

doubtless her mother was anxious that there should be no triangular struggle, being a timid and conventional woman. Eleanor had been about to catch the train to Petersfield, but because of all that was said, she unpacked her knapsack and sent a telegram. She spent the rest of the day alone in great unhappiness.

This is the only occasion in *The Last Four Years* on which there is a hint of dissension in the Farjeon family.

However, Bertie was aware of the problem: that at the age of thirty-four his sister was trapped in a rigid family life, from which there was little chance of escape because she loved a married man. When Joe learned of her unhappiness, he wrote an emotional letter of sympathy, adding, 'I believe in you more than in anything else I know – and there are precious few either people or things that I do believe in, in that way.'[1] So, despite personal troubles, Eleanor was already imparting a special brand of trust which was to mark her relations with people for the rest of her life.

But those dry kindly letters from Thomas continued to arrive, telling of the latest bit of tedious writing, of editors' rejections. Later Helen Thomas wrote that editors of this time had no room for 'such quiet meditative verse, in which the profound love and knowledge of his country were too subtle in their patriotism for the nation's mood.'[2] There were also boils and colds and the children for Thomas to complain of, while the weather always seemed wet and muddy round Yew Tree Cottage.

And then he joined up.

If poetry had been a great release for the melancholy writer, joining the army was another. Bertie was astonished at the change in the man: for the first time he saw him happy. Bertie believed, as did Frost, that it was the lifting of responsibility after years of toil for a family he was unfitted to support. Now the State had to provide for his wife and children. However, depressives who had turned their anger on themselves, often find relief in war, which is a situation where it becomes permissible to express angry feelings. Besides this, army discipline and close but temporary companionship with other men is a far less demanding situation than the deep and permanent relationship with family.

1. Letter from Joseph Farjeon to E.F., 14.7.15.
2. *As It Was*. Helen Thomas. Faber, 1926.

On a visit to London, in soldier's uniform, Thomas one day suggested to Eleanor that they visit Bertie and Joan in their flat off Haverstock Hill. Bertie opened the door, delighted to see his friend, and informed them that Mr Earle was in the sitting-room.

George Chester Earle was a master at King Alfred School. He had taught both Joan and Rosalind Thornycroft English and carpentry, he had a passion for words and wood.

So they sat down and Thomas took out his clay pipe, as Mr Earle puffed a briar and continued his interrupted thought. Whether he talked of William Barnes, Whitman or Isaiah, the doctrine of the Trinity or the Cerberus myth – and he talked of all these often – Eleanor did not remember, but presently he began to speak of Traherne in his rich voice and quoted a passage.

'Edward stopped puffing his clay to say quietly, "Have you got it quite right?"

Mr Earle stopped as though struck by a stone from a catapult.

"Isn't it," said Edward, "so-and-so and so-and-so?"

Mr Earle thumped his knee. "By God! you're right!" He stared at the soldier in the ranks who could correct him on Traherne.' [ET]

There followed a conversation between the two men which is described as 'one of the most wonderful hours of give-and-take that can ever have created itself between two men to whom poetry was the breath of life. The alertness of Thomas's mind shining through the drawn pallor of his face afterwards made Earle exclaim, "By God, what a man! He calls to mind that description of Carlyle's, 'wearied yet unweariable'."

The Thomas family now moved to Laughton in Essex. Before they left Steep, Thomas burned papers and many books, so that none of Eleanor's numerous letters survives. His to her, when he arrived in France in 1917 have a new tone: they are alert, with the tendency to complain gone. He described ruined houses, the lowering skies and his own feelings with the clear-headed astringency of his poetry. 'I keep feeling that I should enjoy it more if I knew I would survive it. I can't help allowing it to trouble me, but it doesn't prey on me and I have no real foreboding . . . it is worse for you and for Helen and Mother, I know. I wish I could keep back more of what I feel, but you mustn't think it is often fear or even dread for more than a moment.' [ET]

'In those two words "for you",' wrote Eleanor at the end of *The Last*

*Four Years*, 'he laid by his reserve for the only time in our friendship and allowed me to know that he knew how much I loved him.'

Her sonnet XLII on their parting has the same twist.

> *When we had reached the bottom of the hill*
> *We said farewell, not as it were farewell,*
> *But parting easily, as any will*
> *To whom next day meeting is possible.*
> *Why, it was on a scarcely finished phrase*
> *We made our clasp, and smiled, and turned away –*
> *"I might meet you in London in three days."*
> *The backward look had soon no more to say.*
>
> *You might. I thank you that you would not, friend.*
> *Not thanks for sparing a pain I would have dared,*
> *But for the change of mind which at the end*
> *Acknowledged there was something to be spared,*
> *And parting not so light for you and me*
> *As you and I made it appear to be.*

At the start of the war Joe and his wife had moved away from London dangers with their baby daughter Joan, to Gilman's Cottage, outside Billingshurst in Sussex. Here Eleanor rented a room and wrote, read and walked and enjoyed those aspects of country life of which Thomas and his wife had taught her so much. Here she went over his letters from the front line by candlelight. He asked for news of his first book of poems, now going into print, and reminded her of the dedication that must not be left out: To Robert Frost. There were hidden clues to his whereabouts: 'Tears doesn't rhyme with care, does it?' he asked, and questioned his wife, 'What do you think of Armed Men in Tears as the title of my next book?' She thought it a bad title, but Eleanor knew at once he meant he was going to Armentières.

From Billingshurst Eleanor wrote back, not knowing that news of his death had already reached Helen. It was in Fellows Road that she opened a letter from Viola Meynell which began, 'My darling Eleanor, I can hardly bear this for you.'

Upstairs in the bedroom her mother joined her. 'I heard myself saying to her very clearly, "Mother, it was never as you feared with

Edward and me." I say *heard myself* for I seemed separate from my body's movements and words and actions. I remember her saying "Nellie – " pleadingly. After a little while we went back to the dining-room, and I sat down with the others. I never forgot Harry's quiet injunction the day our Father died: "We've got to eat, you know", at times when I've known I mustn't break down.' [ET]

This self-control stood her in good stead when she met Helen at Liverpool Street Station ticket barrier. 'I was waiting for her there when she arrived, not with the laughing face and hurrying steps with which she always ran a little to a meeting. She was very pale, said "Eleanor" in a faint voice as we passed through and found a corner seat in a carriage. She sat in it, I by her, between her pale face and the incoming travellers. We held each other's hands. Suddenly in a great burst came her sobs and tears. "Don't let me cry, don't let me cry," she sobbed. I put my arms round her while she wept, and nobody looked. Presently she whispered, "I asked you to come because I thought I could comfort you – oh Eleanor, you'll have to comfort me." ' [ET]

Eleanor stayed two weeks, looking after the children, sleeping with Helen at night, shopping and making meals.

# Sussex

IN JANUARY 1917 Captain Victor Haslam, serving in the Royal
Garrison Artillery and Royal Flying Corps Balloon Company, had
written a fan letter to Eleanor Farjeon praising one of 'the most
delightful books' he had read: *Nursery Rhymes of London Town*, published by Duckworth. It consisted of verses that played upon the
names of districts or monuments in London. The two became
acquainted by letter and then, as Eleanor commenced a new book,
she posted the chapters one by one to the soldier in the trenches; and
very fresh, remote and whimsical they must have seemed by contrast
to his grim surroundings.

When Haslam returned to England they met, and for a short while
it seemed as though a romance might develop, but three years later
Eleanor explained to George Earle: 'For more than a year our friendship and affection seemed leading up to the gift of all I had to give,
and when I found he wanted so little of it, it fell back on me heavily
for a while. (It had blown away like thistledown before April two
years ago.)'[1]

One result of this rebuff was *A Walk in the Dark*, at first planned as
a novel but terminating in a short story of great sensibility and
tragedy. It is about a young woman and her feelings towards the man
who has lately left her to marry another (as Haslam did). The man
flirts with his new wife, fondling her and parading his happiness ssin
front of the cast-off woman, in the knowledge that she still loves him.
His egotism and the wife's embarrassment are most delicately

1. Letter from E.F. to George Earle, May 1922.

described, with the heroine's troubled attitude towards the couple creating extraordinary tension. Beyond the agonised humiliation there shows that ability to accept emotional pain which was one of the enduring strengths of Eleanor's character.

The joyful *Martin Pippin in the Apple Orchard*, whose success set the pattern of a prosperous career, was the book whose chapters were sent to Haslam at the front. Its prologue begins: 'One morning in April Martin Pippin walked in the meadows near Adversane, and there he saw a young fellow sowing a field with oats broadcast. So pleasant a sight was enough to arrest Martin for an hour, though less important things, such as making his living, could not occupy him for a minute. So he leaned upon the gate, and presently noticed that for every handful he scattered the young man shed as many tears as seed, and now and then he stopped his sowing altogether, and putting his face between his hands sobbed bitterly. When this had

*All the way to Alfriston*

All the way to Alfriston,
From Chichester to Alfriston,
I went along the running Downs
High above the patchwork plain,
With coloured squares of grass and grain,
Earthen russets, duns and browns,
Charlock-yellow, clover-green,
Reddening wheat and silvery oats;
Fantastical as Joseph's coat,
And rivers coiling in between,
And roofs of little peopled towns.

Eleanor's handwriting

127

happened three or four times, Martin hailed the youth, who was then fairly close to the gate.

"Young master," said he, "the baker of this crop will want no salt to his baking, and that's flat."

The young man dropped his hands and turned his brown and tear-stained countenance upon the minstrel. He was so young that he wanted his beard.

"They who taste my sorrow," he replied, "will have no stomach for bread." '

The young man goes on to explain that he loves Gillian who is locked up in Old Gilman's well-house, where she weeps beside the well. Six milkmaids, all sworn virgins and man-haters, keep the six keys of the gate, and live in the orchard outside. So Martin the minstrel finds the orchard, tells the girls six love stories and, overcoming their hatred of men and their prudishness, wheedles and tricks the keys from them. Finally the freed Gillian goes off, not with the tearful sower of oats, but with Martin Pippin himself.

This fanciful tale was written in a mood of delight: a caprice set in the Sussex countryside, where the flowers and woods, the downs and valleys, had become personal to Eleanor, with place names like Hawking Sopers, Open Winkins and Pillygreen Lodges full of wayward meaning. Adversane was one that seemed to her to have been taken from Malory, and evoked the world of troubadours which had so intrigued her on holiday in Brittany before the war.

*Martin Pippin in the Apple Orchard* was not written as a children's story, although it is now known as such, being a neatly patterned, whimsical pastoral, the main theme dovetailed with songs and stories improvised by the minstrel hero, in a way which Eleanor herself would have improvised for anybody in her company. The affected, antique mannerisms of language are not what Thomas or Lawrence would have approved, but they would have suited brother Harry in a game of TAR. The book is vivid and coherent, its artlessness full of craft, while the picture of this English Arcadia is curiously individual. Descriptions of munching apples in apple trees, of the spring grass which grew 'high and full of spotted orchis, and tall wild parsley spread its nets of lace almost abreast of the lowest boughs of blossom' are pictures full of Eleanor's light poetic vision.

Martin's lilting roundelays are wrapped about the names of wild flowers; there is wit and wrangling in the coy conversations, where a girl will jib at the word 'kiss'. But the converted milkmaids at last climb up and down the double apple-picking ladder over the hawthorn hedge and away with some last minute lovers, while Martin takes Gillian to his cottage hidden in a lush Sussex valley where 'all flowering reeds and plants that love water grow' and the 'pussy-willows bloom with grey and golden bees'.

It was before the completion of this book, when the moon was full and Zeppelins came over London, that Eleanor took her nervous mother to join Joe's family at Gilman's Cottage. Here she enjoyed her niece Joan's company, and recorded interruptions from the next room while *Martin Pippin* was in mid-song.

'But I must shut off most of my thoughts and get on with "Spring-Green Lady" –
"Lady, lady, my Spring-Green Lady
May I come into your orchard, Lady?"
"Pussy-cat, pussy-cat, where have you been?
I've been up to London to visit the Queen.
Aunty Nellie!"
"Yes, darling?"
"Isn't that a *nice* little song I sang just now?"
"Very nice. Go to sleep now."
"I made it up for you myself."
"Oh, Joaney!"
"But I did."
"Do you know what? I sang that song before you were born."
"You mustn't say that, Aunty Nellie – I *did* make it up."
"All right. Go to sleep."
"Teddy's telling me a story, Aunty Nellie. Teddy's roaring like a hunter, Aunty Nellie. Oo-ooo-grrr! Stop roaring, Hunter, or I'll smack you! Grr-rrr!"
"Shut up, Joan."
"You *mustn't* say shut up, Aunty Nellie."
"I'm sorry. But you keep quiet."
Prolific growls from the bed. "Ooo-errr-grrr! Shut up, Hunter! There, I've smacked him, Aunty Nellie."
"Oh, poor Teddy!"
"But I wanted to smack him. Oh, he's tumbled out of bed."

"Has he?"

"You come and pick him up for me."

"I thought as much, Joan."

"So did I. You come in."

What chance for concentration in Joan's rest hour?' [Memoir]

But Joe's wife found the extra work of relatives too much. The Zeppelins came less often and Maggie Farjeon returned home, while Eleanor found a place of her own: The End Cottage, Mucky Lane, Houghton.

A rutted way, scarcely a cart track, led to this primitive dwelling, two-up, two-down, thatched, with a seven-sister rose bush beside the porch and a well in the garden.

Here Eleanor lived alone for nearly two years. She wrote that these may have been the most important years of her life. As a child

she had feared almost everything: death, illness, torture, ghosts, burglars and humiliation. Now she walked the downs at all hours of the day or night, sat before the fire smoking the clay pipe Edward Thomas had coloured for her, and here she wrote and went to bed leaving doors and windows open. It seemed to her an almost perfect way of living, filled with natural and necessary things, like collecting wood and fir cones, picking flowers and mushrooms from the fields, watching the seasons change, learning to grow vegetables, and above all learning to lose fear.

She wore the coarse linen dress of a Russian peasant which had been bought before the war at the height of the ballet craze, when many Russian garments were imported and sold at Polunin's shop in London. Eleanor's garment was simple, quite straight to mid-calf with long sleeves. Two red medallions were embroidered just above the breast and two red stripes ran down from shoulder to hem, which was also bound with red tape. For wood-gathering expeditions she

put on brown stockings and sandals, with a rope harness to drag her rough sledge up into the woods. On this, dead branches were piled and tied; then she set off at a run down to the cottage. She lived by no timetable, eating, writing, walking as the mood took her.

When neighbouring children gathered in Mucky Lane to skip beneath her window and sing old rhymes handed down for generations, she went out and asked them to explain the intricacies of their game and recite the words. Elsie Puttick was the deftist of all the skippers and years later became the heroine of one of Eleanor's best fairy tales, *Elsie Piddock Skips in her Sleep*.

The ability to fascinate children never failed. One of Alice Meynell's grandchildren described her visiting Greatham around this time, running about and playing, till her mother said, "Eleanor, you must stop playing with the children and have a rest." It had never occurred to the girl that Eleanor was not one of themselves and as tireless. 'I remember in 1919 she invited us over for the day for a picnic and after we'd all sat down and had the picnic, Eleanor suggested we should go and paddle in the river. And we went down to the river and there were the reeds, and suddenly among the reeds we saw a bottle. Eleanor pounced on this bottle – "Here's a bottle," she said, "I wonder what's in it." We opened it and in it we found a letter from an old sailor. And it described some hidden treasure which we would find nearby, in a cave, guarded by a dragon. Eleanor was absolutely thrilled at this find and we all followed the clues and eventually got to a cave in the chalk cliffs which border the river Arun at that point. And in this cave there was a bottle of acid drops guarded by a green toy snake. That was so thrilling. It showed how Eleanor always added something extra to any occasion. No occasion was ever quite enough. Something exciting, something creative, something that you would always remember was added.'[1]

In Mucky Lane friendly neighbours taught the town-bred new-comer how to stew a rabbit and roast chitterlings, how to bake and how to mull ale. She learned quickly, eager to absorb all this domes-tic knowledge which her mother had never mastered.

In Arundel, shopping twice a week with a knapsack on her back, Eleanor got to know the local cobbler, who one day asked if she would like to go upstairs and make his bed for him. On being told no, he was not offended, nor was she, and they remained friends. To have begun to cope with this kind of advance at the age of thirty-seven, which most girls have to cope with at seventeen, was an odd state of affairs.

Doubtless during the two years in End Cottage she suffered a great deal, mourning the loss of Thomas, but the loneliness was soothing, while the writing of prose and verse for children filled her mind with visions.

1. Christian Hardie, BBC radio programme, 16.1.81.

# 19

# George Earle

BACK IN LONDON in 1921 Eleanor, aged forty, rented a mews studio up the hill in Hampstead Village: 20 Church Walk. Originally this had been a stable at the bottom end of one of the smart Church Row gardens where horse and carriage were kept, but for some time now, converted, the hayloft had served as a studio for Arthur Watts, the *Punch* artist, and then Joan Thornycroft, until she married Bertie in 1914.

After a while Eleanor altered the stable area into a front room – this must have been when she bought the property – behind which was a kitchen. A few steps led up to a poky bathroom and workshop at the back, then out into a square of garden with an apple tree in the middle and a fig tree in the corner. The brick walls all round were a soft red colour. Upstairs, with a thick rope instead of a banister to pull yourself up by, was a study living-room and a bedroom, the latter looking on to the cobbled mews. On this first floor the walls were lined with tongue-and-groove boards, which kept the place warm and gave a cosy country atmosphere. In the study the boards were stained brown, above which a sloped ceiling, once white, had turned musty yellow with age and smoke. Facing the garden was a lead-paned window opening right into the branches of the apple tree.

Into this little home, after doubts and difficulties, Eleanor brought her lover, George Chester Earle.

George Earle, the man who had talked of poetry so enthusiastically with Edward Thomas in 1916, was the son of a Somerset rector, himself a learned man who had edited *Beowulf*. Here is Earle's story of how his lifelong passion for English literature began.

'When I was a schoolboy of fourteen years old, I was always very far down in the examination lists in my class, and after one very bad term I determined to do something about it. It was the Christmas holidays and I was going home in the train when it occurred to me that I had a father who knew something about the subject, and as soon as I got home I had a talk with him and told him how badly I'd done and what a trouble it was to me. He cheered me up at once by saying "All that can be easily remedied, my dear boy. Just tell me what the subjects are, and I'll tell you how to tackle them." So I told him it was all English language and literature, Shakespeare, grammar and essay writing. "Well," said he, "there are just two things you must do." I remember my heart gave a leap of delight at this quick way out of my difficulties. My father went on, "The first thing to do is never to let a word pass you that you feel you only partly understand. It isn't enough to know *of* a word, you've got to know *it*." '[1]

The rector then advised his son to look words up in the dictionary, to ask his teacher, to find out whether they had a Greek, Latin, French or Anglo-Saxon derivation. It became apparent that this entailed more than five minutes' work, so Earle asked his father about the second thing. "I've told you what to do with words taken one by one. But words are put together in sentences, in all kinds of figures of speech. This means that you must study the nature of a metaphor, my dear boy, for there *is* nothing else."

Besides benefiting from this solid Victorian guidance, the boy made friends with a local carpenter who taught him his craft. So it came about that Earle's adult life was spent inculcating with enormous enthusiasm the virtues of wood and words. From 1901 to 1920 he was assistant head to John Russell at King Alfred School, Hampstead, teaching English and carpentry.

This establishment had been started by a group of liberal-minded parents, Joan and Rosalind Thornycroft's mother among them, who considered the rigid and often brutal education provided by the English public school unfit for their children. King Alfred was a co-educational day school, whose curriculum aimed to be broadly based, high toned and intelligent. It was not geared to the passing of examinations, but to the development of character and talent.

1. G. C. Earle, Papers.

Earle also sought the pure and noble, which he expressed in rhetorical prose. The quality of his high-flown thought rings out typically in a letter to the furniture designer, Barry Parker: 'My dear fellow, for all our sakes you must keep up your spirits – bear in your heart an Olympian scorn of all material obstacles – the spirit, tho' dwelling in time and in matter, must own a realm beyond their pale.' His youthful marriage had been a failure, but his teaching was a success. One of his classes built a navigable boat which, manned by the children, was launched on the pond in the Vale of Health. Rosalind Thornycroft wrote to Eleanor late in life, 'I think he started me off on nearly everything that I love now.' While another pupil, Roderick Garrett, said, "I revered him with something very much approaching love. His introduction to Chaucer was magnificent."

In school the high tone was set, not by conventional Christian morals, for there was no formal religion taught, but by something more like William Morris principles. Joan Thornycroft and her cousin Ursula Cox disapproved of corsets for women as a symbol of female constraint, so they set about a plump fellow pupil, Vivien Haigh-Wood who later married T. S. Eliot, and forcibly removed and hid her corsets. A democratic example was set by the balding headmaster, who one morning at Assembly asked the children to decide on the matter of his appearance, and from a box took a wig which he put on. A vote was taken for or against. The wig won.

This kind of unconventional rationalism suited the new self-reliant Eleanor. She and Earle became fast friends.

In 1920 Earle's career came to a crisis, for the bewigged John Russell was retiring and suggested his assistant should apply for his place. Earle responded with a doubting letter. 'Indeed,' he wrote, 'it is only because I feel that education opens the only ultimate solution to international (as well as other) problems that I can rightly consider further devoting myself to it.'

Earle was not appointed, but J. H. Wicksteed. Earle was affronted.

The following letter from A. S. Neill, another pioneer of the modern free schools, shows that the pipe Earle always smoked had become a bone of contention.

My dear Wicksteed,
I think I now understand why old Earle [he was aged 49] took

umbrage at your letter. You say things in a letter which are much better said by mouth. Why didn't you give me your views on smoking at school? Smoking is so unconscious a thing with me that I can't definitely recollect smoking at school. Moreover in J.R.'s day the whole staff smoked every interval.

But I am not Earle, and I don't mind your belated "vote of censure". That is one of the agreeable things resulting from analysis. In the old days I gasped and cried: "I've put my foot in it!" Nowadays I smile and say: "I wonder what's at the root of Wicksteed's tobacco complex?"

It was a little before this upheaval, in April 1920, that Eleanor came to know Earle well. He was a small, bearded schoolmaster who wore whiskery tweed suits. His vivid conversation was marked by apposite quotations and a sonorous wit and wisdom, something in the style of Dr Johnson. Eleanor described him 'as ardent a perfectionist in the matter of dovetails and inlay as he was in his choice of words to fit a phrase.'

One April evening they had met at Margaret Radford's lodging. As usual the talk had been on literature, when Earle suddenly jumped up saying, "Well, you're two very nice girls, but I must go." Eleanor recalled in her memoir:

'I rose at the same time; I had to walk back to Fellows Road. We three stood together saying goodnight. Mr Earle removed his pipe to kiss Margaret, remarking that it was good to have friends. I said, "I'd like to feel that I'm your friend too," and instinctively leaned forward as he replaced his pipe. He pulled it out again quickly – "Oh, did I burn you?" – we kissed, and he said to Margaret, "I am going to see this lady home."

'We left Denning Road together. When we had turned into Rosslyn Hill I found that my hand was in his coat pocket, warmly held by his. He always insisted I put it there, and there it remained till we reached the gate of 137 Fellows Road. Except with Edward Thomas, I had never exchanged thoughts with greater happiness or so much ease, for George Earle's tongue was uninhibited by Edward's reserves. That April night we spoke each other's language. Before we separated he told me he was going next day to Ireland to stay with the parents of one of his pupils, who is now the Irish writer Arland Ussher. He would write to me from there, and hoped I would dine with him one night in town, when he returned for the summer term at King Alfred's, perhaps his last.

'But when he kissed me again as we said goodnight, I knew I must not pretend to myself not to know what was happening. I must look at it very clearly in his absence. I was just thirty-nine, he would be fifty in May. He had had the best part of a lifetime of experience; I had had a lifetime without any. I had loved once more fully than I felt I could ever love again (and this had remained true throughout my life). I also knew that very few people fall in love once only, that I was on the verge of doing so, and that in middle life, when the fall is not headlong, there is sometimes a moment when one can draw back. Mr Earle was married, and had a family. I wanted love and children, but not at the expense of other people. On his return to England, while I could still command myself, while parting might be a wrench for both of us, but not, I hoped, a tragedy, I asked him to tell me about his home life as honestly as such one-sided things can be told. He did so simply, without excuses or blame; what he said convinced me that no one would suffer personal unhappiness if I made a home for him and lived with him as his wife. He would soon have to find a new post by which to maintain his family, for Wicksteed had been chosen for King Alfred's; I could maintain myself now, and would take nothing from him except himself. I would not live furtively; but discretion must be used concerning the school authorities wherever he might be teaching. For myself I had no religion to trouble my conscience with a sense of sin, and I was prepared to meet the social consequences.'

During a subsequent visit to Sussex a letter to Earle shows how easily Eleanor expressed her feelings to him and how taken up she still was with country experiences.

*A secret valley in the Downs*
*Thursday teatime, but no tea.*

I've just been sending a telegram.

How do you send telegrams in London? I rather forget. I suppose if you get a letter by the first post which says "Wire by return" you go round the corner and do it, or perhaps have to walk for five or even ten minutes to the inconvenient post office.

Here you have to walk three miles, so you might as well make a day of it. When I have to send a telegram in Greatham I begin by putting bread and cheese in my knapsack, and then I'm equipped.

To-day has been heavenly hot. And it's one of the loveliest walks in the world, to Amberley across the water-meadows, all little bridges and stiles, the grass tall and flowering and smelling its sweetest, cows knowing what a hot day it is by being very quiet, and larks by being very noisy. Then a footpath up through a cornfield rising from the flats to the highroad under the Downs that goes to Amberley, which is as lovely as its own name, and in the same way – grey and half asleep, with thatched roofs you want to stroke like a purring cat. You can't do things quickly in Amberley, not even telegrams. Really important telegrams may not take more than a day and a half to arrive, however.

I had to amble about the village, talking to the baker and the postmaster and his sister who are some of my cronies, and eventually the telegram got sent and I set up on the Downs. I can't imagine why the Downs are always deserted, even on a day like this, when they are better than woods and seashores or any other place to be. Perhaps they aren't deserted but have the power to make their lovers and wanderers invisible and so keep themselves to themselves. They are so much beyond human beings to me that I can almost not talk of it – I don't mean I love them more, and yet in a sense I think perhaps I do. Anyhow, I'm theirs, and if ever I vanish from the face of the earth it will be because they've drawn me in, and if you walk there any green hummock or shadow in a great round dimple in their sides, or tuft of thyme, or breath of the wind that is perpetual on them, might be me. They've healed me more, and given me more strength and certainty and peace, than any other living thing.

My bread and cheese was practically Welsh Rarebit by the time I got to it, and there wasn't nearly enough of it at that. So I went half-asleep for an hour by way of dessert, and then wandered on and found half an empty cottage, and knocked on the other half to discover if I would be allowed to live in it. But the first condition was that I should be a shepherd, so I said I'd call again in a year or so. Then I got on a Downside full of tottergrass, orchis, and the tallest lady's slipper I've ever seen, gold and blood-red. I think perhaps I'd no business there, as I had to climb a locked gate to get into it, but it was too lovely, and nobody wanted it but me, and I found a very deep nest in the middle of the flowers where the farthest shepherd couldn't see me, and took off half my clothes and had a sunbath. Then I went on a bit more and got into a plantation of flowering pea where I *knew* I'd no business, but I was careful with it till I reached the hedge, which I had to break through a little; and then I was in one of the loveliest of all the valleys I know, with a tiny coppice in the cup of it, so I went there and had another sunbath, a whole one this time. I can't think why people talk about being clothed and in your right mind. I believe our clothes put us in our wrongest possible mind very often. Anyhow we have foregone entirely one utter joy that we were born with. I wish to goodness on hot hot golden days like this it were possible to shed everything man has made, and walk on the hills as God made us. The story of Eden is a wonderful invention and a perfect nuisance.

Now I am out of my copse, and the birds are beginning to forgive me. The wood pigeons and the daws were in a great way about it. A carter with a horse has just curled up a far little track up the hollow. It's still so hot and dreamful and green and solitary that I don't know how I'm ever going to make myself move away, but I'm beginning to feel very hungry, and it will take me an hour and a half to reach food, and in ten hours I'll only have had that insufficient sandwich of bread and melting cheese.

I must put on my stockings and shoes and go. Perhaps there'll be a letter from you on the floor when I get in. The afternoon postman shoots them there when I'm out.

This is how we send telegrams in Sussex.

The four unsigned pages of this letter are torn from a small lined notebook and written in pencil.

And still, even now, Eleanor knew almost nothing of sex in theory or practice. She told me that it was on a visit to Paris, sitting in the Luxembourg Gardens, that Earle discovered this fact. Beside her on the bench, with children bowling their hoops along the arid neat paths, he explained, drawing in the sand at their feet diagrams of the male and female parts and how they worked with the tip of his stout British walking stick.

Back in London, in July 1920, they decided to elope. It must have been to the west of England, for they were to meet at Paddington Station and catch a certain train. Eleanor arrived early and waited. Ten minutes before the train left Earle had not appeared. Five minutes, no Earle. One minute, nobody – and the train departed. She sat down on one of the benches. The next train came and went, but no apologising lover disturbed her. An hour passed, two hours, three hours, and it was growing late. So Eleanor went to the buffet, bought herself a sandwich and returned to the familiar bench. By now the station was almost empty, but as she gazed short-sightedly about, she perceived a small bearded man seated alone on the very back bench, head bent, engrossed in a book. It was Earle. He had been there all the time, reading. So they eloped and, as she wrote, 'sealed as true a marriage as could be without benefit of clergy.' [Memoir]

# Italy

AMONG EARLE's serious and formal love poems written to Eleanor is this one in a lighter vein.

### TO RIPE BACHELORS

*Pretty girls you'll meet in plenty*
*Round about the age of twenty;*
*And at thirty you'll find*
*Many girls of charm and mind;*
*But if you would have her true,*
*Warm, and wise to comfort you,*
*Lover leal and comrade sporty*
*You must search much nearer forty!*
*Hear my word, unmarried men,*
*Few the girls who last till then,*
*Few they are, though ripe and fit;*
*Hear my word and ponder it!*
*For it comes from one who knows*
*Life and its deceiving shows,*
*Who at last has found a love*
*Sweet-and-twenty far above,*
*Far above such charm and mind*
*As at thirty you may find;*
*She is rare, you understand,*
*Even in that selected band*
*Who at forty ripen still*

*Body and mind, heart and will,*
*Who are growing as they grew*
*In their youth – alas, how few!*
*Charm, mind, spirit, yes and more*
*I have found in Eleanor.*

However, a serious difficulty soon arose between the lovers. Eleanor's desire for a child of her own was not anticipated with any pleasure by Earle. From the previous marriage he had to support three children: he had had enough of screaming infants. This matter is mentioned with careful tact in Eleanor's unfinished memoir, where she explains that she did not know how powerful would be her reaction when, in September, it became clear to her that Earle's vocation was for teaching not fatherhood. And she was pregnant. The early miscarriage came as a blow. It was her only conception. The sonnet "Farewell, you children that I might have borne" was written at this time out of her sorrow.

'When I came to my senses and realised that I must uproot the hope once and for all, I found it impossible to readjust myself. By now our love and need of each other was deep, but I could not bring joy to our meetings. Instead of being happy with him I was strained, and of course he knew it. I foresaw the danger of a life charged with secret resentments if I could not conquer myself and begin again; and believed this effort could only be made at a distance, disentangled from our intermittent meetings, and from my home ties, where my feelings must be dissembled.' [Memoir]

Five years later she wrote about this episode in rather cryptic terms to the poet William Ibbert: 'I am not a complete woman – I was once, very nearly, but something went wrong.' The loss of her baby, combined with Earle's indifference, upset Eleanor considerably. It was a subject, like others which gave her deep pain, of which she rarely spoke and only to intimates; more superficial sorrows were enlarged on with something like gusto.

Then Rosalind Baynes sent an invitation from Italy. On October 28th Eleanor said goodbye to Earle and the first part of the incomplete memoir ends: 'He thought I was breaking off our relationship for ever. It was never in my heart or mind. I went away to save it.'

On this holiday Eleanor continued to write 'Tomfool' verses for *The Daily Herald* which were printed daily. A description of the Channel crossing may still be appreciated.

*I am not going to think about being seasick.*
*I am going to think*
*Hard*
*About the sea,*
*And the horizon,*
*And the eleven gulls*
*Flying round the boat,*
*And the Seaman with the nice face*
*Who says he will look after me like a Mother.*
*I am not going to think about*
*Being seasick.*
*The sea is green and white*
*Like that lady's complexion*
*Over there.*
*The horizon is round*
*So of course*

And round.
The gulls go <sup>up</sup> and <sub>down</sub>
As though they did not mind
If they were <sup>up</sup>
Or <sub>down</sub>.
Some one ought to tell them
That if they don't keep still
They will soon feel
Far
From well.
The Seaman's face
Is <sub>not</sub> a <sup>bit</sup> like my Mother's.
My <sup>Mother</sup> never

143

Had a grin on her
Face
When she looked after me
Like a . . .
Damn!
I am not
*Going*
*To* . . . *think about*
*Being* . . .
. . . . . . Seamen*!*

At this period Rosalind, now separated from Godwin Baynes, was living in some poverty on the side of the hill above Florence, in Fiesole. Her father, and brother-in-law Bertie, were helping financially. Baynes could no longer be looked on as the blue-eyed god of Eleanor's earlier fancy.

The holiday turned out a great pleasure. There were Rosalind's three little girls, Bridget, Chloe and Nan, who adored their mother's friend. In her collection of children's stories, *Nuts and May*, which was dedicated to the girls and illustrated by their mother, one of Eleanor's methods of amusing the young is explained. 'This was a Choosing Story. Sometimes when I have told stories to Bridget and Chloe and Nan all day long, and really can't think any more, I say, "Choose what shall be in the story." Then everybody in the room chooses something.' So sitting round they would tell in turn, waiting with great excitement for their own thing to come into the story, and she never forgot one. *Nella's Dancing Shoes* was the result of one such occasion. And here, in the Villa Adino, Chloe made a crude book of wobbly houses and wobbly words which Eleanor kept throughout her life.

The Tuscan countryside and Italian way of life were enchanting. In Fiesole in 1920 this is how the village market was seen: 'All the things they sold in the little shops in that market-place on the hilltop were brought up from Florence, miles away, in carts drawn by white oxen. The oxen were as white as milk or marble, and drew the carts in teams side by side. Their wide horns were adorned with red tassels, and so were their tails. They had collars of little bells, which rang like silver and shone like gold. When the beautiful oxen appeared in the village with their cartloads of red wine and white, and oil, and fruit, and cheeses, and sausages, and sweetmeats, the most important thing they brought was the Pasta.'[1] In this market, under the big bright umbrellas where the cook, Anina, bargained so expertly, Eleanor revealed herself an innocent. 'Tomfool's' experience explains:

### In the Market

*"Buon' giorno, Signora!"*
*"Buon' giorno, Signor!"*
*"How much this elastic?"*
*"Two lire, no more.*
*Two lire the metre."*
*"Two lire? Too much!*
*One lire!" "For three*
*You could hardly get such –*
*Signor, I am giving*
*My living away*
*In selling so cheaply!"*
*"Signora, good day."*
*"Signor – un momento!*
*I must if I must!*
*I'll sell at one-fifty."*
*"The price is unjust.*
*One lire a metre*
*Is all I will give."*
*"Non possibile, Signor!*
*A woman must live!"*
*"Good morning, Signora."*
*"Ah, have it your way –*
*One lire the metre!"*
*She measures. I pay.*
*But when I get home*
*With a laugh for the sport,*
*My elastic I find*

---

1. *Nuts and May: A Medley for Children.*

*Looks uncommonly short.*
*For elastic's too plastic*
*By half, I'm afraid!*
*One lire the metre –*
*She measured. I paid.*

On returning to England Eleanor had recovered, although it must have been hard for one so insatiably affectionate and protective to accept that her maternal instinct would never be fully satisfied. But her remarkable will, almost as strong as Harry's and far more intuitively intelligent, won. There was no secret resentment, and she sublimated her desire to hold her own child in her arms by holding other people's. Resignation was made more easy by the knowledge of her power to gain their love.

So she and Earle set up house together in the Church Walk cottage. At first he stayed weekends only, but refused to leave on Sunday, which entailed rising very early Monday morning in order to get off to his new school on time. Eleanor was the one to set things going. She wrote:

'I always got up first, a little before six, to make the morning tea, for which he was loth to sit up, and when I dragged him sternly into position he would flop back on the pillows like a small boy. So I invented one morning, on the spot, an "Ancient Rune, from one of the Counties, well-known to have effect on slothful lads in the mornings." It went like this:

*"Now zitty-oop, my vitty lad!*
*An' zitty-oop, I zay!*
*Vur thou must dree the barley weird*
*Avor the breake o' day!"*

*Then down ee vlopped, the vitty lad,*
*Azackerly as Oi veared –*
*"Oi will not rise at breake o' day*
*To dree the barley weird!"*

The first time I rolled this off, as a genuine bit of country lore, he would hardly believe I had invented it then and there off my tongue, and took it for the genuine article; then he roared with laughter, and this rune became part of our household joke.' [Memoir]

Of course there were problems with the family. Since that row over Edward Thomas it seemed unlikely that George Earle would be acceptable to Mrs Farjeon: again it was a married man with three children. So she was not told. Harry was extremely upset and shocked when he discovered that his sister was living with Earle, so Eleanor told Alice Meynell. There was inevitable jealousy for, though Harry respected Earle's talent for teaching, he was too much the dictator to resign himself to his sister's emancipation.

For the rest, Joe would accept whatever his brothers or sister did, over-anxious and loving always, though his wife could not approve of a sister-in-law living in sin. Only Bertie was delighted. In Church Walk he and Earle would settle before the fire upstairs on the shabby sofa and puff their pipes and discuss Shakespeare and Milton and Keats and Chaucer – their subtleties, oddities and beauties. Then Eleanor was happy.

# The Invalid Mother

LIFE WAS NOW DIVIDED between the top and bottom of Hampstead hill, and Eleanor would take a taxi or hurry on foot down the steep mile to Fellows Road where her mother's chronic cystitis grew steadily worse. The old lady sat in her rocking chair dressed in a neat black Victorian gown, one foot tucked under her, a black shawl round her shoulders, and rocked. She played patience with Harry, alone she fitted together giant jig-saw puzzles, which might take weeks to complete. Every morning the cook came up for orders, for her mistress never went down to the dingy kitchen. When granddaughter Joan stayed in the house, as quite often happened, she was warned not to go into the basement – there might be rats.

Harry's eyesight worsened, and so, with walls papered in dark colours, doors and woodwork painted brown, and heavy velvet drapes half-drawn across the net-curtained windows, the house grew gloomier and gloomier. In the dining-room the glass doors of Farjeon's bookcase had to be opened at breakfast, lunch and dinner in order that bright reflections would not distress the musician's sight. His students wrote their compositions on specially printed brown paper.

It was sometime in 1927 that I remember staying the night. There in the narrow hall lay my uncle's shiny black rubber galoshes, waiting at the bottom of the hatstand beside the ferrule of his big black umbrella. Above hung his black overcoat, black hat and a spare brown eyeshade. Eleanor welcomed me in, gay and loving, keen that her shy eight-year-old niece should not be alarmed at spending the night in strange surroundings. This poem, illustrated by Robin Guthrie, shows how a child's commonplace fear was put to use.

"No," the little girl said
As she snuggled down in bed,
"I don't have a night-light lit,
I'm not afraid a bit.

"But when you've got to go
Leave the door open _so_
With just a crack of light —
Yes," she said, "_that's_ right!"

Down the stairs I went
And left her there content —
But oh, what happened then
She never told again.

She for her secret kept
What happened while she slept,
And hid what came at night
Through the crack of light.

Having had high tea, wriggling about on one of the tall-backed chairs round the dining-room table because spikes of horse-hair stuffing would protrude through the plum-coloured rexine and prickle my bottom, having helped my sweet-spoken grandmother with the giant jig-saw and been praised for my quickness, I kissed her softly crinkling cheek goodnight. Next I had to kiss the dry harsh cheek of my sprightly but always sinister uncle, and then Eleanor took my hand and we went up the red Turkey stair-carpet singing. We unpacked while the bath ran and then I did begin to feel some apprehension: it was such a fusty gas-lit, habit encrusted household, so different from our airy light-hearted home. But I liked the lavatory with its wide seat and handle that pulled up, with a design of purple grapes in the pan. The bath made me hesitate: it was muzzy green. But Eleanor, swishing cold into hot, laughingly explained that Harry had lately taken a bold step and tried his hand at something practical. Because the white enamel hurt his eyes, he had gone to Hardymans and bought a brush and pot of green paint. He had then painted the bath. However, that night on stepping out of the hot water he had discovered that his behind had changed colour – it was a strong bottle green that would not come off.

This undignified picture of the revered head of the household, with Eleanor's ringing laughter, greatly relieved my fears. The offer of a nightlight was refused with some scorn, although I was glad that my aunt insisted on leaving the bedroom door open – just in case it was necessary to call for anything. So I went to sleep hearing the waterfall arpeggios, the titillating trills, the grandiose chords of Liszt and Rachmaninov, which my uncle so loved to play on one of the two pianos in his room. And I imagined that dignified little backside on the piano stool – green.

Conditions at 137 grew more and more difficult, for in those days cystitis could not be cured, and Maggie Farjeon spent more and more time in bed and in agony. Everybody about the house spoke in awed voices, for to the Farjeons illness was a sacred terror. Servants came and went, badly paid and unable to cope with the family problems until, in 1930, Bertha Summerbell arrived; Bertha with her northern generosity, frankness and energy. It was her first job. She gave this impression of her reception: 'I went up in my cap and apron and stood outside Mrs Farjeon's door. She was in bed all the time by then. Her companion went in and said, "She's here." I heard the old lady say, "Tell her to come in." So the companion came out to me, but I wouldn't go in. I said, "Tell Mrs Farjeon I'm not a jug without a handle." So she went back and told her, and I heard Mrs Farjeon say, "Tell the jug with the handle to come in." After that we were great friends. She liked me for speaking out. She was a very charming dainty old lady.'

In June 1933 Bertie wrote to his sister with suggestions for a change in the organisation of his mother's household:

. . . It is about the working arrangements at Fellows Road, which are now so expensive and seem, what with one thing and another, to have got out of proportion. The idea is that it ought to be possible to do with one less helper, which would mean, I suppose, a saving of about £100 a year. Categorically, the suggestion is:

(1) That there should be a working housekeeper to do the work of the companion.

(2) That while the nurse is resting in the daytime, the parlourmaid should be with Mother.

(3) That the shopping in the morning should be done by the cook or over the phone – we don't go out to shop here at all in the mornings but arrange orders with the tradesmen when they call.

I know that it is all very difficult and that for anyone not on the spot it may seem a little simpler than in fact it is. But the domestic arrangements at present are those of a very rich woman, and I thought I would write because Joe, in common with everyone else, is now in pretty low water, and although this isn't his idea, it might help him, and Harry, and everyone who is giving assistance.

I put this down rather badly, but you will take it in the spirit in which it is written.

Always affectionately,
   Bertie.


So it seems that in the early thirties this ailing mother was cared for by a companion, a parlourmaid (Bertha), a cook and a night nurse, with considerable assistance from Eleanor, who now had to earn her own and her lover's living. Earle had had a slight stroke in 1930 and from that time gave up work.

It was Bertha who became the backbone of the household, taking the place of the companion and ultimately cook, though her wage remained officially at five shillings a week until Harry died in 1949. It must be said that some time before his death, Eleanor added another five shillings, asking Bertha to keep the matter quiet. My mother always said that domestic help was shockingly paid at Fellows Road.

Soon Mrs Farjeon became so attached to Bertha that she did not like her to go out on her one day off. These mornings she would come over dizzy, but immediately Bertha agreed to stay, perked up. The kindly doctor would come at any time of the day or night to hold her hand when he could not relieve the pain. Every morning Bertha and Eleanor would count the number of cottonwool balls she used – they then knew how often she had been up during the night, and sometimes it was twenty.

Almost always Maggie Farjeon was a kindly conciliating woman, but there is a recorded moment of bitterness against her daughter, whose lover in Church Walk was still officially secret. By 1930 Eleanor and Earle had been living together for nine years. It is not surprising that some rumour, combined with Eleanor's happiness, should have apprised her mother. One day when Bertha was with the old lady, they heard the front door latch click and knew it to be Eleanor arriving from her other home.

"Here comes the hypocrite," Mrs Farjeon remarked.

Moral outrage was felt even more strongly by Earle's brother, John, who was a fashionable doctor hoping to become King George V's physician. In 1930 Earle had his first minor stroke and received a visit from his brother. When Eleanor opened the front door he brusquely demanded to know where the invalid was and, brushing by, went upstairs. On coming down Eleanor stood waiting. She asked, "How is he?" to which the doctor made no response. Imagining that he must be overcome by emotion, she laid a hand on his sleeve, with some sympathetic word. At this he snatched away his arm as though he had been stung, and left the house of this scarlet woman.

Eleanor still kept her room in Fellows Road. She worked and slept there when needed and, still writing the daily Tomfool rhyme, topical or nonsensical, now composed one dedicated "To a Perfect Woman".

> *Bertha!*
>    *You're worth a*
> *Dozen tidy wives*
> *Who bring despair into their husbands' lives!*
> *You gather from my floor the shirts and ties*
> *I have sown broadcast there – but, being wise,*
> *You leave my work piled up at every angle*
> *Upon my desk. Yet even there you wangle*
> *An air of order that has no disparity*
> *With my disorder. Then, with what sweet charity*
> *For my unpunctual sins, your head peeps round*
> *My door, which you have opened without sound –*
> *"Do I disturb you, Mr Tom? And can*
> *I do your room?" The heart of any man*
> *You'd win, as with your duster and your broom*
> *You still respect the litter in my room.*

*Ah well! some day some lad, I'll stake my life,*
*Will find that Durham breeds the perfect wife,*
*And but for certain cogent reasons, I*
*Would be that lad, or know the reason why!*

The last years of Maggie Farjeon's life were painful. Eleanor continually organised for her comfort. She hired nurses, sat beside her, brought down invalid foods cooked in the cottage, phoned bulletins to her married brothers: nothing was too much trouble. Yet everybody, including the invalid herself, longed for the end. Harry did what he could to enliven his mother's bedridden existence, but he equalled Earle in his incapacity to boil an egg or empty a waste-paper basket. Relief came at last in 1933 when the old lady died with her two elder children beside her.

On this occasion Eleanor did not put off a visit to the Ballets Russes at the Alhambra Theatre, where she was to meet Clifford Bax and other friends. Arriving in a rush into the crowded foyer, she hurried up to the party and announced in ringing tones, "Isn't it marvellous – Mother's dead!"

# 22

# Collaborator's Honour

WHEN IN 1921 *Martin Pippin in the Apple Orchard* charmed the public, a professional career was established, and by 1928 twenty-two books of verse and stories, mostly for children, had been published. This average of over two publications a year would be satisfactory for any author. It seemed as though the store of ideas which had piled up in Eleanor's imagination for forty years now flooded out.

One of the important results of living alone in Sussex had been that in losing fear Eleanor emerged resilient to the buffets of the world. As with her father, a natural optimism kindled continual hope, and although her judgement sometimes went astray, she could now accept failure and learn from it rationally, without disenchantment. When selling her work she became almost immune to disappointment, each manuscript going off to a publisher as on a journey, from which, if rebuffed, it would be welcomed home with her faith in its worth unshaken.

In the early 1920s Eleanor was asked to write some hymns and readily produced three for which the fee was nine guineas. After her death the hymn called *Morning Has Broken* was taken by the pop star Cat Stevens and sung on records and at concerts. The three guinea hymn soon became 'Top of the Pops' both in Britain and the United States with a blast of notoriety and royalties that would have amused and delighted its author.

When writing verse Eleanor liked to discipline herself within some definite form. In the sonnet she achieved a mastery which was in danger of becoming facile, as Lawrence discerned; with light-hearted rhymes the alphabet became a favourite framework. The

Drawing by Edward Ardizzone of Eleanor's cottage in Perrins Lane

Town and Country Child, the School, Sussex, Magic, the Seaside, Twins and the BBC each had its own ABC. A pipe-smoker's ABC was planned which might have been dedicated to Thomas, Earle or Bertie with equal warrant. Most of the ABCs have charm and wit, but in the hurry of composition and the effort to earn money, poor quality work could pass uncensored.

But *E for Express Messenger* shows how effectively and simply the chosen form was generally mastered.

> *The Postman comes at eight and twelve and four and nine o'clock,*
> *He's certain as the night and day, and steady as a rock;*
> *But the little Express Messenger has unexpected hours,*
>   *Like nightingales, and shooting-stars, and showers.*

> *The Postman up and down the steps upon his patient feet*
> *Will plod for hours and hours until he's done a single street;*
> *But the little Express Messenger will flash through London like*
>   *A zig-zag streak of lightning on his bike.*

> *The Postman brings advertisements, and catalogues, and bills,*
> *And notes from Aunt Priscilla that describe her latest ills;*
> *But the little Express Messenger, like carrier pigeon, flies*
>   *With a letter that is always a surprise.*

*W is for Waves* can be appreciated by a four-year-old as well as an adult, and in some of Eleanor's short poems there glows a clarity that approaches Blake's vision of innocence. Her stories for children are lucid and to the point, while the best have an underlying complexity, with the moral not forced but gently and firmly stated.

'Tomfool's' topical rhymes, which appeared in the *Daily Herald* for over ten years, were another discipline to which Eleanor responded. Here her facility was a great asset, the styles being so varied and lively that it was no wonder she acquired fans. These would sometimes call at the *Herald* office asking to meet Tomfool, but the staff never gave away his whereabouts or sex. When going on holiday Eleanor would run off verses in advance: she was always reliable, for the professional standard required by journalism had been firmly imparted by Ben Farjeon to all his children. This *Herald* job gave Eleanor a regular income which, starting at half a guinea per rhyme, rose to a whole guinea, after Alice Meynell announced that nobody should ever take less for a poem. Later the fee was doubled. In the 1920s and early 30s twelve guineas a week was a very reasonable basic income for a freelance writer.

During this period Eleanor was also working for the weekly *Time and Tide*, owned and edited by the wealthy and strong-willed Lady Rhondda. The paper was staffed and mostly written by women. A monthly poem, illustrated by Gwen Raverat, appeared under the pen name of 'Chimera'. I am sorry to say that Chimera's poems were a throwback to the days when trees were temples of Pan.

It was not until 1929 that Eleanor and Bertie began to collaborate once again, this time on a series of verses about the kings and queens of England. The following letters show how brother and sister worked together, with the maxim of 'collaborator's honour' which, Bertie told his sister, meant that neither ever revealed who wrote what. Manuscripts were posted back and forth between Hampstead and Sydenham, where Bertie now lived with Joan and three children: Joscelyn, myself and Gervase. My father was earning a fairly steady income as dramatic critic for *Vogue* and the *Sunday Pictorial*, editing Shakespeare for the Nonesuch Press and writing satirical songs and sketches for theatrical revues. The *Kings and Queens* verses were written, as usual, without a publisher or deadline in view.

Dear Bertie,

Here's my morning's budget, spurred on by yours. I won't do any more till I hear whether these are more or less in the vein, and anyhow I'll leave you to choose the next; I hope I haven't seemed to pick all the obvious ones, I think the others are just as easy when I have the history book by me to light on some salient point (George II is a little vague, for instance). One doesn't want to try to crowd too much, or anything in the way of real information; that is why I've left your Queen Anne as a sort of extension of the first verse only, which I like immensely. I agree that William the First has got to be striking, and I like your idea of the eight strokes, and what happens on them, but they would be ruined if they ran on in long lines, and what goes before seems to me to have a general effect of being too long and too explanatory, though taken line by line it isn't so. I'd like to leave this one a bit. As to pictures, big heads and shoulders only, unless very cleverly and distinctively done, will not be quite enough to suggest the differences to the child, especially in the older kings. I'm rather for single full-length-figures, in colours, with nice details of costume; and, if it would run to it, perhaps tiny thumbnail black-and-white up in a corner, or down in a corner, of the next page, either touching on an incident such as Eleanor Cross, the Tower, or a Bluecoat Boy. But this is only a suggestion. Do you think, as another suggestion, (but I'm not sure whether it's the best quarter for the book) Francis[1] might see it as a popular line, or would he have to do it too expensive? I think [Jonathan] Cape would consider it.

Nine months later she wrote: 'I'm glad you like the "candlelight" verse; it's always nice to please you. Here's George II to look at.' The letter continues with problems in her mother's home.

Alas, I've had to give the new companion notice on the obvious grounds that she simply is not healthy enough to stand the strain of this place. She knows it too; but, like most of the poor creatures who are so eager to come (and so eager to go) she is between Scylla and Charybdis – Scylla, a job she's unequal to, Charybdis, a home

1. Francis Meynell of Nonesuch Press.

with a mother dying of cancer and a drunken stepfather who beats them both. Really the inside stories of these girls – their different reasons for being driven in shoals to apply for companion's places, are past contemplating. A play, a book, called The Companion keeps on forming in my background. I believe a good one could be done, though I dare say not by me.'

The return letter from Bertie is critical: 'I look at Henry VI and Edward IV sometimes and still don't like them much. They are fair, and might pass in the crowd, but are really below the level of most of the others I think.'

Victor Gollancz accepted *Kings and Queens*, writing to Bertie:

My dear Farjeon: do forgive my horrible delay about this. The trouble has been that, while I think that the verses are perfectly charming, I have not wished to go ahead until I could feel pretty certain in my own mind that I could handle them to advantage.

Immensely difficult though this market is, I now feel that, in view of the originality of the idea, we may be able to get away with special treatment, in which, if I may say, we specialise! Even so, however, these things are one in a hundred gambles : and if we fall down badly and sell only a few hundred you must not blame us.

Shall I write to you direct about terms, or have you an agent?
Yours sincerely,
    VG

The next problem with the book was to find an illustrator; so Bertie devised a typically Farjeon competition. Three artists were short-listed and asked to make specimen designs. These artists were Mary Potter, Ivy Mackusick and Rosalind Baynes. Discriminating friends, who included Francis Meynell, Richard Jennings the bib-liophile and leader writer for the *Daily Mirror*, with Mary Allen, producer at the BBC, were asked to give judgement. Voting was arranged on a points system and came out narrowly in favour of Rosalind, who was already preferred by Bertie and Eleanor, though they did not wish to say so because of their relationship. Her portraits of the kings and queens were in the bold Pollock tuppence coloured style of theatrically posed figures, with a panel at the bottom depicting some event, such as Lambert Simnel sitting before his spit or Edward VII at the races.

This popular, unceremonious history book was admired by the royal family, even though fun was poked at their antecedents. Bertie had written to his sister: 'Let's have no nonsense about it. The Bad Kings are Bad, and the Good Kings are Good, just as they were when we were children.' Diana Cooper remarked, "I learned all my history of England from Bertie and Eleanor Farjeon's *Kings and Queens*."

At about this period the first memoir, *A Nursery in the Nineties*, was begun. It entailed re-establishing links with Farjeons and Jeffersons in America, which gave Eleanor great joy, for every tentacle of the family was sacred to her, its pivot always being Harry-Nellie-Joe-and-Bertie. There was also information about her father to be gathered from New Zealand and Australia. And every letter she wrote, with ebullient energy and affection, established new connections and friendships.

Adulation of family is the drive behind the memoir, Eleanor's most interesting piece of adult writing. And although sections are confused by her exasperating habit of leaping back and forth in time, certain scenes and the emotional reactions of characters have a vivid impact. That hot-house nursery in South Hampstead, those eight thousand books flooding the house, the children's intensive imaginative life matched by their artistic energy, are all exposed with humour and sympathy. That the two ruthless men, father and son, who ruled the home, one with his heart, the other with his head, never came into conflict can hardly be believed, but it is greatly to their credit that Eleanor emerged from under the weight of their combined domination such a spirited woman. In springing prose she gives insight into the ways a child's imagination may be stimulated, with never a word of analysis or strained discussion. She understood that it was best to educate by way of enjoyment and that her father's dictum, 'Don't teach them anything they don't want to learn' was no argument for idleness.

Now in her fifties, Eleanor knew that she was strong in spirit and that her energy would not fail. Yet, despite the affection of family, of Earle and many many friends, the need for more and more love grew with time. Endearments and kisses flowed out to almost everyone she knew. One day, to the shocked delight of us children, she greeted my father's astonished chauffeur with a hearty hug and kiss. The gas man, the tax man, child and lord were all gathered into the circle of her arms, thereby becoming extra special to themselves and her. Maitland Radford's early warning about friendship had been to no avail. But these people were not taken up momentarily and then dropped, although her affections did swerve from one favourite to another: there were always presents, copies of her books with special inscriptions, sympathetic letters neither hackneyed nor short, gifts and cheques. Only when recipients grew too greedy, thinking her to be softer than she was – she was quite aware of her own softness – would they suddenly be cut off from her favour.

The ability to dismiss unwelcome thoughts at will was remarkable. Where most people revert in their mind to some unfortunate circumstance or relationship, waking in night hours to go over and over the problem, Eleanor was able in a most practical way to wipe the matter from her mind when she felt no longer empowered to help herself or others. In a truly Victorian manner certain persons who had offended were never spoken of again, and if referred to by others the subject was quietly cold-shouldered. The technique of this effective ban had probably been learned from Harry, though his more aggressive nature made embargos more numerous, so that his life moved in a narrower circle. Eleanor's life seemed limitless in range: she was continually stretching out to humanity all over the world, as though there could never be enough love to satisfy her need.

*Kings and Queens* turned out such a success that Victor Gollancz suggested another book in the same vein, and soon the collaborators were working on *Heroes and Heroines*. But Bertie now had a new plan and wrote:

Dear Nellie,
  I have had the germ of what I think is a good idea and one that may appeal to you. It's only a germ, but here goes. In the first place the idea is that we should collaborate in writing a very light, sentimental opera, probably in three acts. In the second place, although I have no plot, I have (what is so much easier) the atmosphere, which is, for period and weight, the Henley scene as *originally* conceived. That is to say, Victorianism in about the seventies: Frith.[1] In the third place, I suggest that we can do

1. William Frith, painter, 1819–1909.

entirely without a composer, and that we should dig for our melodies among the albums of the period, putting new words to the tunes where new words are required for the purposes of the story, which will be, I should think, in most cases: this will keep the music absolutely 'right' – and cheap. I have now told you almost all I know.

Of course, there must be no laughing at Victorianism: at the same time, the thing should be sharp as well as sweet, with gaiety and festivity. The first scene might be the sitting-room of a very Victorian house; the second scene might correspond to the Henley of yore; the third might be at night in the garden (cf. last scene of *Figaro*). I see some daughters – perhaps three – and a heavy, rather ominous father, who is the oppositional force to the love interest, looming a little, like the Count in *Figaro* again. But a story is very important. Let us remember fireworks . . .

Now Eleanor's ideas flowed. The neat complications of two bouquets presented to the wrong girls by a feather-headed young go-between were cleverly plotted. Had not that bouquet been presented by Wyndham Albery to the wrong little girl in her childhood? Eleanor well understood the consequent chagrin. In family albums of music the brother and sister re-discovered songs which their mother had sung, accompanying herself on the guitar, when they were young. They remembered her loveliness dressed in satin and lace for a ball or a first night. Tunes were chosen, words fitted. The light-hearted wit and sentiment suited Eleanor perfectly, and her whimsical webs were disciplined by Bertie.

Morning, mid-morning, afternoon and evening posts would bring sheaves of dialogue to our house from Hampstead, which Bertie would approve, discard or rewrite. It was out of the fertility of his sister's imagination that his own often blossomed. There were many times when she was hurt by his criticism, but she gave way, so that her sentimental effusions were generally curtailed. He relied on her boundless enthusiasm for impetus, enjoining her in a letter: 'Write as much as you like, as much as you can, write much too much. I'll use what we want and fine it down.'

*The Two Bouquets* was accepted by a theatrical manager, Sydney Carroll. He was not a man for lavish productions and no expensive stars were chosen to lead the cast, but actors and singers with good voices, lively personalities and acting ability. It was put on at the Ambassadors Theatre.

Eleanor was excited, over-excited, by this first full venture into the theatre world of kisses and tears, exasperation and euphoria. She had known the backstage atmosphere from childhood, had experienced those three operettas at the Royal Academy of Music in her teens, but never before been professionally involved. Bundled in a baggy coat, stray bits of greying hair sprouting from a much pinned bun, she looked like a spectacled White Queen sitting plumply in the darkened stalls. Beside her, under the next seat, lay capacious bags which contained comforts such as sandwiches, a thermos of hot tea, aspirin and even a hotwater bottle for anybody in need. But her mind was not in the least like that of the White Queen: it leaped nimbly forward devising necessary changes and ingenious additions, her criticism was positive, while with lavish optimism she encouraged actor, director, conductor, designer, scene-painter and stage-hand.

Bertie would also sit in the stalls watching rehearsals, well away from his sister, for Eleanor's public effusions embarrassed him. Hunched, shy, dry and witty, his criticism was more devastating, he was more determined to have his own way and was always jotting down notes for improvement to be gone through with the director later. He was more experienced in production, having written satirical revues, and comedies with his friend Horace Horsnell, in one of which Sybil Thorndike starred.

In an introduction to the projected fourth part of her memoir Eleanor wrote: 'Dear Bertie! you taught me more than I taught you. It was you who directed, I who took direction. We both built the coach, but while I galloped away with it, you held the reins. I was fluid, and could pour myself into the channel you dug for me; but it had to be *your* channel, you must be the initiator, you could not enter my imaginings and create something out of what you found there. It was wonderful to be able to enter yours, and I have profited by what I found there ever since.'

This was, of course, playing TAR all over again. She now poured herself into her younger brother's imagination with the same verve, the same instinctive sympathy as she had done with her elder brother.

On the first night of *The Two Bouquets* in August 1936 Eleanor presented the leading young ladies with exquisite Victorian fans

# THE TWO BOUQUETS

A Comedy with Music
by ELEANOR & HERBERT FARJEON

Photo by Sasha

**GEORGE BENSON**
London's New Comedian

## AMBASSADORS THEATRE

*The Two Bouquets* : programme

from a collection bought from her friend, the antique dealer, Mrs Pyatt, in Hampstead High Street. The fans were for the ballroom scene, but proved too frail for hard use and soon fell to bits.

George Benson, as the feather-headed masher who muddled the flowers, was the success of this excellent production. His gaiety and dash, his absurdity and charm, were irresistible. The newspaper reviews were good and predicted a long run.

In 1937 a sequel to *Martin Pippin in the Apple Orchard* was published: *Martin Pippin in the Daisy-Field*. This was in the old style, with more fanciful convolutions of conversation. It is significant that although seventeen years had passed since the first Martin Pippin, although Eleanor had now experienced a varied life knocking up against the world and earning her living, the youthful concern with playing mothers and fathers, with games and rules, fair and unfair, revived as fresh as ever; and with it the child's astute single-mindedness. Here is one of the chit-chats between Martin and his six new little girls – daughters of the six old little girls in the apple orchard. They sit in a Sussex field making daisy chains and urge Martin to tell them stories. The question is who shall have her story first.

Being first has sometimes its advantages, but not when it is going first to bed. None of the six was eager to get her story over while the light lay on the land. They went on threading their chains, and Stella looked haughty, and Selina looked dreamy, and Sylvia looked mischievous, and Sue looked obstinate, and Sally looked somewhere else entirely; so Sophie looked round, laughed, shrugged, and said obligingly: "Me if you like."

"I do like," said Martin.

"What do you like?" asked Sylvie, for now it was safe to come in again.

"I like Sophie."

"Why do you like her?"

"She laughs. That's one reason."

"She cries, you know, sometimes," said Sue very solemnly.

"I like her for that too."

"How peculiar of you," said Sally. "Laughing and crying are *other sides*."

"There are two sides to everything. If you took one away the

164

thing wouldn't be there. And if you like one, you'd better like both."

"*I* see," said Sally.

"I don't," said Sue.

There is a sprung rhythm to this dialogue, to the whole of the Martin Pippin fantasy. The minstrel's flirtation with the girls remains curiously sexless despite innuendo, much like that which Harry adopted in real life, a philosophic banter that showed off his ability for word-spinning. *Martin Pippin in the Daisy-Field* was yet another success.

*23*

# Cat and Elephant

THERE WERE CATS walking along the top of the brick walls that enclosed the garden, and along the alleyway and the backs of the Church Row properties, in a criss-cross cat ghetto. Wild cats and pampered cats trod the gutter of the low cottage roof, peered through the window and came in or passed on. The book *Golden Coney* relates the story of these cats, about whom Eleanor grew lyrical, especially when tackling the subject of feline masculinity.

'Below him drop the dark wells of the gardens; above him shines the moon. Threading his way between Nos 16 and 28, he brushes now a supple branch of fig leaves, now dripping laburnum fronds; the poplars' silvery rustle fills his ears, a soft wash of water on the shores of the night; the arabesques of a creamy rambler rose, that spreads to three gardens with its roots in one, strive to detain him; odours of night-scented stock and tobacco plant, sunk in shadow among stone paving and cobbles, rise with Cicerean charm to lull and stay him.

'Lull him! detain him! the God on his pursuit?

'Broad as Hercules his chest; gold as Apollo's his hair; like Vulcan's his sinews. His eyes are small and humorous as a pig's. His ears are bitten, one of them hangs in rags, and in his shoulder a raw wound bleeds a little. His nose is bashed like a heavyweight's. But he does not emulate beauty; he hunts it, and his passions are Jupiter's.'

This work was about to be dedicated to the publisher and fellow cat lover, Michael Joseph, when Eleanor changed her mind; it had to be inscribed to her own cat, Bunny. In a letter to Michael Joseph, Eleanor explained that her home carried on under a matriarchy and that she could do no other than dedicate the story to the mother of its hero. The letter records: 'It was our habit, yours and mine, to compare notes three or four times a year. As I remember our telephone talk of those days, we spoke first of litters and second of editions. The litters greatly outnumbered the editions.'

The cats who resided at 20 Church Walk were as important as anybody; they were never spoken to in baby language, but conversed with; their fads and fancies over food and cushions were attended to. The vet was as essential as the doctor, and more often called in, honoured as all Farjeon physicians had to be until found out, when another infallible medical man would be discovered. The matriach Bunny had come as a kitten from Mrs Pyatt's antique shop and, as soon as she became pregnant, hints about lying-in and cat obstetrics were passed on to Eleanor by Mrs Pyatt, the expert. Eleanor's excitement over the birth of kittens, which now occurred several times a year, never diminished, while many poems show her amused delight in cats.

> *Cats sleep*
> *Anywhere,*
> *Any table,*
> *Any chair,*
> *Top of piano,*
> *Window ledge,*
> *In the middle,*
> *On the edge,*
> *Open drawer,*
> *Empty shoe,*
> *Anybody's*
> *Lap will do,*
> *Fitted in a*
> *Cardboard box,*
> *In the cupboard*
> *With your frocks –*
> *Anywhere!*
> *They don't care!*
> *Cats sleep*
> *Anywhere.*

When in 1935 the Sussex cottage, Hammonds, was bought, half and half with Earle, infinite trouble was taken over the cats' transportation to the country. There were four at this time: Pickle, Nonny, Bunny and Golden Coney. They travelled down with Eleanor and Earle in a chauffeur-driven car. To steady the cats' nerves sips of water from a spoon were provided as, released from baskets, they leaped about the back seats in a frenzy and wailed. But they soon acclimatised themselves to country life and could be trusted to go out and attend to their own business. This is a description from *Golden Coney* of how the two neutered males managed:

'These two, deprived of love's pangs and pleasures, consorted on a plane of mutual understanding. To see him go off for the evening with his foster-father, like a young club-man put up, seconded, and elected by an old one, was to understand the freemasonry of the male from which the uninitiated female is excluded. Together they strolled their estates, and Pickle, grown plump and rather indolent, introduced the youngster to his holes and haunts. There was a special mouse-hole in the larder, gone to earth below the cupboard under the stairs, to which Nonny applied himself diligently on each return from their town to their country house. He would sit there hour after hour, as still as a sportsman waiting for wings to fly or fins to rise. In a few days the hole was cleared.'

In a short story, *Spooner*,[1] written long before Eleanor had a cat of her own, the observation is acute. 'Cats are more fluid than solid, they can pour themselves through any sluice like water.' And again: 'I have never yet known a cat who could not make its commands imperative, even if not explicable. Spooner stood on his hind legs, stretched himself like elastic as high as the keyhole, and laid a paw on either side of the key. I turned it and opened the cupboard.'

Hammonds stood outside the village of Laughton. It was a proper cottage with a steep roof, low ceilings, a Valor paraffin cooking stove, open wood fires and beams on which you were likely to bump your head. It was a delight to be living in Sussex again, comfortably near Glyndebourne Opera House, which was visited in state every year. On such outings Eleanor wore a dark full-length silky dress, rows of long beads dangled over her full bosom, mother of pearl opera glasses were held in an old-fashioned velvet purse which hung

1. From *Faithful Jenny Dove and Other Tales*.

*Eleanor and George Earle*

from a chain on her wrist. She drove over with whoever had been carefully chosen to accompany her, with a hamper of equally carefully chosen wine and delicacies to be eaten beneath a pergola in the gardens during the interval. Mozart was the ideal, but a variety of classical music was always an important part of life, her memory being so retentive that she could play the symphonies of Beethoven mentally to herself from start to finish, and so accurately that the particular style of some favourite conductor would also be memorised.

Eleanor, Earle and the cats went to Hammonds mostly in summer weather. At other times the house was lent to friends or relatives in need. There were luxuries in Laughton difficult to come by in town: a village woman always ready to clean, an asparagus bed dug by Mr Fradd the gardener, the downs always in view, for now, with bad bunions, Eleanor did not often walk far.

It was at Hammonds that Mr Fradd's mother was scandalised one hot morning. The elderly countrywoman knocked at the door and was invited to come in. As usual she found Earle sitting in his tweed suit with a newspaper. Then a figure appeared on the stairs which led straight down into the room: it was Miss Farjeon stark naked. Descending, she wished the old lady good morning and began to discuss the weather and other matters, as though this was the ordinary way to welcome a visitor. The astonished Mrs Fradd left as soon as possible, expostulating to her family when she got home, "I wouldn't have minded so much, only there was the old gentleman sitting in his chair smoking his pipe."

However, Eleanor and her old gentleman were still considered nice people, despite other nonconformities, like not being married and allowing cats to walk at all times on the kitchen table.

Bertha Bettesworth [Summerbell], who was now married but still living in Fellows Road looking after Harry, also reported that Eleanor would discard her clothes readily. "I remember her dropping them off and standing there stark naked. I'd never seen anyone naked in my life before, and I blushed up like anything. And I remember her just standing there laughing, the way she did when she saw me blush up."

The absurdity of physical modesty had already been the subject of one of those 'Tomfool' rhymes in the *Daily Herald*.

# THE DECENT DRESS

*Not only in the times most recent*
*Was modern clothing thought indecent.*
*Appalling were the household scenes*
*When ladies first dropped crinolines;*
*In Paris, in Directoire days,*
*The followers of Fashion's craze*
*Were mobbed before the public eye*
*And ducked for their immodesty.*
*And has it not been ever thus?*
*Clothes which were too voluminous*
*So obviously could conceal*
*What clothes too scanty would reveal.*
*From the vast Turkish-towelling gown*
*Which hides Ma's bathing-costume, down*
*To Eve's first fig leaf, dress intrudes*
*Either the point of view of prudes,*
*Or else insists too consciously*
*On what we may or may not see.*
*It seems to me in Nature's name*
*All forms of dress might be to blame,*
*Except the pure and perfect dress*
*Of Adam's God-made nakedness.*

George Earle was himself no prude, though he would never have made so extrovert a demonstration as Eleanor. He spent time, now that he had given up all effort to earn a living, making or mending furniture, and had presented a box of the most wonderful workmanship to us three children. The box had a tray with compartments which you could not push down into place, it fitted so perfectly, but had to allow to sink gently on its own as the air below slowly escaped, like the smoothest lift descending. Though still in his sixties, Earle treated himself as an old man, and Eleanor with her maternal managing nature was not unwilling to encourage his dependence. So he worked at the bench in whichever cottage she decreed, or read and did crossword puzzles, coddling himself and being coddled. He was pleased to talk to whoever was introduced into the house, his almost invariable opening to a stranger being, "Do you know Keats?"

When in London he would go out to do a little light shopping, not the heavy shopping which Eleanor managed in voluminous bags that bumped her ankles, and then he would walk across the Heath in order to view Keats's house once more. He would return for lunch with a flower, or a story of some adventure over which they could laugh. Eleanor was a great one for mirth: a full note of happiness rang out when she laughed, as though the fun of life burst through, topping all the other emotions and sensibilities which so obviously moved her.

With her the morning would often be spent in bed, the eiderdown an up-and-down sea floating letters, cats, proofs, books, paper and the black Remington typewriter. From her bed she talked for hours on the telephone, soothing and encouraging distraught friends, or booking theatre tickets, discussing a book with an editor, or a job for somebody, and her cats and her triumphs with everybody. Although by now bronchitis was a regular trouble, she seldom complained and, unless extremely ill, was never idle. People came first always. 'Writing gets done at odd moments,' she wrote. However there must have been a good many of these for, besides all the published work, there remains a considerable mass that was never published or acted. Before her death she destroyed some unsaleable material, but I have found twelve plays and operettas among the papers, as well as the unfinished memoir.

Eleanor was never in debt and paid bills immediately. She continually gave away large and small sums to the indigent, or to those she felt were in need of a treat – she so loved giving treats. But during the 1930s, after Earle stopped work and gave her £1 a week for the rest of his life, money was at times a worry, for children's literature is traditionally ill-paid. So she turned out stories, poems and plays as fast as possible, reusing and rehashing old material, in order to make ends meet.

Of the Farjeons during the 1930s it was Joe who earned the largest income, with his popular detective novels. He worked with perseverance, refusing to leave his study each day until two thousand words had been written. Bertie also worked at home for most of the day, visiting the theatre at night as a dramatic critic. His income fluctuated, but at its peak our household expanded to two maids, a cook, a gardener and the part-time chauffeur kissed by Eleanor. As time went on the expense of three children to educate curtailed the number of maids, for at this period there was no question of middle class families taking advantage of free education: it would have been of no advantage at all.

Whenever work was scarce the brothers and sister were ready to help each other. They also shared in the keep of their governess, Miss Newman, and sent money to their old nurse, Fanny Dodd.

Eleanor had invested in Bertie's revues, which by the late thirties he was managing, as well as writing, for the Little Theatre. The amounts she gave were never large, because Bertie did not wish anybody to lose a substantial sum, and most backers invested £100. The business was run on a co-operative system he had devised, all the company receiving the same basic salary, on top of which each member was allowed a percentage of the profits according to his or her rating, from star to chorus. This meant that when the theatre was full everybody did well, but when it was empty each received the basic £5 a week. So the interest of the whole cast to make the show succeed was ensured, while everybody was concerned about box office receipts from day to day. Up to now Eleanor had profited by investing in Bertie's shows.

Now money was needed for a new operetta, *An Elephant in Arcady*, which she and Bertie had written. It was a comedy set in an Italian palazzo garden where an eccentric count kept his menagerie, period the eighteenth century with contemporary music, in the choosing of which great help was given by the conductor Ernest Irving, whose fastidious and often ferocious demands had so contributed to the high musical quality of *The Two Bouquets*.

In June 1937 Bertie wrote to Robert Solomons: 'We are out for £2000 backing of which we already have offers of £1750. I am wondering whether you would care to have a small finger in the pie and write to you just in case. Whether it is a success or not – of course, we all believe in it – I feel sure that it will be a show such as you would like to see succeed, quite apart from finance and friend-ship. We propose to run it on the same co-operative lines as "Nine Sharp",[1] of which, if you should be interested, I will send you particulars in two or three weeks. The virtues of that co-operative system have not, I consider, yet been tested, they being designed to tide over trouble rather than to aggravate success.' The P.S. to this

1. Little Theatre revue.

letter runs: 'The success of "Nine Sharp" really has been great fun –
there have been moments when I have almost felt contented.'

This rare content felt by Bertie made an extraordinary contrast to
his sister's continual complacency with the world.

There came a favourable response to Bertie's appeal:

My dear Bertie,

I am really very interested in your letter of the 17th June, more
especially because your new venture is to be run on the same
co-operative lines as "Nine Sharp".

There has been criticism and although I do not know the details,
I have always said, on hearing this criticism, that you deserved a
hearty vote of thanks from all the artists concerned and that if the
stars have not received their full pound of flesh, the result,
nevertheless, has been a run which in the end will bring stars more
than they could have expected elsewhere. I have also heard that
the starlets have been earning more than they have ever earned
before, and this, I think, is very much to the good.

At any rate, you seem to have found a way of preventing
landlords and stars between them from ruining revues financially.
For this reason, I should very much like to have the details of your
co-operative system and you may take it that I should like to be
interested in your next venture to a small amount; and I see that it
is only a small amount that you will still require.

Will you come to lunch with me as soon as you are ready to take
the matter further?

With best wishes to you all, Yours,
    M. R. Solomons

Eleanor was not involved in the business side of the show, but she
appreciated the worth of Bertie's radical system. As far as politics
went she was a socialist and voted Labour at elections: her politics
went as far as a general belief that the spread of wealth should be
equalised and that many people were misguided in their greed. From
the following letter the difference in attitude between brother and
sister may be seen – the one so difficult to please, the other so easy.
To Bertie she did not use endearments.

Dear Bertie,

A lovely morning, working out the enclosed in four parts; I have typed the exact things each voice has to sing, and the variations occur because it is in canon, and they aren't all singing at once, or in equal lengths; but it is a superb number, and the interleaving of the exclamations ought to be a joy. For the script we must get out something general and shapelier, of course, based on the Soprano part.

It is typed in three sections, so that you can combine the four parts more easily as you read. At the end the three extraneous ARCADIANS can rise during the last lines, and limp off, variously, leaving the scene free for ORTENSIO, BETTINA, and GUILIA.

Ernest [Irving] really is a gem when it comes to knowing what will fit a scene effectively. This is quite different from any other thing in the piece, and we couldn't have found it ourselves, as it is a bit of chamber music I think – anyhow it has never been sung before.

Love from N.

The lyrics were more original than those of *The Two Bouquets*, and musically the requirements of Paisiello, Scarlatti, Mozart and the other eighteenth century composers were more demanding than those of Victorian drawing-room songs. This time operatic artists had to be employed. For leading lady they were lucky enough to engage Irene Eisinger. She had sung Susanna in the Glyndebourne production of *Figaro*, and no more charming actress or lovely voice could have been found. The lover was Eric Starling, who had been with Sadler's Wells Opera Company, while the eccentric Count Pomposo was sung by Frederick Ranalow, who had been at the Royal Academy of Music when Harry was a student and could be welcomed as an old friend.

Here is Count Pomposo's opening song as he introduces his menagerie, with its new, most important inhabitant.

> *My darling little dingoes,*
> *My rosy red flamingoes,*
> *My crawly crocodile*
> *Imported from the Nile –*
> *I sweeten their captivity*
> *In every way I can,*

*My pets are my proclivity,*
*I am a happy man!*
*My birds and beasts and fishes*
*Fulfil my fondest wishes,*
*My cockatoos and curlews*
*I visit in their purlieus,*
*And I rise at break of dawn*
*To gambol with my fawn,*
*I ponder why my marmoset*
*Likes swinging on a tree,*
*And wonder what my lamas ate*
*Before they came to me.*
*With sugar plums I humour*
*My porcupine and puma –*
*My jackals and hyenas*
*Rejoice in your arenas,*
*And sing this cheerful chant –*
*Pomposo has an elephant!*
*When I think of his immensity*
*I quiver with intensity,*
*I've got an elephant –*
*I have never had a vaster piece,*
*My elephant's my masterpiece –*
*Pomposo's elephant!*

For artistic refinement, for exquisite music and originality *The Elephant in Arcady* was of high quality. Certain of the audience came to see the show fourteen times, but in days when opera was not popular in England *The Elephant in Arcady* was hardly appreciated by a large public. Financially it failed, although the co-operative system kept it going far longer than would have otherwise been possible. Eleanor and Bertie considered it their best stage production.

The *Evening Standard* critic (6th October 1938) saw the situation clearly: 'I fear that from the point of view of popular appeal this elephant is a white one. But of the beauty, originality and charm of the production there can be no question. Mr Irving's score is a masterpiece.'

Bertie grew more thin and nervous with the strain of half-full houses, but Eleanor took defeat, and the paying out of extra hundreds of pounds which she could ill afford, in her stride.

# Other Authors

IN 1936 A COMMITTEE was formed in order to raise money for a memorial stone to Edward Thomas, to be placed on one of the Hampshire hills where he had so often walked. The committee included Walter de la Mare, Lascelles Abercrombie, Clifford Bax and Eleanor, but the chief mover of the idea was Roland Watson, a civil servant who had long been an enthusiastic admirer of the poet, though they had never met. Eleanor used her powers of persuasion among journalists and authors to publicise the project. Besides Ezra Pound, Bertie was one of the few who refused to subscribe, explaining to his sister that his feeling was anti stones and monuments, though he would give willingly to any scheme which entailed reprinting Thomas's work.

A huge stone, brought from Avebury, was winched down the steep slope into place on Stoner Hill, and into its top was set an octagonal plate which read:

'This hillside is dedicated to the memory of Edward Thomas, Poet. Born in Lambeth 3rd March 1878. Killed in the Battle of Arras 9th April 1917.

'And I rose up and knew that I was tired and continued my journey.'[1]

In October 1937 the Poet Laureate, John Masefield, was among the writers, old friends and relatives at the ceremony, when the melancholy quotation was revealed. From this time Roland Watson became Eleanor's friend and it was to him that she ultimately presented all her letters from Edward Thomas.[2]

1. From *Light and Twilight* by Edward Thomas, Duckworth, 1911.
2. These letters were subsequently given to Battersea Library, London.

So there was renewed interest in the man whose writing, although always appreciated by the few, had never become popular. A biography was begun by John Moore, following Helen Thomas's more intimate book about her husband, *As It Was*. When Moore's manuscript was half written he sent it to Eleanor for comment, and the following letter gives her judgement, one which points out many of the pitfalls that may overset those impertinent enough to expose on paper another human being.

*5th March*, 1938

Dear Mr Moore,

I hope I haven't kept this too long. I find myself in a difficulty in giving you my frank opinion of it, because you have treated it in a way which seems to me the wrong way, and I know, as a writer, what a thing it is to be told this half way through a work of importance. But this does not feel to me like an authentic biography of Edward Thomas so much as a story about him, skimmed off the top of others' writings and sayings, a novelist's biography, rather too facilely running its course. The easy references to Edward and Helen by their Christian names produces the effect of their being persons in a story written by you, rather than actual persons of whom you have been a student. It is hard to say what one wanted in a biography of E. T. produced at this time; but I think it was something of more depth and less surface, something that, with greater gravity, could take its place among the lives of our distinguished writers, a book to be turned to by future generations, both for enlightening and particular reference. I am not asking for something heavier and duller, for such subjects don't lose in interest by gaining in depth. It is a question in my mind whether a public, unfamiliar with Edward, may not wonder whether this man and his life were of enough interest to account for the present record. You have been reading and reading omnivorously in the past year, and, for me, the result is a compilation out of your mass of material, rather than a revelation from it. It is true there is much to come. But the manner of treatment remains, which troubles me from the first page.

Is this rather awful for you to read? It is, for me to write; and where it will land you, goodness only knows. No writer can tell another how to write his book; but every reader can say how he has

178

read it, and that is all I can do, with sad honesty, now. One thing that troubles me a good deal (which may be mitigated by your later chapters, but, I should think, be apparent in your first as well) is the presentment of Edward almost entirely on his unhappy and neurasthenic side. It is time, I think, and of great importance, for some understanding of his other qualities to be published, unless he is to go down to posterity as a morbid, cruel and even dislikeable figure. That is a danger I forsee as one result even of Helen's beautiful book, from which it is easier for a reader to grasp how much he made her suffer than how much he was worth suffering for. That she bore the suffering magnificently, and was magnificently happy in between, is likelier to be put down to her being a woman great in love, than to Edward's being what he was. (A woman friend of mine and Helen's, who never knew him and has read her book, thinks of him as cruel, whom she would have disliked had she known him – I have never told Helen this, it would so much distress her, and I only tell you now because it may help you not to make your book another nail in the coffin.)

What Edward was, is your problem. He doesn't, like Keats, translate into his letters all his moods, from black pessimism to hilarity. But his intimate friends had them all (except the emotional expression which, in his life and his letters, was probably reserved for Helen alone). But consider this: Why did those who knew him well, love and value his society almost above that of any other man? Why do some of the men who loved him still ache for him, as the greatest loss in their lives – the best friend gone? Why, though he detested playing cricket, did he join willingly, and why, though he played it execrably, was he asked to join those radiantly-remembered cricket-weeks of Clifford Bax's, which included some of the gayest spirits and the wittiest minds of the time? It would be impossible, and false, to present Edward's nature and character without the self-torture from which he suffered so terribly. But remember that when his moods weren't on him like a sickness, when his nerves weren't harassed by overwork and anxiety, when something in himself and in his company had released him from his own constraints and boredom, he was, among other things, the best company in the world; the best talker, the best thinker, the most humorous (his humour scarcely ever is referred to, but it was the finest brand I've ever known, I think), the best man to walk with, to dig potatoes with, to sing in the evening with, to share a joke or poem with, or to come away from feeling the every vestige of pose or sham had been wiped off the slate while you were with him. He had a charm that was never exercised, and an integrity that couldn't be questioned. His power of friendship was as great as his need of it. What made Horatio love Hamlet? Some of the same qualities, I believe, as made his friends love Edward – things that can't be brought to light, that he himself would have rejected if they had been uttered, things that could not save him from his own suffering, and that made us who loved him ready to share everything he was. I have spent single days, and whole weeks, with him, in his own home and others, when the companionship was of a kind that happens seldom and is remembered for ever. Nobody would have borne with him, I think, if he had been only, or chiefly, a sick tormented bitter disappointed figure. Men like Nevinson, Hudson, Garnett, and Frost would not have delighted in him, or country folk talked at ease with him, or young men on holiday been eager for him. No picture of him is true without these things. I wish you could have talked with the men who knew him.

I will end with a plea for your forgiveness, if you feel I need it.
Yours always,
Eleanor Farjeon

Next day Eleanor sent a copy of this to Roland Watson with a simple condemnation.

Dear Watty,
You'll be reading this perhaps before John Moore does; but I feel you'd like to see my effort in the cause. Nothing will make a good book of it now, I fear; but some harms may be avoided, perhaps, against the day when the right book is written by somebody else . . .

Eleanor's attitude to other writers was mostly generous and never pretentious. It was about this time that I showed my aunt the verse of a serious young poet whom I admired. However, she made nothing of his work, frankly admitting that she did not understand his kind of poetry, which was abstruse somewhat in the manner of Eliot. She did not undertake contemporary poetry, or not much, I would say, beyond de la Mare and D. H. Lawrence. There were no collections of Eliot, Auden or Pound on her shelves and she never mentioned them to me. Her taste remained, I think, old-fashioned. Late in life it emerged, to my surprise, that she had never yet read Manley Hopkins. He came as a revelation and her delight and excitement at his discovery gave us mutual pleasure. Modern novelists, on the other hand, were widely read, among the women authors Rosamond Lehmann, Storm Jameson, Katherine Mansfield and Virginia Woolf being thoroughly appreciated.

By contrast to that cool estimation of John Moore's biography was Eleanor's earlier response when Rosalind's eighteen-year-old daughter, Chloe, sent her three short stories. Of course, in this case there was no personal emotion involved, but every appeal for literary help, whether from child or adult, was taken with equal seriousness and her considered opinion given.

Dearest Chloe,

This all seems to me very promising. These aren't by any means the average short-story, but something much more difficult to succeed in, because, being slight and subtle, they want real art to bring them off; and I think you nearly do in each case, and perhaps you quite do in "Intruder", which I like the best of the three. It was hardest to bring off too, because its effect can't be assisted by such obvious touches as point the other two; there is a real sense of beauty in it, to heighten the self-consciousness of the Intruder; the description of the funeral procession is perfect, and moving. I have really very little criticism to offer; if this is going to be your vein (or one of them) you will go on making it better yourself, finding out (as Katherine Mansfield so marvellously did) how to make every sentence contribute to the effect you're after, so that the whole thing is acute and unmistakeable. If I were you I'd start in at once sending these round to magazines like Lovat Dickson and Adelphi; hoping very little, and expecting nothing. You've got to get used to returned MSS, because they are so likely at the start; and you needn't be disheartened by the returns, and can feel jolly bucked up if once in a way they stay put. Don't try sending these off if, in these early days, you feel their return will discourage you, and cloud your own criticism of yourself. I wish you'd have a shot at it though.

I've made one or two faint pencil marks, easily erased, in the stories; most of them are only queries about things I'm not sure of myself.

## INTRUDER

Page 2, line 6; I don't like the sentence I've marked. I'd rather have it turned round quite simply : "Suddenly a rent of scarlet split the sky." But if you like it, and did it on purpose, and want to keep it, don't change it because I don't like it. Don't ever do that for anybody. Only consider whether you agree or not with what has temporarily pulled up your critic . . .

This final advice harks back to the time when Ben Farjeon insisted on changing 'mefrom' to 'from me' and Eleanor gave in, although only till he was out of her room. She had understood very early that it is generally sound to stick to your own opinion.

# New York

ON MARCH 8th 1938 a Western Union Cablegram arrived at 20 Perrins Walk (as Church Walk had now been renamed). 'Please communicate with Curtis Brown London [Eleanor's agent] regarding our inquiry immediate production here Two Bouquets do you own American rights cable address Marconel. Marc Connolly'

Marc Connolly, actor, playwright, director, and film maker, had met Eleanor back stage at the Ambassadors Theatre in 1936, during the run of *The Two Bouquets*. Eleanor described him as a big bald-pated evanescent American, tickled to death by the show, and her half-Yankee heart went out to him. He described her in Joyce Barbour's dressing-room. 'She burst in bearing a market basket overflowing with groceries and vegetables of all sorts from carrots to scallions [onions] and also the proofs of her novel. Before she could put down the basket, I informed her that I wanted to produce *The Two Bouquets* in America.'

By 1938 the rights of the play had reverted to its authors and a contract went through without procrastination. On March 11th Eleanor wrote:

Dear Mr Connolly,

My brother and I have signed the contract to-day, but I am not weighing all the pros and cons for coming over until the question of Edward Gill [the role George Benson played in London] is settled. But I am catching the mail to-night with a few questions, in case all's well by the time you get this.

(1) I don't want an advance on royalties, though it is kind of you

183

to suggest the additional £350 to help me out; but much of this would ultimately be due to my brother, Ernest Irving, and the London Play Co. So may I rely on the fare one way, which you suggested over the telephone, and which I took to be an offer without liabilities? If this is right, what would it amount to?

(2) Even with this assistance, a trip of 7 or 8 weeks would be difficult for me to arrange, because of domestic matters here, work put aside, and the cost of living in New York during rehearsals and production. So, if my fare was given to me, on the assumption that I was coming to give an eye to details during the production, would it be fair and square for me to arrive early in April, instead of late in March? That is, to be there during the first three weeks of rehearsals, or thereabouts? (Longer, if production can't take place on April 25th.)

(3) Do you know any place convenient to the theatre, where I could get a room for a fairly modest sum? And a basement rather than an eyrie. I have to own, with shame, to an appalling complex about heights. One day I shall die of imagining I've fallen over a precipice; I may be standing in the middle of Holland at the time. If you do know of such a place, can you give me a notion of the price of a room by the day (without meals).

If the situation warrants it when this arrives, can you cable me brief answers to these questions? I have a copy of them, and can supply intelligently any brevities you indulge in. Then I *will* make a decision, and cable you a Yes, with a date, or a No. In the event of No, my brother and I will send you a letter with certain points which you may find helpful; there was an attitude we strictly preserved during production, which I think was valuable to the thing as a whole, and contributed to its success.

Yours always,
Eleanor Farjeon

At first the domestic difficulties appeared insuperable. What should be done with Earle and the cats? Earle needed constant care – or at least he was accustomed to it – and for eight years had never been left alone by his devoted Nell. But friends urged her to go; some promised to look after him, others to look after the cats. She was persuaded: after all she had not had an adventure for years. So she wrote to cousin Harry Russell Farjeon, son of Uncle Israel, who lived sumptuously in New York, asking him to put her up for a short while. He cabled back 'Your American home is with me'. Now, with the household cared for and free board and lodging in Park Avenue, the adventure was on.

Connolly sent 400 dollars for expenses, the passport photo was taken and a tourist class shared cabin booked on the *Queen Mary*. Wardrobe and grooming were organised by Joe's elegant Bostonian wife, who admonished, "Nellie, if you go to America, you must take yourself in hand. You simply *cannot* go about New York as you do in Hampstead."

On the strength of Connolly's cheque, which came to £80, a manicure, hair trim and water wave were arranged, face cream, a box of powder and a few pretty clothes were bought. But two days later Eleanor was in bed with a sore throat. The doctor promised to pull her through in time, yet she very much feared she would be cancelling the passage. Next day she was up for a bit of packing, but the following day grew worse. However, by March 29th she was better and wrote in her diary 'A full last day – Pod[1] very dear – oh dear, how we shall miss each other.'

On the 30th she was seen off on the train by Earle, Harry, Joe, Bertie and Gervase. At Southampton the size of the Queen Mary seemed staggering, while her stateroom was filled with flowers, telegrams and chocolates.

In *The American Adventure*, which was planned as a part of her memoir, Eleanor wrote: 'Super luxury on the *Queen Mary* soon palled. The drink-bars, Cinema shows, beauty-parlours, smart shops, and overwhelming menus for too many meals a day (with steward-borne trays to support life in the intervals), seemed to have nothing to do with the sea. "Tourist Class", crowded with passengers bent on squeezing the last ounce out of their trip, was like a five-day non-stop cocktail party; and peace was wanting in the superb stateroom-and-bathroom I shared with Marion King, who turned out to be a writer of children's books like myself. The "restless little thing" kept up a stream of high-strung chatter, obsessed with her own restlessness, her need of happiness, her desire to do something "big" for children, her dislike of women, her incapacity for listening, and her capacity for talk. She had the spoiled-child

1. Pod was George Earle's childhood nick-name.

185

outlook of many of the American women I was going to meet, was afraid of life and dirt, and vowed, "I am going to wear *jolly good clothes* all my life." Famous names thrilled her, and she was enraptured by an invitation to tea in the Saloon with Jascha Heifetz and Mrs Scott, whose horse Battleship we had just seen win the Grand National on the ship's cinema. "But there's something curious about her that I rather like," I wrote in my day-letter to Pod.'

This tolerance was one of the admirable characteristics which Eleanor took to almost every human encounter. She found it hard to dislike anybody. Like so many others, Marion King confessed intimate details of her life to her cabin mate, a compliment which was not returned.

Waiting on the New York dockside stood six-foot cousin Harry, Marc Connolly, doing a sort of St Vitus dance round the luggage in his eagerness to get it through the customs, his partner Bela Blau, his press agent and others. Eleanor explained that she would not be photographed, interviewed or televised, and was immediately whisked off to Connolly's hotel with all the details of production problems in her ears. In a second taxi she was returned to cousin Harry, where she met his daughter Grace and the Canalettos down the hallway. Having been installed in a rose pink suite 'overflowing with flowers and mail and telegrams as though I were Claudette Colbert', she was off again to lunch with Connolly at the Algonquin, and then on to the theatre to meet the musical director, the designer and pianist. An audition for the chorus parts followed, which went on for hours, at the end of which nobody was cast but everybody was calling her honey and sweetie-pie.

Returned to Park Avenue for dinner, she was off again in a fourth taxi to see *Hurray for What?* with Connolly; then back stage in Ed Wynne's dressing room eating and drinking things, for half-an-hour bosom pals, never to meet again. Connolly next took her back to his hotel where, over beer and sandwiches, he began to describe the new play he was writing: a semi-mystic theme of a lost race in the Appalachian Mountains. He jigged up and down and round and round the room explaining scenes, acting them, flinging notions and incidents and scraps of character and dialogue about. 'Marc in these hours at his most remarkable, and his work at its best, stops jigging, munches a last sandwich, gives me the time and place for tomorrow's, no today's, auditions.' [*American Adventure*]

So began a continuous whirl of New York life, intensified by the frenzy of theatrical production. Eleanor was included in every branch of the activities, consulted and deferred to. In the enthusiasm sustained over the next two months, between audition and production, friendships developed on all sides which were to last her life. She commented shrewdly, 'Perhaps we were enjoying ourselves a little too much for the good of the piece.'

It wanted Bertie's dry critical eye. But for his sister this was an intoxicating revel.

When writing the play my Farjeon blood is flowing, but during the rehearsal period the Jefferson in me seizes its chance to sit in a playhouse at any time of day or night, preferably shrouded in dustsheets which I have the right to drag aside and sit where I please. Whatever is taking place I must be there. The worries, the set-backs, the delays and catastrophes, the quarrel that always boils up in the third week when nerves break, are as integral to the drama of production as the kaleidoscope variety of interest, the conferences with the producer, the cutting of a speech and re-writing of a scene, the surprises the actors can give you as they bring their parts to life, the dress parade in which they become other people entirely, the settings in which your play becomes another play, the replacement of the pianist by the orchestra when the songs become magical music, the network of fears and hopes leading to the excitement of the first night – from first to last I must be there, whatever is taking place.

'And whatever is *not* taking place, I must be there. I can sit contented hour after hour in an empty theatre, waiting for the next activity to light it up, idly hearing a hammering in the wings, a voice shouting from the flies, glancing through my blue pencilled dog-eared script, jotting down a few notes, munching a bar of chocolate, exploring the circles, haunting the gallery, coming to know the stage-door-keeper, the wardrobe mistress, the cleaners, the firemen and the stage cat. [*American Adventure*]

Although guarded from reporters, a long article in the *New York Herald Tribune* explained how Miss Farjeon followed none of the traditions of visiting English writers, giving no lectures or interviews and never posing for pictures. Coming over she had escaped attention by the expedient of travelling tourist class. This very American sleight of mind, by which the shame of being too poor to go first class had to be explained away, could not have pleased the nonconforming writer. Another example of different conventions, which must have amused her, was at a dinner party arranged by Grace Farjeon for her father's birthday. All went smoothly until the meal ended, when Eleanor said she would join her cousin Harry in smoking a cigar. Following what must be American etiquette, the eldest daughter, Virginia, believed that Eleanor should not be the only woman smoking a cigar and so followed her lead. Eleanor, of course, was quite comfortable, having always enjoyed cigars, but the girl looked awkward, though inwardly satisfied that she had saved Eleanor from embarrassment.

Another episode in the apartment remembered by Grace Farjeon was the one moment when she saw Eleanor angry, ('and anger is too strong a word') she wrote in her letter to me. Eleanor had returned to the rose-pink suite to find that her work table had been tidied up. Cousin Harry, almost obsessive in his neatness, had done this, imagining it would be helpful. So, while she was out, he organised what seemed dreadful litter into neat little piles, expecting his cousin to be delighted. His consternation when told that she never wanted him to touch the desk again, that she was very upset and would brook no further interference with her work, was considerable. His contrition immediately appeased the lady and all anger evaporated.

The effort to smarten Eleanor up had been vain. One evening she was invited to a reception as the guest of honour and arrived at an expensive apartment block with her usual bulgy bag and petticoat wavering below her dress. The hall porter looked askance at this shabby character and demanded where she was going. On being told he responded, "Oh no, you can't go up there! They are giving a party tonight."

"But," expostulated Eleanor, "*I am* the party!"

The streets of the city fascinated and bewildered her. She did not know how to catch a bus or subway train, she crossed roads against the traffic in a dither, but was saved by passers-by. However, 'I had never felt so alive. I could go round day and night from seven in the morning till the small hours: go from letters and breakfast and telephoning in my room to ten hours of theatre work and daytime appointments, a show in the evening, supper in a night club, an hour in a glaring bowling alley, a drink or a party in somebody's fabulous apartment, still more fabulous than somebody's the night before: then back to Cousin Harry's safe apartment home where everyone was in bed but the fatherly porter, and where, after another hour letter-writing, I fell asleep at four or five o'clock: sleep so profound that I woke invigorated for the day-and-night round again.' [*American Adventure*]

To Earle she wrote a long almost daily account of her doings, but – 'Yes, if it weren't for you, beloved, I'd be having the time of my life; but without you I never never can.' In these letters to Earle her affection often became passionate.

To Bertie there were analyses of each artist in the operetta and how they fitted their roles. Leslie French was going to be perfectly charming, easy, dapper and roguish – Connolly recognised the artist in him. Leslie was full of ideas, rehearsed firmly and sweetly with never a trace of egotism. Mary Westcott, a golden girl who turned up at a crucial moment, was perfect for her part, exactly the right size, with the feel of a very young and spoiled child. And so on, with hardly a demur.

To brother Harry she gave a description of a visit to Dr Rosenbach. 'The best Chinese lacquer is nothing to the fine glaze on Rosenbach himself.' He was a man of infinite wealth and impeccable good taste, who took her into his inner sanctum 'and for 20 minutes I was shown, and allowed to handle, things that made me dizzy to see and touch – first editions of Chaucer, Milton mss, Shakespeare Quartos – oh God! that was a room. During this time he began to see me as somebody, and not anybody, and a little bit of himself peeped through the lacquer. I find Bertie's Shakespeare[1] is known and possessed here by most of the fine collectors . . .'

Altogether, she described how deliciously spoiled and loved she was. The cast at the theatre adored her – two of the actors would always have a silver stemmed magnolia for her button hole when she arrived at rehearsal each morning, for the streets of New York were full of magnolia sellers.

Then, three days before the opening night at the Windsor Theatre, Marc Connolly lost his nerve and began a series of last

1. The Nonesuch Shakespeare.

minute changes that destroyed the play. Bits of business were invented to underline every joke; a maid could not carry a tray without some farcical piece of mime. It was exactly what Bertie had banned in his original letter: 'Of course, there must be no laughing at Victorianism.' Rehearsals lasted from four in the afternoon to eight-thirty next morning, the singers' voices began to give way with strain, and everybody's nerves were on edge. This coarsening of the operetta was its ruin. All charm, elegance and light-hearted sweetness were lost in vulgarity.

Although the first night appeared successful, although Eleanor toasted the company in a specially composed song to the tune of 'Here's a Health to Mama', and went to bed elated, the newspapers next morning gave bad notices. The show was condemned as arch and silly.

# Tony Kraber

BEFORE ELEANOR sailed for England she fell in love.

I have used her own account of this rapturous experience (which in some kind extended to the cast of *The Two Bouquets*), because it gives a picture of her ability to act out the glowing feelings which burgeoned within her, and were so often returned in a sort of boomerang reaction by recipients. What she wrote was typed out in duplicate. She was not one to waste an adventure.

This falling in love came as a climax to the American visit. It was a sensual experience, something Eleanor had hardly enjoyed before. Doubtless, twenty-five years earlier, she had longed for the handsome Edward Thomas, but he was so untouchable that there was no chance of her being roused by reciprocal ardour. This time was different.

To make the sequence of events clear there must be a prologue. So soon as *The Two Bouquets* was launched and the bad notices unwillingly digested, Eleanor, with a few days to spare before she sailed for England, told cousin Harry that she wished to visit Paradise Valley, the home where her mother had been brought up, before Joe Jefferson became wealthy and bought his estate in Buzzard's Bay. Nineteen-year-old Grace Farjeon was delighted to drive her there, beyond the Delaware Gap into Pennsylvania, and they arrived at the weekend through a forest road at the old wooden farmhouse. To greet them were the Jefferson cousins, Connie and Dot, who had decided to show the place which, although now inhabited by a stranger, Lelia Hill, still seemed redolent of the past.

It was a sentimental journey of the most satisfactory kind and led to a friendship with the woman who now lived in the house. An effusive letter, sent three months after this visit, shows the impact of Eleanor's personality.

> *'Hillbrook' P.V.*
> *Oct 18th, '38*

Dear, dear, Eleanor Farjeon:–

It was all I could do not to write 'Nelly', I have so learned to love her, – and to love all those delightful children who romped thru' the pages of your charming book [*A Nursery in the Nineties*].

I am not a demonstrative person, yet I was drenched in tears while reading your opening and your closing chapters, and have rolled out of my chair, laughing at the million and one humorous incidents that were chronicled betweens.

When I first read it, – and I've done so more times than you will believe, – I thought to myself 'How I love her!' – I wanted you back here, there were so many things I wanted to tell you – so many things I *should* have told you, and shown you.

One of them was the 'Tiddy' tree, a mulberry, just to our left, as we sat in the porch. I passed under it as I went to the tulip tree; and just out of sight, around the corner of the house, is the companion tree, another mulberry called the 'Charlie' tree. Both trees were planted in 1863, and I do not know whether your grandfather planted them, or gave them to Jachen [?], or how they were named after the two Jefferson children, but they were, and there they still grow.

My sister Marion, the authoress, born in 1868 was always called 'Tiddy' after little Tiddy Jefferson.[1]

Why these things never entered my head while you were here, I can't imagine, – but your visit was so sudden and so short. 'So like the lightning which doth cease to be,' etc.

You hadn't driven fifty feet down the road, before I wanted to call you back.

I didn't know then, what for, but I did not want you to go. While I was reading your book, I suddenly knew why. As I said before, I am undemonstrative, and did not realise, until you had left, how I had been drawn to you. I wanted you back. I want you

1. Margaret Jefferson's childhood nick-name.

back. Oh won't you please come, and bring the brother who likes fishing? While we talk, he can fish, altho' he may not catch any fish. If it is just sport he is after, 'Hillbrook' doesn't lack for game. I have rats in the cellar, mice and bats in the attic, gophers, moles and skunks, *everywhere*. A veritable hunter's paradise.

'Hillbrook' is just as it was, when your grandfather was here, – only a little more so. Paradise Inn has been modernised, but Hillbrook has sunk into a state of 'innocuous desuetude'. We wash at the pump and sit in the sun until we dry. Lamps and candles shed their little beams, and *little* beams they are, but I wouldn't give it up for a palace.

When I received your 'Thatched Cottage',[1] which I enjoyed and thank you for, I wandered round looking for something from 'one of *my* shelves' to send you, and I happened across a photo of one of your grandfather's drawings of our old barn, long since torn down. I am sending it under separate cover and as it is a photo mailing case, I enclose this, father's notation.

Please forgive my delay in writing. I never write, – after wading thru this, you will readily see why.

Just believe me when I say I love you and want to see you again. I haven't begun to say half what I want to say, so you must come back.

Affectionately
Lelia Hill

After the visit to Paradise Valley, meeting Lelia Hill, after staying with her Jefferson cousins on the way back, Eleanor returned to the Park Avenue apartment and found a letter waiting.

This is her own story called *The American Adventure*:

Tony Kraber's letter: written on Saturday, June 4th, 1938, while I was in Paradise Valley. I was to dine with him and Willy (his wife Wilhelmina) on the Monday, to see Fritz his little boy of three, and the letter was written to tell me how to find his place; but I had not received it on the Monday afternoon when I left, and only found it waiting for me, in my room in Park Avenue, when I came home late at night, after dining with Tony, going on with him and Leslie to the theatre for the show (the worst and flattest performance I saw of it in

1. The Thatched Cottage was probably a postcard of End Cottage.

193

Tony Kraber

America – Jess Gale had flown from Boston, with Ebb's wife and
Mother to see it –), and then on to Macklin Marrow's[1] and Julie's,
where Leslie, not well, with a bad sore throat, also turned up, and
was followed by a very smart party of men and women. So Tony's
letter reached me too late for me to speak of it to him, or let him know
how much I felt it.

It is written on the note paper of the Group Theatre, of which he
was one of the first members.

1. Macklin Marrow, conductor and musical director of *The Two Bouquets*.

Dear Eleanor,

I wish there were time for us to know each other, for without that, I think you are one of the most adorable, sweetest, and most enchanting persons I have ever known, and you must admit that time helps to improve (?) those qualities, not in you but in one's knowing them. Since that day I unwittingly made you cry about the cats in New York you have owned my heart, fully and completely, and since that day, as I have known you better, I have wanted to make a bigger and completer heart, to make you know how I loved you. I am delighted to read about the hummingbird,[1] whose story seems so much like yours, or like you, should I say. I've only read 90 pages, but the reason is I can't tear Willy away from it, who has only 30 or so to go to finish it and who thinks it is lovely.

Your book is beautiful, but you are wonderful. Really, Eleanor, all politeness aside and any compliments in this illegible note also aside, I not only love you but adore you. And I long to see you and feast on your sweet personality which makes people happy.

Of course the essential part of this is not to tell you how I love you, which I could only tell to *you* but to tell you where you are dining Monday night, which is 44 Jane St. which is near the corner of 14th St. and 8th Avenue.

I love you
    Tony Kraber

How quickly can things happen – what makes us suddenly aware of them? They have been happening long before the moment of awareness. When I read this letter I knew all at once what had been happening to me as well as to Tony, though he had begun to love me first. I honestly did not know what had been happening to me for perhaps two weeks. I knew that when the darling company kissed me, coming and going, as most of them did, Tony had once or twice put his arm round my shoulders with more strength than the others, and kissed my cheek and neck with a special eager affection, and always with that bright look in his honest eyes, and the vivid smile that is his characteristic. But I took it as *his* expression of the affection with which the whole company treated me, and only knew, as the

1. *Humming Bird*, a novel.

195

time grew short and my departure close, that I too wanted to know him better. I had always been aware of him from the first as a keen, alive and unusual personality, a man with a real view of his job, though besides being assistant stage-manager, he was only leading the chorus, but doing it so well that, at one of the dress-rehearsals somebody said, "The best performance in the show is given by Tony Kraber." When off-stage conducting for the Finale was required, it was Tony whom Macklin Marrow entrusted with it – he has music, rhythm, acting and dancing in him, and had played a part, and proved himself invaluable I gather, in Marc's previous production "Having a wonderful time". There was no part for him in the Bouquets (though he understudies Leslie), and the job was a small one, but he is poor, and couldn't afford not to take it. I learned this later, when he was telling me of his part in the Group Theatre, which he seems to have left when he saw them becoming commercial.

At night, at the end of the rehearsals, when I had always lost some belongings and a general hunt was begun for them in the different seats in the theatre, the lounge, etc. Tony was always first to run down the wooden stairs into the auditorium and look about for me, sending me off at last with his expressive smile, nine parts confident, one part shy. Perhaps the first time I was specially sensible of him-and-myself was on that queer Wednesday night, May 26th, when Marc kept us all in the theatre till half-past eight on Thursday morning, while he exhausted the company, already worn out, by keeping them there for the lighting of two acts. All sorts of things happened that night; it was like a muddled dream; sometimes we were in the audience, sometimes those who weren't wanted trudged down to the dear little smoking-lounge where coffee and sandwiches were kept going through the small hours. We came up again, and reformed in different groups, and dozed and woke – I always seemed to be waking up on somebody else's shoulder. Part of the time Leo Carroll was with me (but I didn't doze on his shoulder, I respected his English circumspection, the darling), but Bela was once my support, and Alan Saalburg, and Bob Chisholme. Then somewhere about 4 a.m. on the Thursday, as I was sitting and drooping rather on an aisle seat, Tony suddenly jumped off the stage (the little wooden stairs had gone by then) in an interval when he wasn't wanted, and came and knelt by me, and put his arm round me and held me up, and for five minutes or so I dozed on *his* shoulder, till he was wanted, and left me to climb on to the stage again. I suppose I ought to have known then, but it is the truth that I did not. I took his affection in the same light as Winston O'Keefe's, between whom and myself a very special love existed, without the disturbance of sex, though I dare say a little sex was in it somewhere, sweetness without trouble.

The next time I particularly marked Tony was on the Sunday before production, May 29th, when the horrid little fuss blew up between Gabrielle and Ben Kranz. I was in the wings when it began and suddenly was aware only that loud and angry words were passing, Gabrielle protesting rather overmuch about some point (I don't know what it was) and Ben suddenly crying rudely "Well I'm just not interested!" and Gabrielle: "Well you needn't shout at me" – and Ben: "I shall shout at you as much as I choose" – it was the tones of voice that were hurtful and horrid. Gabrielle controlled herself, but was awfully upset, and every man in the company was furious with Ben. As if she had not had enough (they all had, and that was why nerves were breaking, Ben's and Marc's as badly as anybody's) she was told to come back after supper to rehearse a new idea for the Finale of Act Two. She took this nicely; several of the rest of us were going back to sup at Joe Moon's (this I'll tell elsewhere); myself, Joe, Leslie, Winston, Alfred Drake, and Pat Morison. In the passage outside the stage-door Tony came up to me and said with distress, "Eleanor, I want to apologise to you, for all Americans, for the way Ben Kranz insulted Gabrielle." I think he added, "This wouldn't have happened if I had been stage-manager." "Oh Tony you mustn't think of it like that," I said, realising from his tone how terribly wounded he was, as a man and an American, on my and Gabrielle's account, as women and Englishwomen. Gabrielle came up and said something nice rather shakily, and I asked her what she was going to do – "I wish you hadn't been asked to come back," I said. "Oh I don't mind, of course I don't, I'm ready to work if they want me to," said the poor tired thing; "but I can't help trembling all over, I feel so upset. I think I'll go back to the apartment and see if there are any letters." "No, don't be alone," I said. Bob Chisholme was there, and I said to him, "Take Gabrielle back to your place, and make her a cup of real tea, and let her lie on your lounge till it is time for you both to come back – don't let her be by herself." The kind fellow carried her

197

off, to look after her, and we went on to Joe Moon's, little Leslie hot with rage and hurt delicacy, and insisting that if there wasn't a public apology from Ben next day he wouldn't go on with his part. These storms! They always happen, but it's a pity when they happen so near to production.

On Wednesday, June 1st, when I was thinking what to do after the performance (for one never went to bed at once) I felt I wanted to know Tony better and would rather sup with him than anybody; so I spoke to him at the stage door and asked if he would wait at the end of the show and come and have a drink with me. He nodded quickly, with that flash in his eyes which says much more than his words; and after the show, and of course some more behind-the-scenes rehearsing from Marc, who can't leave them alone for a minute, Tony and I went round the corner to the Child's restaurant in 7th Avenue. We were hailed by Joe, Pat, and Alfred, and joined them, sitting on one side of the table while they sat on the other, and "guyed" us as a pair of strangers that had butted in on them. Joe sneered (*at* me), "That Moll of mine has got a new gangster." We had beer and something to eat, and kept up a pitched battle, but through it all Tony and I were talking about other things, as though to make up for lost time; I think it was then he told me about the Group Theatre work, and once, without anything to lead up to it, he looked at me and said, "Where I have given my love it never changes" – and the look in his eyes, straight into mine, had his heart in it, in a way I've seldom seen (once in Rosalind, and it is the last communication of feeling that is past the tongue's telling). The others rose to go and we sat on. "Shall we have some more beer?" asked Tony, less because we wanted any than because we wanted not to go too, I think. So we sat on alone, talking for a long time, and he said, "I wish I could have taken you home, I'd like you to have seen where I live – I could have made you an omelette." I forget now what we said, but it brought us nearer, it was our first real talk together. Outside, I said I would cab him back – he wanted to see me home, but I can afford cabs and he can't, so I said I'd drive him to Jane Street, and take the cab back alone. In the cab I told him, "I've got a boy in England," and told him about Pod, and our not being married; and he was glad for me, and said marriage meant nothing when two loved each other. "I hope you've got a girl, Tony." He nodded. "Yes, I have Willy – we're married, but we know we're free to do as we please. I can't understand possessiveness. You know my wife, you've seen her often, it was she who made tea for you at night in the Lounge – Bela Blau got her in to do it." "That sweet person? But why weren't we told?" "Somehow she never got introduced properly," said Tony; then he told me, "We've got a little boy, Fritz; he's three. Leslie has been to us and seen him. He was a success with Fritz. That's why I wish you could have come to my home, to see him too. But there's so little time now, and you're going away till Monday." "I'll come on Monday," I said, "to dinner before the theatre." "Will you?" he looked delighted. The cab had drawn up at his poor street, and we sat talking in it for a few moments. "Come early," he said, "before six and you'll see Fritz in his bath." Then he put his arms round me again and kissed me with his eager joyousness, as though there was so little time to express all he had to say, and he could only do it so. The queer thing was that there was no sense of pain in it all. I think the moment itself means much to him, more perhaps than most or for me. He is instinctive with quick feelings and intelligence – at least I think so. I know him very little, but feel him very strongly.

The Thursday, June 2nd, was my cousin Harry's birthday, and this was all Family Party; the Friday I drove with Grace to Paradise Valley, and on the way back, on Saturday, we slept at my cousin Dot's in Morristown; and on Sunday we came home in time for the big party I was giving at Andrea Beren's. These three events I shall describe separately; but on the Sunday night Winston O'Keefe brought his guitar, and sang, hauntingly and excitingly, a group of cowboy songs – things I had not heard before.

On Monday, June 6th, two days before I sailed, I was busy with seeing business friends for the last time; I cut my lunch with Jacob Wilk, to lunch with Leah Salisbury and Jean Dalrymple – Jacob was there, as it happened, and arranged to lunch with me next day at the Astor instead. Jean left, and Leah and I sat on and on till nearly four o'clock, making me miss an appointment with Ann Watkins and Margot Johnson (my literary agents); but Leah and I went deeper and deeper into each other's lives and hearts, till she cried "What IS it, Eleanor, what IS it you've got that nobody else has?" How could one answer that, for I don't even know what it is that she thinks I've got; and these records can only be put down, without comment and explanation from myself – I can only write down what I heard them do and say in relation to myself, however terribly it is to *do* with myself. It is true that the expression of love from my friends over there was almost overwhelming, and the whole time – the whole two months seemed like an unimaginable flowering of America for myself. I felt above myself most of the time – I doubt if it could ever happen again like that, but out of it I have made friends who will be mine till death and after.

From Leah's I went on to Stoke's office, and saw my darling Helen Fish; we talked friendship and business, and I signed several books to be sent to friends, and brought away "Portrait of a Family" for Willy, and "Over the Garden Wall" for Fritz. When I reached Jane Street Fritz was in the bath – Tony and Willy greeted me with great affection, and while they busied themselves with the supper I went to splash and be splashed, and give Fritz the Easter Rabbit which sweet Florence Williams had brought me in April. The child is glorious, such a splendid firm and perfect body, very excitable and vigorous, and full of fun. The rooms are poor, and practically all the furniture in it came out of the play "Men in White", in which Tony had acted; when he married the play was ending, and he was allowed to have the curious double-tiered table that had been used in the hospital dining-room, and the canvas-seated chairs, some of which he was stringing for his guests, because this was the biggest dinner party he and Willy had given; they had no money for furniture when they married, so this funny stuff was a godsend, and I loved their poor rooms better than any I had been in. A real life is lived there. She cooked, he strung the chairs, and mixed a lovely apple-cider drink, Fritz rushed about, the child and his noise was part of the place, Leslie arrived, then four more friends, all nice, we drank, Fritz drank too, nothing was thought out of place, it was just lived, and neither Tony nor Willy made a bother of anything. She was sweet. Then Tony fetched his guitar, and began to sing some of the cowboy songs Winston had sung the night before; and others as well. His singing was rougher and more exciting than Win's, less beautiful perhaps, but stronger and more native; he had a good voice. As he sang, his eyes and face seemed all on fire – his blue eyes snapped, and his excited smile was part of the queer music and sounds which only men can make in their throats. Willy came in to say supper was ready – he shook his head, and went on singing chiefly to me as I lay on the bed, laughing – you had to laugh. Then he sang one song quieter, "Nelly" was the girl in it, and it was a song of parting and remembrance; I said I would take that one for myself. Presently we did go in to supper, rather late, a lovely dish of chicken and wild rice – there were other things, but in the end we had to hurry because of the theatre – "If Leslie isn't there in time, who is his understudy?" I asked. "I am," laughed Tony.

I cabbed them there, and left them. Marc was on the stage and beckoned me; he had thought of some new business for Amelia interrupting the girls' first scene. He rehearsed it then and there, with the audience coming into the house on the other side of the curtain. I hated it; it is one more spoiling of the opening scene. The show seemed too boring for words to me, especially the first half of Act One; I saw it from the top balcony, out of the way of people; but in the interval went down and saw Jess Gale, who loaded me with parcels for myself and Fan and Joe and Joan.

After the performance I waited for Macklin Marrow and Julie, who drove me to their apartment. He really is awfully ill, and very angry about the whole ruination of the piece and the music, which he had so looked forward to. It seems that Marc, on the last dress-rehearsal, had thrust his head into the orchestra, during the perfor-mance, and screamed at Mac that he was playing too slowly. Mac said to me: "Honey, I have had to decide whether to walk out of this, or to do it for your sake; for if he had got somebody in at two days' notice it would have been worse still – I decided to stay, for you." And whenever I've seen him lately, he asked, "Did we play well for you to-night?" as though I was the only ears he counted in the audience. Their apartment is lovely, very white, and curious, and sensitive, like wonderful Julie herself. I was in my old clothes, and sat there drinking whisky and eating sandwiches, till Leslie came, his throat really very very bad, but as sweet as ever. He has become like a real younger brother to me – so I must some day make it be with Tony. A small party of ultra-smart New Yorkers swept in an hour later, really terribly smart, the sort I am seldom at home with; but the two months had built my confidence, and I sat on in my old rags and unkempt hair, and unvarnished nails (Tony said, by the way, how glad he was that "Willy didn't like nail-polish either") and they were all interested enough in me to take me as I was. Presently Mac asked me to tell the "Mr Snag" story, which I did, with great success; they all roared, at the end the smartest woman turned to her hus-band, asking discontentedly: "WHY don't such things ever happen to me?" Her husband murmured: "Well, my dear, I don't suppose you would walk down Forty-fifth Street with a man with a shabby bag."

I left between two and three, as I had letters to write, and did not expect to get to bed that night; and when I got home, there was Tony's letter – and that was when I entirely knew that he loved me, and I him, beyond the common. It only gave me joy, and I knew that it must mean nothing but joy to us both; but I wanted him to know that I had not had his dear letter when I came that evening and I wrote to him first of all, a letter to leave in the theatre for him next day; I felt too that I must see him for one real goodbye before I left, I could not let him go without. I sat up all night writing letters to the darling company, and to Harry and Grace and everybody who had been so wonderful to me.

In the morning, before going to my appointment with Jacob Wilk (which his secretary has re-arranged by phone), I rang up Tony – Willy answered that he had just left for the theatre; but would be back for dinner. "I'll ring him up then," I said; "but will you tell him I hadn't had his dear letter last night, when I came?" "I'll tell him – it was such an honour, you here," said Willy. But that hurt me. "You mustn't call it an honour, Willy – we are friends who love each other." I can't bear this "Eleanor Farjeon" business, ever, as though I were special. We spoke a little more, then I rang off. My appointment with Jacob Wilk failed – I waited an hour in vain, owing to a mistake by his secretary. Then I went to his office to leave a book for him and his wife. I had a last lovely talk with Rachel Field, in the children's room at the Public Library; and on to Ann Watkins, for a farewell – Margot Johnson took me to tea at the Vanderbilt, and we had hoped for Joe to appear, from an audition at which he was accompanying Alfred Drake, but he couldn't "make it". So two more goodbyes were said.

Home to continue packing, and have my last dinner at 1185, with Harry, Jean, and Grace. I gave Merilda her 25 dollars, to her delight. Harry etc. had been asked by Marc to my farewell party after the show in the lounge – they were to come after eleven; I packed till nine o'clock, and dressed in my dark blue evening dress and silver coat, hoping to escape the whole of Act One. I got in during the second act, and felt that it was going well; quite a different performance, and a different "house" from the previous night.

I felt excited and moved. After the show I went behind to the dressing-rooms – oh I have left out, above, my ringing Tony up before dinner. I said, "Tony, I wanted you to know I hadn't had your letter when I saw you last night – I would have said something about it, if I had." I forget what he said, before I added, "I want to see you alone to-night, to say goodbye, we must have a little time alone if it is only five minutes." "Oh yes," he said "we *must*. Eleanor, when I sang those songs last night – I didn't know you had already heard them. I wouldn't have sung them if I'd known." I think he wished he had been the first to sing them to me. But I told him they were lovely, and that I had not had my "own song" sung to me. "To-night, when Fritz got into his bath," said Tony, "he asked 'Where's Eleanor Farjeon?'" I said that was the loveliest thing he could have told me; then I said, "Will you wait for me after the party, however late it is?" "I will," he said, then "Goodbye – sweet." He has a curious voice, with double notes in it. The "sweet" came on the double note in his voice.

The party.

After the performance I went behind the scenes, to see several of them in their dressing-rooms. I think it was then I gave Tony the letter I had written the night before, and he put it in his pocket, to read later. I don't remember now what I wrote, beyond telling him how dear his own letter was to me, and that leaving him would be the thing that made leaving America hardest for me.

I went down from the stage on the Prompt side, into the passage that led through the "catacombs" to the darling lounge; and here Melville Hammet met and stopped me. "I shall see you inside there, I dare say," said he, "but I'll say goodbye to you now, while we can have a moment to ourselves." He then kissed me with warmth, and I knew he was among those who wanted to make me feel, before I went, that I meant something to him. I don't mean that all these people were "in-love" with me, or I with them, but it is true that a great flood of feeling seemed to envelop us all, during those five or six weeks; Leah Salisbury said, during the evening, when people were flocking round me, "I've never seen anything like this; Americans *don't* kiss and express themselves in this way, Eleanor; it's something you've done to them." It was not the men only, but the women too. Much of it I can take as responsive perhaps superficial affection, liking-and-propinquity, desirous to evince itself as long as I was there, not necessarily with roots; others came from deeper stirrings, and in a few cases, for me, and I think for some of them, the feelings were rooted. To hold back from any of it during this strange time would have been, for me, a false thing; and when, out of it, that strongest love for Tony appeared, I could not have tried to deny its presence, without the sense that some sin against truth had been committed – the misconceptions and falsifications of feelings that come of deliberate actions create worse troubles than the difficulty of seeing a thing clearly *together*, if that is ever possible. But at least one must try, and, unless one is living by an entirely selfish rule of life, one can try to act fairly to all the circumstances, as well as to see clearly and feel truly. Only, in the passage of any such experience, there are bound to be moments when feeling exists beyond the power of thinking and doing. But if anything I felt has resulted in hurting Tony beyond what couldn't be helped (for what he felt, he felt, beyond my say in it), or has hurt Willy, when it *might* have been helped, I must try to see clearly that part of it too, and do either something, or nothing, about it, whichever is necessary.

The people were gathering in the lounge, several from outside, like Harry, Grace and Jean, Margot Gilmour, Jane Crawford, and others; and the company assembled as it got itself dressed in its day-clothes. A long table was set with a swan in ice, like glass, and all sorts of wonderful food about it; and champagne and beer in quantities. Marc was almost in tears, however – "Sweetie, I had something you were to be given to-night, and it isn't ready – honestly, sweetie, I can't tell you how I feel about it." He told me to ring him up in the morning, at twelve, and arrange to see him and receive it, but his disappointment at not presenting it to me that night was very great. Mac was not at the party, he had kissed me goodbye by the orchestra, as his illness made it necessary for him to go home. I think his last words were the old – "Did we play well for you, to-night, honey? Were you pleased with us?"

Somebody filled my glass with champagne, I could hardly drink it, or eat; the glass was filled again before I had finished it, but I put it down somewhere. It was not like the party of a week before, the excitable first-night, when I only felt gay; there was too much else choking me. Wherever I went, people wanted to keep me, tell me things, and embrace me. Joe Moon got me to himself, at one end of the room, holding my hands, trying to say things – "Eleanor, I do want you to know that I love you – honestly I do – I want you to know how much it meant to me that night you sat and talked to me when I was so down, and almost ready to kill myself – a fellow gets like that – Eleanor, honestly – " His kind face and blue eyes were eloquent, while his tongue stumbled.

Marc came to us in the middle of this, but while he talked to me Joe clung on to my hand, and obstinately would not go; when Marc moved away, he made another effort to finish his goodbyes. I kissed him like a darling son or brother, and told him to remember that his "Moll" was ready to write and help him in any way at any time he might need it. Then Leslie came up – he was still ill with his bad throat, and was leaving early. He had said to me, weeks before, "Eleanor, when you go, I shan't come and see you off at the boat – I shouldn't have a lump in my throat, I should have a goitre." But luckily, in any case, my sailing was on a Wednesday, a matinee day, so that none of the company could possibly come, except Gabrielle and Bob, who don't appear till late in the piece. And darling Pat Morison, trembling and loving and excited, had said she would be there at one o'clock, before the show, if I was going to be there early. Of the girls in the company, she is the one who most clung to me, she and Gabrielle; and after them, perhaps, Harriet Henning, the dancer.

When Leslie came to say goodbye, it was too much – I simply turned away, into the corner by the telephone, and began to cry. His eyes were full of tears too, when I turned back, and we embraced closely; he did not love America, was not happy over the play or his treatment, and I think longed to come home. Well, him I shall see again. After this I think I went to find Leo Carroll, who, with his usual modesty, had not made himself evident; he was sitting talking with Harry and the two girls, and when I came and sat with them he brought out the lovely photograph, a large thing, which, by courtesy of the Players' Club, he had had made for me of the David Garrick poster, of 1773, with my great-great-great grandfather's name on it – HAMLET by Mr Garrick, THE KING by Mr Jefferson – this was Thomas Jefferson, the Yorkshire farmer's son, and father of the first Joseph Jefferson, who emigrated to America and founded the family there. Leo had inscribed it, as a memento, to both Bertie and myself. Then several of the chorus came, and drew me to the table, where they were drinking; Tony was standing there, drinking beer, looking very nice in a sort of linen suit. He put his arm round me while the others talked and kissed me, and Ann Ayers and I sparred a little. I said she would be known as "The woman who stood between Farjeon and Publicity" – Tony laughed with the others and said, "Oh that's *won*derful" – which it wasn't so very, dear Tony. Then each of them, men and girls, preparing to go, took me, one after the other, kissed me, tried to say something special – Marcy Westcott was very sweet, and Pat incredibly so; Alfred was lovely and Winston unbearably so – he nearly broke me down again – Bela, of course, while moved, kept his smile, and a few were left – Harry and the girls went off, Leo, who lived in the Berkley (I think) on the same block, still lingered, and a few others – somebody got my silver coat and said it was raining – we went upstairs to the foyer – a cab was outside, and Tony and I got in; if it had not rained I would have walked with him, but this was all we could do. The others waved to us; I said to Tony, "Shall I tell him to drive about Central Park." Tony nodded, I think he said again, "That would be wonderful", but what we said from that moment hardly mattered, nor did the driver – I have no notion what he was like, and I think his little glass slide was open, but neither of us took account of it.

What came then was the very sweetest hour in all my life. It may have been absurd, or wrong, I really don't know. It can't be reasoned out, it was the meeting quite simply, of the feelings which had grown in the last few weeks, and the hour was like a tiny island in time, a dream island, which we visited that once, and departed from.

I don't remember clearly, just words, and his kisses, and his arms round me, and mine round him. He said "I love you," and I said "I love you," and "I couldn't go without telling you, after your letter."

Next day Eleanor was in a state of great unhappiness, yet on leaving the Park Avenue apartment with her cousin and his daughters everything was held up while she said goodbye and thanked the elevator man and the doorman. Like Johnny Townmouse she carried a rolled steamer blanket secured with straps, through which was stuck her umbrella. But of course she was not as spick and span as the mouse.

She sailed away from New York that afternoon in tears, remembering the sweetness of kisses and the ecstasy of that midnight drive round and round Central Park, and back and forth from Jane Street to Park Avenue three times when they could not bear to part. In her diary she recorded that Tony Kraber had said, "You are so real. How can you be so real?" And how she had asked him never to compromise with life; how he had picked up the handkerchief she dropped and kept it. Both of them knew they would return to their regular lives.

# War

FROM THE SUSSEX COTTAGE, Hammonds, on October 13th 1938, Eleanor wrote a letter to Tony Kraber:

Dearly beloved Tony, Oh your lovely second letter this morning – and now I don't know what to say except that I am happier in having it than I deserve to be.

Then, after going over moments of her rapturous experience in New York, she begins to discuss the present state of affairs in Europe.

What is going to be the end of it here? I was a Socialist when to say one was a Socialist was like saying one is a Communist now. Now I believe in many things I want to see come to pass, but the trend of things from the [1914–18] War on makes it appear impossible for any big changes to occur without violence and its aftermath. And I am more violently opposed to violence than to anything else, I think, for even when it has, or seems to have, the ideal of justice behind it, once it is let loose on its object ideals get lost in the melée, and the results of victory and defeat are difficult to applaud. We made a pretty good mess of it in 1918–19. We helped to create an impossible situation. We shouldn't have crushed Germany like that, and now the boomerang is returning on our own heads. A Hitler was almost inevitable; I detest his aims and methods, but all he wants is not entirely unjust. I long to see the Dictatorships disappear, and I think if we were now at war there [would be] a big chance that internal revolutions in Germany

208

and Italy would have helped to bring this about more immediately. It will take longer now. But war itself is just Moloch. Perhaps it *has* to be, perhaps all the believers in fine and noble things *have* to be martyred for it. But the martyrs are on both sides, *always*. After the first year, or sooner, it just rolls on sickeningly, horrifyingly, wastefully, and helplessly. Afterwards, nations that called themselves just, make unjust terms, with fear or greed behind them. I can only think of one war in which the victor earned the right to stand with Christ. When Alfred and his nation looked like being vanquished by the Danes, and then in turn vanquished them, the Danish leader met him to ask his terms, and Alfred took his hand and said, "Peace for England." If only in 1918 we had all said "Peace for the World" – but there were too many of us building Babel once again.

I don't know *what* I believe, Tony, except that I'd rather be shot than shoot, and that there is an *idea* of Peace which may end the idea of War, and an idea of Love which I know can vanquish the idea of Hate. But what all this has to do with the politics and operations of the moment I can't dimly see. I hate much that we have done, and most that Hitler is doing; and I dare say if I came face to face with him I wouldn't be given cause to like him much. But I don't throb with hate when his name is mentioned. He seems to be an inevitable result of our own mistakes. I am utterly against him and all his kind – and if we could do no better, by fighting him, than make the same mistakes again, I am utterly against us. Hope for the world may mean a lot of deaths on the cross in the next generation.

Luncheon interval
and a rest from politics.

A picture instead. A long low room, barred all down the ceiling with 400-year-old black adzed ships' beams. A fireplace like a small cabin, with an oak-log fire roaring up the big chimney; and a great gale roaring down it. The small leaded window panes weeping with rain. The last red apples, and the last yellow roses, holding their own outside in the teeth of the storm. Inside, in her snug basket, little tortoiseshell Bunny curled on top of her newest family (her second since my return – on the date of production of our play, as we had to postpone it, she decided to produce instead), occasionally lifting her soft brindled throat to be tickled.

209

Pod in a deep armchair sucking his pipe and tackling one of the
brainier crossword puzzles. Books and papers on most things that
are meant to be sat on, so you sit on the red brick floor instead;
brown wooden walls, a brown piano, some creamy garden
chrysanthemums, and the fire flickering on a row of old
horse-brasses hung along a beam. On one side a door leads into a
small glass-house crammed with flowers in pots, a screen of
tomatoes, and a curtain of grapes; on the other side of the room,
sounds from the kitchen of Alice[1] (the Best Person in England)
getting tea. Golden Coney stretched languorously in one of the
windows. Nonny, her gold half-brother, in one of the fireside

1. Alice, her London maid.

seats. Pickle the tabby crowning the top of the piano. A little old Swiss musical box with a bird on it singing the "Rang des Vaches" in a far away voice whenever you lift the lid (it is our signature tune at Hammonds); and Nellie – no she's not there, but up in her pented room under the roof writing something or other to someone or other somewhere or other. She sends him her love; please see that he gets it.

Dear Tony.

Eleanor

By the end of December 1938 depression overwhelmed Eleanor. She put this down to the menopause which, as she said, should have happened years earlier, but there was also the aftermath or reaction to her American adventure, with anxiety about money coming in from her work. 'About money,' she wrote to Bertie on New Year's Eve, 'it seems to me that either one gets into the habit of being awfully careful about it, in order to feel secure in the problematical later-on, or else one mustn't be careful at all.' She was never too careful, but did worry, explaining, 'My advances grow smaller, and my sales never reach them; in the last two years I have produced eight books of various sorts which, evened up, with percentages and taxes knocked off, average a clear £225 on the year. All the rest is made up of all sorts of things, a crowded scramble of work done badly – ' The books that she had to do had, apparently, become a nightmare, while there was nothing in view save a book for Dent, which would mean £30 in the autumn. The financial failures of *The Elephant in Arcady* and *The Two Bouquets* were a disappointment, though the production of *The Elephant* was never to be regretted.

And then on September 4th 1939 war with Germany was declared. In England there was immediate apprehension that Hitler's planes would arrive the same night and bomb the cities flat. Those with friends, relatives or houses in the country left town hurriedly, children and property were bundled from one place to another. However, nothing happened. The first bomb did not explode on British soil till October, up in the Orkney Isles, and it was not until six months later, after the fall of Holland in May 1940, that air raids on the mainland began in earnest. By September 1940 London was being bombed almost every night.

Hammonds had almost been sold in 1938. There had been an offer of £1,100. The £550 Eleanor would have received, after halving it with Earle, would have kept the household going, so Eleanor told Bertie, and relieved her of having to earn for six months. She knew that she would not get more than the £1 a week from her lover, who seems to have been tight with his money. But now that war had come it was lucky this deal had not gone through, for here was a country home for those in need. On September 9th 1939 Eleanor wrote to Bertie from Hammonds:

> This will tell you as briefly as I can what has happened. Alice has gone for good, to her sister in London; but she managed to get dear old Miss Newman here; and Miss Newman is bewildered and blissfully happy, and amazingly useful, and just lovely to have in the house. She and Pod get on like anything. I had arranged a room for a Mother and two or three babies, but none are being sent to Laughton because of the water question (we've no main drainage or water). And I've lost my job at Reynolds,[1] and am high and dry. Meanwhile things are bad at Ditchling [Joe's home in Sussex]; their maid gone, Joan held tight, Joe at his wits' ends, and all near a crash. I rang up and told Joe that he and Fan could have my spare room, and he my hut to write in; and Joan could go to Mrs Fradd's (a big room for 6s a week). And his money and Harry's will help me run this place for them all; I shall housekeep and cook breakfast and supper and get space for writing in between; Ma Gander comes now at 7.30 for the heavy early morning work, and a nice village woman can come as long as I like for the cleaning jobs; and with Miss Newman to manage the mending and laundry, and Fan to sew and lay tables, I shall get my jobs apportioned so that each can do what he does best, and none too arduously I think.
>
> It has meant a terrific move about; I have carpenters to alter rooms, to ensure privacy, well-cleaning men to clean wells, and umpteen things to see to, in re-storing my stores; but in two days I'll be clear, and Joe and Co installed; Harry a little later.

It was with the advent of Miss Newman that Eleanor began to map out her next novel, *Brave Old Woman*, which was to be a life of the

1. Writing 'Tomfool' rhymes.

governess. In it the Farjeons (Farrars) are easily recognised, with the delicate demure Mother, bouncing Father and four children. Auto-biographical scenes abound, with Eleanor's optimism pressed out of life's tragedies through the strong-minded heroine (Miss Newman). Admiration for the stoicism of old age is expressed in severely moral terms. 'Ah, if life loses its enchantment, it is because time and experience have lessened and not increased you. Waning sensation matters so little if you have a waxing vision.'

The patches of sentimental glue are cleverly mopped up by the dryness of the heroine's attitude, which Eleanor, with her chameleon-like nature, readily understood. It is an annoying book, soft at the centre, and yet surrounded by so much intelligence.

One of Eleanor's concerns at this time was her niece Joan, sleeping at Mrs Fradd's, but living all day at Hammonds. Eleanor saw how a sense of duty was holding back the girl's ambition as a theatrical designer, how her parents made restrictive demands. Joan had already been in trouble with Joe over taking one job scene-painting – this was seven months after a successful operation on Fan [Frances] when they still had a nurse living in. Joe had demanded, "How can you do this to your Mother?" The fact was that Joan was expected to stay at home until she married, in conventional Victorian style. It was a situation only too familiar to Eleanor and she determined to free her niece one way or another. She watched her washing-up at the sink, as decreed by the household order of the day, and wrote a letter to Bertie, who was in London preparing his latest revue, *Nine Sharp*, for the Little Theatre. The letter explained that there was nothing to keep Joan in the country, and asked whether it might not be possible for him to make use of her – even as a scene-shifter in these days when strong men were in such short supply. Sorrow at the prospect for young people born to suffer the effects of war was some small consolation for the loss of her own child, who would now have been nearly eighteen, Eleanor wrote.

Next day a telegram arrived offering Joan a job scene-painting for Bertie's new revue.

Immediately Eleanor ordered her niece to go off and pack, while she doubtless talked the astonished parents out of protest and into good sense.

This early wartime household soon dispersed in any case. Harry refused to budge and continued his work at the Royal Academy of

Music throughout the war; Joe and Fan returned to their Ditchling home; Miss Newman went to live at the Fradds'; while Eleanor felt the necessity to return to Hampstead with Earle and the cats.

But it was hard for anyone with Semitic blood to escape from a sense of menace at this time, as it became clear that the Nazi aim was to annihilate the Jews, and as one after another the countries of Europe fell to German domination. Hitler's armies had now conquered Czechoslovakia, Austria, Poland, Holland, Belgium and part of France: it seemed an ominous prelude to the conquest of Britain. So in June 1940, as one with a part-Jewish family which was eligible for the gas chamber, Bertie wrote to his cousin Harry in New York:

My dear Harry,

I expect you have been wondering sometimes how we are getting along over here during these heavy times, and I am writing to you now because, if things go badly, it may be that we shall be gravely in need of help and that you would generously do what you could to give it to us. Of course, if the best comes to the best, there is likely to be no geographical change, though there are bound to be many other changes in our way of life. But if the worst comes to the worst, and if there is a set against anyone here with Jewish blood in their veins, our great hope would be to get somehow or other to America and there start a new life as best we could. This might be difficult; but if it were possible, I trust and believe that you would do what you could for us in the initial stages, and I can promise you that we would do our utmost to be as light a burden for as short a time as possible (though I've a suspicion that you will regard the word "burden" as badly chosen, for Eleanor and Gervase have already brought home evidence of your unbounded kindness when they stayed with you). We Farjeons have many American ties, and it is likely that our Harry and Eleanor could be helped by the Jeffersons, that Joe and Fan could be helped by Fan's relatives, while we – do you think that you could take us in tow for a bit? I have made no specific enquiries as yet, but I gather that the inability to take money into the U.S.A. would mean that we would have to be financially guaranteed. And though restrictions make it hard nowadays for people of one country to get jobs in another, Harry, Eleanor, Joe and I are all in the fortunate position of carrying our businesses in our brains as creative artists. So many Americans have seen my revues over here, and have been so enthusiastic, and there are so many theatrical people I could get in touch with, that I have confidence that I should soon be making something of a living . . .

The letter ended: 'I write all this with emotional restraint, for one dare not relax the emotional restraint necessary in these times. But if the need should come, and if you could then help us, I cannot express what we should feel.'

This appeal took over a month to reach Harry Farjeon in Park Avenue. He replied that of course he would, without any question 'go to the bat' for these cousins of his, and quoted a letter from Marc Connolly: 'If the war were to force Eleanor and Herbert to move to America, I can't imagine them having any difficulties making livelihoods. Their talents are so unusual that everyone in the theatre would be eager to give what little help they might need.' Connolly also gave the assurance that on the date they arrived they would already have been made members of the Dramatists' Guild of the Authors' League, thus ensuring their right to have theatrical productions shown on Broadway.

It did not come to this. None of the Farjeons fled to their American relatives. After the Little Theatre was bombed, Bertie put on a show called *Diversions* in Bronson Albery's Wyndham's Theatre, for which, as so often, Eleanor provided material, this time a charming translation of *Vienna Woods* for Irene Eisinger to sing. After Bertie's house in St John's Wood was bombed he slept with other homeless theatre people on the floor of The Players' Club basement in Albemarle Street. But Eleanor's cottage in Hampstead never came to harm.

Against the brick wall across the cobbles of Perrins Walk, and almost opposite the front door, Eleanor had a concrete and brick air raid shelter built, conforming to the pattern advised by the government. She went into the matter of survival thoroughly. She learned that if a bomb dropped nearby its blast might burst the eardrums, therefore on such occasions it was wise to keep the mouth open. But in order to keep the mouth open it was also wise to keep some rubber object at hand on which to bite. After careful thought Eleanor decided that a dog's toy bone would be the thing, so she went to the pet department of John Barnes. Having asked to see the rubber bones and choosing a moment when the saleswoman's back was turned, she surreptitiously sank her teeth into one, only to be caught in the act. "Is your dog very small?" asked the saleswoman. "No, not really," the author replied, standing there in some embarrassment, big and bulky, a large rubber bone in her paw. She later allowed a young friend, Francis Thompson, to photograph her at the ready, gas mask on wrist, bone between teeth. In this photograph she wears the same Russian garb which had been bought before the First World War, and which remained her favourite summer dress.

At night when the siren wailed its warning and the loaded German bombers droned heavily overhead, as the ack-ack guns on the top of Primrose Hill made the air vibrate with cracking explosions, or the whistle of a descending missile ended in the crescendo bang, Eleanor and Earle lay secure in their little stronghold. Eleanor was not afraid, busying herself with practical aids to make life snug. There were two beds, blankets, eiderdowns and pillows, there were deck chairs, a table with books, writing materials, playing cards, aspirin, boiled sweets, torch and the little travelling clock Bela Blau had given her when she left New York. Under the table were a first aid kit, candles, plates, water and washing bowl, there were electric plugs for the kettle and light, there was the radio – it was compulsive listening to learn how the battles raged, in news broadcasts five or six times a day.

After an early supper in the cottage, Eleanor would fill hot water bottles, turn off the gas main, feed the cats and leave them by the coal fire with her coat to sleep on. The window was opened, for this lessened the effect of blasts and, anyway, the cats hated being shut in and did not flinch at the strange nightly hullaballoo – 'a barking gun sets their fur quivering less than a barking dog, the scream of bombs excites them less than the caterwauling of the ragged tabby tom who roams the yard.'[1]

With Earle settled in the shelter beside her, Eleanor would light a cigarette and begin a dud patience. 'I reserve the brainy game for the time when the planes are really overhead; it amuses me to prove to them that all their humming can't spoil my calculations. At nine o'clock I turn on the news, and boil my kettle. Somewhere between ten and eleven I undress, put in my wax ear-plugs, roll myself in my pink blankets and quilt, and switch off the light.'[2] Later there was a scratch at the door – 'I would hear it through a thousand wax ear-plugs' – and the cat Bunny came in to lie across Eleanor's chest with a soft chin over her wrist. When there was a big bang the shelter shook, then came the sound of tumbling masonry, the high tinkle of glass. At such times every sense would strain to mark the direction of the calamity, while overhead the sky took on a salmon-pink glow, as fires roared up to light the path for fresh waves of German bombers.

Next morning it was the milkman who would tell of local disasters. After one raid there came a call from Bertie's house. It was the daily maid.

"A landmine last night in St John's Wood, miss. The house is indescribable. I've tried to telephone Mr Gervase at the architectural school, but he hasn't come yet. And I can't get 'Telegrams' on the phone, or a call through to Mr Farjeon."

"I'm going out now, and I'll send a wire from the post office."

"Oh thank you, miss, I thought I *must* tell somebody."

On this morning there was another air raid warning, but by now no one took much notice of daylight raids. In the shops there was

1, 2. *Sample Day and Night* (unpublished).

more to be learned about local damage. When Eleanor passed an unexploded bomb sunk in the road it was roped off and guarded by a policeman. He said she need not evacuate, but had better keep away from the windows until it had gone off. It hardly seemed a bomb worth boasting about.

So down the hill Eleanor went to Fellows Road with a jar of calves-foot jelly for Bertha's baby, because there was no gas down there and they couldn't cook. In College Crescent, where her father had bought trinkets the day he became ill, there was a bad sight: two shops gone, one the greengrocer, an old friend. As yet no one knew whether he was under the ruins or not.

Bertha met her with the baby in her arms, a baby who minded the nightly disturbance no more than the cats. 'Babies and animals, who know no difference in the world to-day, are an immense joy and comfort to us who do.'[1]

Eleanor returned to the mews to find a couple wandering about looking for rooms. Last night they had been drinking tea before going to bed, the woman explained, when "Suddenly, quite quietly, the house parted on each side of us, and we were drinking tea in the open air. I couldn't help laughing."

They were filthy dirty and had been searching for rooms all day. Eleanor ran a bath, put out clean towel, soap and powder for the woman, then went off with the man to try and find a lodging.

As Bertie wrote at the end of a wartime letter to his sister: 'Who says history is dull?'

1. *Sample Day and Night.*

218

*28*

# Otto Lampel

IN 1939 ELEANOR had been made a member of the PEN club executive committee. PEN stands for Poets and Playwrights, Editors, Essayists and Novelists : it is a world association of writers. The main effort of the committee at this period was directed towards those suffering under the tyranny of European dictators: much money and effort was spent helping Jewish and other dissident writers escape from Germany and the Nazi occupied countries, although India, China and Malta were also on the list for assistance. Eleanor worked on the committee for ten years and became a dear friend of Hermann Ould, the backbone of the club.

Hermann Ould, quiet and clever, had acted as the PEN international secretary since 1926, and through peace and war was able to preserve a genuinely non-political organisation. His integrity and tolerance, his gentle friendliness to the distinguished and undistinguished alike impressed all who knew him. Storm Jameson called him 'resolute and unassertive – a force which held together the explosive egoisms of the PEN.' Eleanor looked on him as saintly, her enthusiasm for the club being fired by her enthusiasm for the man.

But the friend with whom she became most intimate early in the war was a Czech pianist and *diseur*, Otto Lampel, whose career in Prague's light entertainment world finished with the Nazi invasion. His wife was in a concentration camp.

Lampel was a large smooth-mannered man in this thirties, who kissed ladies' hands and cajoled unmercifully. He composed his own songs with ready expertise. His self-assurance was of the brassy variety, something of a shock to the society of refined and self-

deprecating English to whom Eleanor introduced him. She was not in the least embarrassed by his travelling salesmanship, but amused and delighted by the badinage and flattery. From her wildly enthusiastic reports of his charm and talent the family soon realised that she was captivated. Lampel was hailed as a genius and Bertie was urged to use him in his next theatrical production.

In a large Boots Scribbler Diary for 1941 – which is one of her few remaining diaries – Eleanor wrote spasmodic reports:

*April* 16. The biggest London Blitz so far. From 9 o'clock till 5 it sounded as though a solid ceiling of planes hummed overhead.

The noise was tremendous. I made Pod come down at 2.30. I believe 600 planes came over in waves.

*April* 17. London is badly hurt. From Oxford Street to St. Paul's – Euston, Waterloo, I don't know what. The Little Theatre smashed and the Shaftesbury. I rang up Wyndham's [Theatre]– "Are you playing today? Yes, just." I was early and had a talk with Bertie in the foyer first. He is contemplating a series of specially 'classy' matinées with Joyce Grenfell, Irene Eisinger, and a third – "Your Lampel sounds as if he may be what I want." Lampel and the Fischels turned up, and Bertie spent the interval in our box, and arranged for me to bring him to Loudon Rd [Bertie's home] to sing and play on Sunday. It was a successful afternoon – Otto fell in love with Joyce Grenfell. Afterwards he and I had half an hour's talk, while he gave the tune of his polka to which he wants English words. It was interesting to watch him through the revue – *quality* gets him instantly.

So on Sunday Eleanor brought her new protegé to St John's Wood. He sat at the piano and sang in French and Czech, his full mouth and heavy-lidded eyes expressive of night-club innuendo, his hands on the notes white, plump, and neat. For percussion effects he knocked his knuckles on the wooden end of the keyboard or rattled a matchbox in an almost spontaneous way. It was an efficient performance, though lacking in what he had so much of in real life – panache.

With a big wistful look, he told Bertie that Eleanor was going to write a special English number for him. It was obvious he hoped her brother would make the same offer.

Bertie quietly explained that English people were so very ignorant of foreign languages he did not think Lampel's present repertoire would be possible. When he had got together songs in English, then it might be good to throw in a couple of French or Czech ones. He must also improve his English to become intelligible from the stage.

Lampel's gratitude was too effusive. He exclaimed on how great the Farjeon name was in the theatre, how honoured he would be to work for a Farjeon – no honour could be greater!

Eleanor smiled and looked encouraging. Bertie looked embarrassed.

Although Eleanor maintained in her diary that 'it was a great success', Bertie was dubious about Lampel's prospects as a performer and did not disguise this from his sister. So it may be seen how Eleanor was able to deceive herself once emotions were involved. It is surprising that her artistic judgement remained generally so sound. However, neither love nor war were able to divert her from work.

> *April* 26. I woke at 6 o'clock, got my Ms, sat up in bed, and finished *Brave Old Woman* before 7.30. Then typed the rest of the copy. It must be corrected and got to Michael Joseph's by Wednesday; but after I shall revise my own copy, while Lusty [publisher] is engaged on the 'book-making' side of it, and hope I can send him an improved Ms before it goes to the printers. Because I think only the first half is what I meant it to be. I have done it – 85000 words, in 3½ months; I needed at least twice that time. But I have to have the money for this spring. In ordinary times I'd have let it go till the autumn – but there may be no autumn. In *which* case, this spring will hardly matter. In short, I've been a bad artist. Otto again last night.
>
> Very tired and flat after the book. It has exhausted me more than I thought, but I didn't know it till now.

In May Eleanor went to the house where Lampel lodged for a 'real Czech lunch' put on by two of his refugee friends, Hatti [Reimer] and Lottie. Both had been good to him. The house was humble, with refugees in every room. Lampel met her at the bus stop wearing a green branch – he was radiant and the lunch became festive, after which they all 'played and sang as though there was nothing to be sad about'. [Diary, 1941]

The blitzkrieg continued. Lampel's ceiling came down and he was shaken, so Eleanor invited him to stay the night at Perrins Walk. He slept in the front room downstairs and when the bombs fell too thickly all three of them moved out into the air raid shelter.

But now, if Lampel was not staying, he had to have a long nightly phone call – his 'bedtime' talk. The main problem in his professional life was lack of a work permit. Eleanor was applying to every influential person she knew or met for help here. And then she and Lampel began a grand scale operetta together, *The Great Alexis*. It concerned Alexis Benoit Soyer, the Parisian chef who came to London in the mid-nineteenth century and designed the kitchens of the Reform Club. After being sent by the British government to organise food during the Irish famine, he went on to deal with feeding the British army during the Crimean War. A general coupled his name with that of Florence Nightingale as one of the benefactors of the campaign.

It was no wonder that this character appealed to both author and musician. Eleanor, Lampel and Soyer were all vainglorious and went in for flamboyant fantasies; besides being greedy they were knowledgeable about food and drink. During the war cooking became one of Eleanor's great interests, and her diary lists in detail many of the excellent meals she made for friends, especially those she cooked for Lampel.

One and a half acts of the three planned for *The Great Alexis* were soon written. There was to be a magnificent opening reception at the Reform Club, with a chorus of club members who included Thackeray, Count D'Orsay, Cruickshank and Lord Melbourne, while the ladies included Mrs Beeton and Countess Blessington. By way of contrast there was to be another huge production number, when Soyer gave a Christmas dinner to the Poor of London. This was to be a scene of Dickensian squalor, with an ox roasting on a spit and cauldrons of soup presided over by the chef himself. The Poor were given the following awful lines to sing:

> *Health and long life to the People's Friend*
> *To the Poor Man's Friend,*
> *Mister Sawyer!*
>
> *May his prosperities never end,*
> *May it never end,*
> *Mister Sawyer!*
>
> *Beef and plum pudden are werry werry good,*
> *They are werry good,*
> *Mister Sawyer!*
>
> *We've never seen such a blooming lot of food!*
> *What a lot of food,*
> *Mister Sawyer!*

Every act was to have four or five scenes. There was to be a great march of soldiers at Scutari where, as night fell, a wounded Russian prisoner played his balalaika, while Soyer threw him a few kindly corny words: "Good music is like good food, it fits every stomach. Sing something, boy."

The opera was romantic, sentimental, and grandiose to a degree. But it was sixty years too late, and should have been staged by Beerbohm Tree at Her Majesty's in 1880. To believe such a production possible in wartime, when wood to construct one small piece of scenery, material for a single costume, or even artists to people the stage were all a scarcity, was a piece of impractical folly which only love could have inspired.

It is easy to understand why the exiled, ebullient, and adventurous Soyer appealed to Lampel, but the Czech musician lacked the stamina to compose music for such an ambitious work: his was the world of light and quick, not ponderous and exotic, entertainment.

Naturally Earle was none too pleased with his Nell's new friend. In May he was packed off alone for a holiday in Hampshire with friends, after which Eleanor brought Lampel home that evening for what she described in her 1941 diary as the 'perfect dinner'. There was 'clear soup, oeufs Parmesan à la Crème en Cocotte, Pomme Perce, Asparagus (heaps from Sussex) and Zabione with almond fingers, and Harry's 1928 Chambertin, in perfect condition, perhaps the best red wine I've ever drunk. O in heaven, (He's always at extremes) praised me for a real chef, adored the wine and went wild over the Soyer couplets. He is going to be a marvellous collaborator – but I must have a bit of me left for Pod and all the world.'

In fact Lampel exhausted her and himself with euphoria on this occasion. Next day he was utterly miserable, and in dire need of mothering and coddling.

At this period my sister Joscelyn was living in the mews three doors away, sometimes sleeping in the shelter and often visiting her aunt, who cared for her during severe sore throats. Joscelyn described how Lampel would receive special treatment at meals and was always given the best and largest piece of meat (of which there was little enough then). After dinner Eleanor would go to the cupboard where food parcels from Marc Connolly and others in America were kept, to extract a special sweet for Lampel. Joscelyn and Earle were ignored. Then Earle would rise from the table and go upstairs in a huff.

In her diary Eleanor excuses this favouritism, of which her brother Harry would have been disgusted to learn, by saying that Otto had a lot of starvation to make up for.

On May 24th 1941 the diary records that she and Earle took Betty Myers to the pub. Elizabeth Myers, author of *A Well of Leaves*, who later married Littleton Powys, was already ill with tuberculosis. She had become known in Perrins Walk after the editor of *The Listener*, Alan Thomas, had brought round a short story for his old schoolmaster to read. Earle's comment on the story was, "By God, it's a little masterpiece." Eleanor wrote a letter of encouragement and became instrumental in getting Elizabeth Myers's first novel published and gaining her the Tom-Gallon Prize, which aims to help struggling writers. She wrote of the first meeting, six months earlier, that the girl turned up one lunch time in Hampstead, walking through the front door which was always open. Earle shambled downstairs with letters to post and they exchanged a keen blue-eyed stare. 'I said, "This is Betty, Pod" – Betty said, "Hallo", and Pod, "I take it you know the letters of Keats." He sat down on a chair facing her, and without waste of time they belonged to one another.

Betty knew Keats well enough to content him (much later she confessed to me that Keats was not one of her chosen, but out of love and reverence for him she never let Pod realise it). She has a mystical intellect (Thomas Aquinas was her chosen Saint), and discussed ideas like a man; her critical genius, like Pod's, was at its best when she was *for* and not *against*. Without losing a moment they were flying away together. A siren wailed. Pod rose, still talking, and led Betty across the yard to the shelter, in which Rainer Maria Rilke and Thomas Traherne took refuge with them. The All-Clear sounded. Betty signed a brick, like all visitors to the shelter, and gathered up her orders to view; Pod ambled to the pillar box with his Crosswords; I returned to my hot-pot.[1]

For the next three years Elizabeth Myers was part of their life, she was known as Pod's Pub Girl. They would go for a drink regularly, while Eleanor joined them intermittently.

On the May evening in 1941 after they had been to the pub,

1. *Elizabeth Myers* by Eleanor Farjeon.

Eleanor recorded that she cooked Earle a lovely meal, but – 'After nine my talk with Otto left me perturbed – he is still "down"; so I rang again later to tell him that he would be in my keeping all night. He said, "I love you terribly." I could only say the same, and he said – "I know it cannot be stopped." We said God bless you. Pod must not be made unhappy. I must try to think as well as feel.'

Next day she wrote in the diary that she had thought of Otto all night. 'I rang O to find out how he was – "A little better. Darling, I cannot *believe* how I love you." I said I'd write him a love letter, and I have done so, as truly as I can, putting *all* my ways of loving him in their places. I hope it will help us *all*.'

Earle was sent off to the country on several occasions; while Eleanor's chief concern remained with Lampel and his work permit. She arranged lunches with Sir Walter Monckton and Robert Vansittart, she pushed and pulled strings.

All the while Lampel was in the middle of a tempestuous affair with Polish Hatti. By June he decided that he must move away from the refugee house in Hereford Road. Eleanor found him a home with a wealthy friend in Egerton Crescent. On hearing this Hatti made terrible scenes and threatened suicide. The emotional saga veered back and forth, with now and then a return to Hatti for the night, after which, to Eleanor's innocent surprise, Hatti appeared much happier.

Eleanor had to restate to Lampel again and again that she did not intend to have an affair with him, that Earle must always come first. There is no doubt that she would never have endured the position of secondary mistress. But she spent days and nights working with and for him on the Soyer operetta, and also on a revue he was to direct for ENSA, the entertainments department of the British Forces.

Her diary records that everything Lampel did was a great success or another triumph. Apparently he was always impressing people with his talent and personality, doing his stuff wonderfully, and yet despite all he did not advance in the world of entertainment.

Another friendship which developed at this time was with John and Isobel Morton-Sale, married artists who illustrated the books of children's verse, *Cherrystones*, *The Mulberry Bush* and *The Starry Floor* with delicate fey drawings. Eleanor's ability to become intimate with people on short acquaintance was remarkable. Sympathy and curiosity were so balanced in her character that it was easy to make immediate friends with strangers, although the friendship was in a sense mostly one way. She did not unburden herself often, in fact she was a reticent woman despite all the noise. True sympathy, intelligent understanding and generous help were given in return for intimate confidences, and for a while she could take over the weight of another's trouble and assuage their agony.

In August the Morton-Sales invited Eleanor and Earle to visit them in their secluded and beautiful Devonshire valley, their home the prettiest little house ever, like an exact setting for Mrs Dashwood and her daughters in *Sense and Sensibility*. They were small, energetic artists, vague in practical matters, but exuding a fairy tale sense of timelessness. Here Eleanor enjoyed rest and peace, reducing her lonely-hearts correspondence by writing ten letters a day before breakfast. There were picnics on the moors and walks through picturesque villages. On August 10th, she was still rather tired, having written over one hundred letters and largely cleared her correspondence. With Earle she had dug up ferns to plant in the walls of the Hampstead garden.

Eleanor returned home alone, to plunge into work for the PEN Club and soothe a niece over a love affair. Yet she did not forget Earle, who was to travel back from Devon in the hurly-burly of wartime transport, and sent the following letter of advice based on her own experience.

Dearest Pod,

To avoid a very uncomfortable and tiring journey observe the following rules.

The train at Newton Abbot will be crowded. Wait for it VERY well forward on the platform, and make immediately for a First Class Carriage. Even those were full, but by luck I found a single place and hopped in. Soon the corridors were crowded with third-class passengers, but our carriage, with only 6 in it, was airy all the way. First point is, don't LOOK at the third class or waste time, but get into any First you can sit in. Perhaps John will help you here.

The train did not get to Newton Abbot before one o'clock, but don't count on this. Be in time.

After Exeter there is no stop to Paddington, and fairly soon a ticket collector comes in and takes your ticket. He did not even say a word when he saw I had a third class. He had too many already of that ilk. But even if you have to pay extra, it's better than not sitting during the long journey.

Get Isobel to give you a packet of sandwiches, AND DON'T FORGET YOU'VE GOT 'EM! At Exeter, during a fairly long wait, the restaurant man comes to take lunch tickets, but you cannot get into the restaurant coach then and there and stay there, and those who ultimately lunched there said the getting to and fro through the corridors was exhausting.

At Paddington it is pandemonium. The taxis are in rows and you cannot take any one you like, and rush along always seeing yours snapped up. It really was terribly difficult. Then a few more dozen cabs are let in and instantly snapped up by the porters. I had to scramble for about twenty minutes before I got one. And left hundreds of waiters behind me. A porter, if obtainable, (but they are scarce) might get you one, and would ease the weight of your bag, but don't lose him in the crush. This is as much as I can tell you, darling. I was lucky, but needed to keep my wits skinned all the time. And I shouldn't have got a seat at Exeter of any sort.

All my love to you and to the three darlings.[1] How lovely it all was. Coney clings to me with little mews, and looks three times as big as Golden Girl. The kittens are enchanting, the apples reddening, and the tomatoes prolific and enormous. Onions also promising.

Till Wednesday, then, with all my love. Your
    Nell

With the cats Eleanor was capable of anything and everything. This year she drowned two of Bunny's new born kittens, waiting until the mother was eating her dinner to take them away, and leaving two alive. She said that had there been only one left Bunny would have noticed and fretted.

In October there was a talk to be given in company with her old friend, Walter de la Mare, at Hampton Court to a group of children. The diary records: 'We found Lady Grant's beautiful Wren apartment and encountered dear de la Mare and Mary Shirley on the

1. Isobel and John Morton-Sale and their daughter Royesia.

stairs. After a sherry all round Pod and Henrietta [Leslie] left to lunch elsewhere, and we had a superb chef's lunch of mushrooms in short pastry, salmon mayonnaise and all sorts of salads, then hot zabione over cherries, white wine and coffee. We talked all sorts of speculative things, due to de la Mare and were late at the Library, but found Pod entertaining the children till we came. De la Mare read first, lovely new poems, after which both he and I were besieged for autographs. Then I talked and read my bits from letters and diaries – it came off well; I felt easy and made the children laugh. At the end, after the extract from Fanny Kemble's journal describing such a toy, I produced my hummingbird box and made the bird sing, which of course brought down the house.'

This hummingbird musical box was the mysterious link which runs through the *Humming Bird* novel, whose heroine was Mrs Pyatt, of the shop where so much of Eleanor's fascinating bric-à-brac was bought. In the book a description of this toy shows why its exposure to an audience of children was such a master stroke. On touching the spring 'a tiny trap in the lid sprang open, and a bird flew up, a glittering morsel of gold and emerald, turquoise and rose. It quivered restlessly from side to side, the feathered throat palpitated, the gilded beak opened and shut, and from it issued a cascade of notes, fairy roulades and elfin trills, sweet, shrill, and liquid as my Kentish nightingales. I sat enraptured. I did not know whether the song lasted for a moment or an eternity when the tiny bird completed its final trill, and disappeared like magic under the trap.'

At this time Lampel acquired a new mistress, an actress much disliked by both Eleanor and pretty Hatti, who was once again living with her Lothario. Even so he was phoning Eleanor all day for reassurance. He had become a full-time occupation with his need to boast and be boosted. Eleanor found it emotionally wearing and tried to stop the calls which broke into her work. Then Lampel sent telegrams: 'Even without the telephone I love you.'

By the end of the year Lampel had been called up for military service and turned down on health grounds. It was then that Eleanor began to plan his great London début. She asked Bronson Albery whether he would consider giving a charity concert matinée for the Aid to Russia Fund at one of his theatres. Otto Lampel was to star, with the soprano, Adelaide Stanley, as support. Albery agreed and the date was fixed for February 9th 1942. 'I went to Otto, and when I told him the news he was nearly speechless with emotion. There'll be heaps to do, but the great thing is, he has his chance, and after this the Work Permit will be a matter of course.' [Diary, 1941]

Lady Playfair organised an audience which included the Prime Minister's wife, Mrs Churchill, and Madame Benesh in a box. The titled and rich filled the rest of Wyndham's Theatre. However, Lampel's stage personality was not powerful enough. Accustomed to the intimacy of cabaret performance, he appeared weak and nervous, according to Bertie's report. This concert was the calamitous culmination of Lampel's career as a solo performer in Britain.

Eleanor's diary for 1942 does not exist, though a letter she wrote a few days later shows how professionalism prevailed over affection for the musician. She had composed the words for five new songs in this show and made translations of most of the others; she had roped in her friends to help; she had supported Lampel's spirits and organised until she was exhausted.

I want you to read
every word of this
letter, long as it is.

20 *Perrins Walk, N.W.*3.
*Feb.* 14*th* 1942

Dearest Otto,

The concert is over for which many of us worked so hard to the exclusion of almost everything else – time, health and our own work and private affairs. Real affection for you, as well as a belief in your gifts, made all the others go on indefatigably after I had to drop out. The great hope on which we were all set was that real professional work and recognition would result from it. When you told me last night that the Phoenix [Theatre] was offering you £30 a week, my heart jumped for joy. When you went on to say that you were demanding double, it sank terribly. Once again I felt that you were inflating your value beyond its real worth. And Otto, my dear, I do not mean only beyond its worth as an unknown artist here; I mean – and I hope you can take this – your *actual* worth as a performer in the eyes of us who know something about it. You are often very very good indeed; you have sudden moments of being almost inspired (when your DAIMON gets you unawares); but you are too often below your best; you can be mediocre, and no £60 artist, who has not made his name here, can dare to be that, or he will soon drop out. After an artist has become a national favourite, he can go on being downright bad for a while (vide Evelyn Laye), but that is a point I hope you will never reach.

Please be clear about this; the concert was not a very great success. You never once 'blew them to pieces'. You were not nearly your best. You had many admirers, some who already knew you and what you can do when you *are* at your best, and other new ones, intelligent ones like Storm Jameson, who, in the theatre world, is unsophisticated. But I have not heard one professional opinion which was hopeful, and I made a point of asking everybody who could tell me the real truth of their reactions and those of the audience; and I have built up a pretty clear idea of what really came across the footlights.

Now listen. You have many times said to me "Don't let me down." Some of us have the right to say it to you. If the Phoenix will not give you £60, or £50, or £40, I shall consider you have let us down if you don't take £30. In these times, in this country, it is a very good offer, not one to shame you in the least; and if you stand out for Star-dom, which nothing you have done here yet justifies, you may find one of two things (a) that you will not get what you want in the way of salary or position or (b) that if you do, the management may rapidly think you are not worth so much after your strong personality has persuaded them that you are. It was your personality that persuaded Holt.[1] But he won't be doing any more for you, dear; you didn't impress him enough. And from the point of view of Bertie and Bronnie Albery, both of whom were seeing what you could put over in a theatre, you did not succeed.

I am telling you these things because, though you will resist them in one way, in another you ought to take them to account. The performance at Wyndham's has the immense advantage, not of producing wonderful notices for you and fame overnight, but of giving you great publicity outside the newspapers, and bringing you into contact with numbers of useful people. Especially through Mary. Wordsworth[2] believes in you and is a shrewd man of business. Don't tell him that you won't take less than £60 if the Phoenix refuses; ask his sane and level advice, and act on it. To me

1. Harold Holt, theatrical manager.
2. William Wordsworth, theatrical agent.

it seems as good an instant result as we could have hoped for; you will be playing regularly before a London audience, becoming generally known (which should mean increasing engagements here and in the provinces) and you will be earning more than your keep. This is extremely important, for you have some bills ahead of you that must be met, and nothing else to depend on for them. It would be dreadful if, by missing good chances, your situation slipped back towards Hereford Road.

Look at it like this; if what you want is to play in a London Theatre before full houses, the Phoenix gives you that, whether you get £30 or £60. If the job itself is good enough, believe me, £30 is not to be sniffed at.

Meanwhile, you can polish your performance, and become so sure of yourself with your material that you will grow easy and gay, as well as grim. You were neither easy nor gay at Wyndham's, and one of your best assets was dimmed. When you spoke to me about your performance on your return home on Monday night, you seemed to me to speak with sense and judgement, but on Tuesday when you came here you talked as though you had given your best show, and swept the audience away. Dear dear Otto, when you do this so excessively, it seems to me you are like a small boy who has no self-confidence, and is boasting very loud to delude himself.

But everybody is agreed on this – that you write delightful and admirable tunes – this includes Bertie and Bronnie; and if, while you are keeping yourself on the platform and stage, you can also go on creating 'Soyer' when I am free again, after my present book is begun and finished, you will be expressing what I too feel is the best of all your gifts, the really creative one.

How much of this can you take? I write it because I am your loving
Eleanor

The Soyer operetta remained half written, and there is no sign of a musical score among Eleanor's papers.

# The Middle of the War

*July 5th* 1941

DEAR OTTO,

Let me say a word or two about the position here, since you expressed your own doubt last night about Pod's feelings. It is better for you to try to see this clearly with me, and necessary for me to try to see it clearly for myself. He is not jealous, I am sure; not only has he no need to be, but he knows he hasn't. He knows that, as a person, he comes first in my life, and that I could never let him down; for twenty-one years I have given him all the health and happiness in my power, and he is my dear companion, still my lover, and very much my child. I have been told by many of our friends, who love him as well as me, that I have spoiled him; if I have, I have had from him his fine mind, his love, and his complete faith. If there has sometimes been *too* much responsibility, too little time to do my own work, too little personal privacy and leisure, there is, always, in every relationship, something which needs adaptation in the two people concerned, if it is going to be a success. I have no doubt at all that he has had to adapt himself to many shortcomings in me. But whatever the drawbacks may be on each side, they are kept in proportion by the loving value we have for each other; it has not become a habit with time, it is alive, and it is what I would not dream of risking for anything that is less than itself.

Well then, of my feelings, I am sure, he is not jealous. I say "I am sure", because he does not in fact speak on the subject, after one short talk I myself had with him, to clear his heart if it needed clearing on the point. But of my time, and my attention, and my

233

personal presence and concentration on himself, he is, in a way always jealous, and always has been; so that writing has been difficult, simply because of the limitations of the clock and one's energy. As for solitude, that has been impossible; and to you, who hate being alone, and to Pod, who can't bear me to be absent, it may seem an odd thing that one of my needs, and secret joys, is being alone. (Of course, one isn't alone, but I won't go into that.) I need it as much as a field needs to lie fallow every two or three years. And more and more, as life mounts and friends increase, and I find it almost impossible to shut out the calls, I see that this precious solitude is what I shall only very rarely have again.

Well, now, darling, let us come to you. I had my Pod already hanging on to one of my apron-strings when you appeared last March to take hold of the other. I don't blind myself at all to what taking Mr Otto Lampel into one's life may mean. He costs dear. But I love him, and am prepared for that to a great degree. But not to the point of pulling things up by the roots which are planted in my life. I think you know that in a friendship, a real friendship, I go forward freely and give without asking, out of myself; what you may have to guard against, Otto, is asking too much, or seeming to demand as your prerogative a concentration of myself and my time and actions for yourself which, if they are anybody's, are Pod's. He is much too sensitively balanced not to be aware if this is in the air, even if he prefers not to face it out; and it is that, I believe, which creates something in the air from him, of which you also are aware. The 'jealousy', if it exists, is because you are tugging at one of my apron-strings, while he tugs at the other. Poor apron! Poor small boys! Both, at this particular moment, needing me 'terribly'.

The last paragraph of this long letter runs:

What a lot of work I might have done this morning instead of writing one letter. How much of it have you skipped?
God bless you –
I love you.
Eleanor

There is a poem written to Earle in the aftermath of some emotional upset which proves how the steadiness of their long relationship was appreciated by Eleanor, despite her wide-ranging heart. It may have been from some other period and incident in their life together, but it suits here, showing her very practical and very sensitive attitude.

*I shall remember, love, as long*
*As I remember love and you,*
*You bore with me when I was wrong,*
*Made me, when I saw false, see true,*

*Remained so gentle, kind, and wise,*
*Though I was spoiling your delight,*
*That when the ill mood passed, my eyes*
*Could not but see with your clear sight.*

*I would undo that hour, my dear,*
*With all my heart; but if I could,*
*I never would have known how near*
*You stand to me, in ill and good;*

*One way, of all love's thousand ways,*
*Would have remained unlearned by me,*
*One day, of all love's many days*
*Would have been kept in secrecy;*

*And I, who thought I could not love*
*You more, would not have known the hour*
*Which made my shaken spirit move*
*Through its own weakness to your power.*

*Even the reproach you will not lay*
*On me, but I would take again,*
*You've shown me I must put away,*
*To spare the pain of double pain.*

*Go then, all shadows of that brief*
*Strange hour, as swiftly as they came –*
*Yet since our acts of joy or grief*
*Can never leave our loves the same*

*Something of this, my dear, I still*
*May change to beauty, light and song,*
*For you, who turned aside the ill*
*And bore with me when I was wrong.*

Before Eleanor's affection for Lampel faded, and it lasted almost four years, she was busy writing a short story about him: *Tiger in a Meat-Safe* (unpublished). In it a sixty-year-old author, respectable and famous, wonders what sort of shock her appearance gives to admirers when they meet. 'Is she older – fatter – plainer than they thought? Do they say afterwards? "No, not a bit good-looking, but *so* amusing, and not a bit stand-offish." ' This must certainly have been the reaction of a great number of admirers to the real woman. Then there begins a description of the writer's infatuation with a young musician from somewhere in Europe. He has a self-indulgent nature and heavy eyelids, he won't get up in the morning. The pair of them go in for badinage and baby talk, which is rather disgusting and, one suspects, true to life. When the lady explains that she only took him up out of pity, the young man retorts tauntingly, "You were never sorry for me. You thought I was an admirable case of deserving genius that would do you glory."

In this story Eleanor was ruthless with herself, in the same way that she never mitigated the humiliations of the child Martha,[1] who had such a bad day trying to make others happy via her fantasies, or the young woman Anna,[2] chasing across Sussex trying to come to terms with her lover's desertion. In the case of the elderly writer doting over a young man, yet aware of her silliness and gullibility, Eleanor was not quite so objective, but mortification marks all three of these autobiographical stories.

In a letter to Lampel in October 1942, Eleanor discussed Peter Ustinov's first play, which Bertie had read in the school exercise books where the young man had originally written it out. Bertie had been much impressed, and recommended the play to his fellow dramatic critic, James Agate, who, a few weeks later, came out with long panegyric in the *Sunday Times*, to the author's astonishment. Eleanor wrote:

1. *A Bad Day for Martha*.
2. *A Walk in the Dark*, an unpublished short story.

Last night was the first night of Peter Ustinov's *House of Regrets*; I longed to be there, for I love Peter, and think he is a tremendous coming man, and I wanted to be, among all his other friends, at his first première. As I was too late for a ticket, I decided to spend the evening in the Arts Club, and see him and all the others in the intervals, and at least listen to the applause; I arrived early, and as I entered the door by the box-office a gentleman was saying, "Well then, I'm afraid I shall have to give you this back", and he handed a ticket in to the girl; I cued up to him like his long-lost sweetheart, and grabbed the ticket as soon as he had disappeared, saying I was the Miss Farjeon who had been pestering them daily since my return. "But there are such a lot of you," said the worried girl, "didn't you send your postal order for a ticket this morning?" "No, that was Annabel, my niece." "Well, we have given *her* ticket to another Farjeon." "Yes, that was her father" – and the girl held on to the returned ticket, fearing new complications, till a second woman appeared and said authoritatively, "Yes, it's all right, she can have it, I've got all these Farjeons straightened out now." "We're all of one family and we don't quarrel," I said meekly, seized the ticket, and sped joyfully to 4 St. Martin's Lane, and had the best steak I've ever had there; then back for the show, where all the Farjeons were gathered in force, and Geoffrey Dunn, and Peter in a state of blue funk, and Alec Clunes[1] who acknowledged the receipt of *These Two*[2] – "You'll send it back, just like *Recamier*[2]," I assured him, "and I have three more to follow, all different; and you'll send them back too."

   Well, Peter's play is marvellous stuff; not quite a perfect play, because the first act, which states the characters, is the best, and after that they talk, and are reacted on by events, and talk, and behave in all sorts of ways, and talk; and just one of them is not quite and entirely himself, but is Peter looking on at the others; this would not matter at all, if you weren't very slightly aware of it. But good heavens! what talk! and what behaviour! all over and under the surface, like Tchekov, with movements of music and poetry and soft poignant sorrows like autumn mist falling over a landscape, and sudden crises of nerves – and this from a

1. Alec Clunes, actor and director.
2. Two plays, never performed.

237

lad of nineteen. There's nothing at all crude or amateurish in the writing itself; in fact Peter is, I think, one of those rare wells of creativeness that just has to dip a bucket into his own deeps and fish up overflowing draughts of the very best water of life. He has written two more plays since then, a novel, and is now on a film; he is barely twenty-one. At the end of the play he looked at me tremblingly and squeezed my hand and said nervously, "Okay?" Max Adrian was very good, though towards the end a little static in performance, and the middle act has a grand situation for him, psychologically, which he doesn't quite rise to; the finest performance, the unaccountable, unpredictable one, and I think the finest-imagined character of the piece, is from Noel Wilman, as an ancient choreographer, on the verge of senile decay. Max is also an ancient Russian General, and the third fine part is an ancient Russian Admiral, also beautifully played. After this, two or three of the women give very good shows, but all the young parts in the piece were badly played, or inadequately; it was, however, an excellent production and set.

At this time Bertie was requiring bits and pieces for a new Cochran revue. C. B. Cochran was a showman whose young ladies of the chorus were the British counterpart to those of the Ziegfeld Follies in the States – they were famed for their charm, beauty and unions with the aristocracy. Cochran, now a flashy impresario, had long ago appeared as a gnome for Joseph Jefferson in *Rip Van Winkle*. The final result of this new revue, *Big Top*, did not please Bertie: he found it vulgar and swore he would never again deal with the big boys of the theatre world.

Eleanor also provided material for *Light and Shade*, another revue which Bertie managed himself. This was a different affair both to the grandiloquent Cochran show or the Little Theatre satires. It was quieter, more poetic and nostalgic for the peaceful past, with here and there an attack on the present that was more serious and intense than anything he had written before. The cast was again chosen for its individuality, with no stars to fight over money or limelight. The sensitive approach and tolerant tone in no way suited the jingoistic mood of the country: critics gave lukewarm notices, Farjeons and others lost money.

As always on such occasions Bertie was deeply depressed at

having failed to convey to the public ideas that were to him significant. Here is one of his sister's three consolatory letters:

*'Hammonds'*, *Laughton, Lewes, Sussex*
*Sept.* 16th, 1942

Dearest Bertie,

Thank you for the cheque to end *Big Top*, First Series. It has paid me much too well, one of life's little surprises. I am happier in having lost about the same amount over *Light and Shade*. It will be, for lots of people, a lovely thing to remember. Pod is continually fed by thinking of it; in a way he may seem to be no criterion, but in another way he is, for he was not fed by *Big Top*, and has never asked to see it twice. In trying to think of whys and wherefores, it seems to me that there was nothing one could or would have considered altering between the 1st and 29th of July, though since then I have assembled a few reasons which have not to do with your beautiful text. Somebody says you say you are not going to write a show for the theatre again. I don't think this is true – in fact, one of the things I find I believe is that you won't be able to help writing for the theatre again some time or other. However, that's your business.

I do hope you're going to have a good holiday, and catches. The other day in Scotland George Fradd, on a little bridge over a river coming down in spate, was leapt at by a 16lb salmon, clasped it to his bosom, and bore it to the mess. His sergeant-major rapidly gave him fifteen shillings for it. Soon after, his Colonel with some annoyance told him to bring the next one to the officers' mess, and he would get three pounds. This is a perfectly true fishing story.

Life is very nice here; too much to do, as always, but things I really like doing; I would like more time for work and letters and myself, but I think I shall get my little cat-book all but done before I go back at the end of the month so that Alice can have her second holiday. I would sometimes like a holiday myself, but I foresee no way of getting one ever again. However, I am sure I will, in some way unforeseen, and I do feel well on this sort of life. I love picking things and preserving and cooking them. I don't like bed-making, or the time-taking fore-and-afters of three meals a day; but I must pull my weight a bit, and I get more than my fair share done for me always, I feel. Jim Toomey has started bricklaying the chicken house; it is nice to see a thousand of one's own bricks, and a yard of sand (not a yardful of sand, you buy sand by the yard, as I don't doubt you know), waiting to aid and abet egg-laying. Yesterday I made blackberry jam; tomorrow I bottle pears; next week blue plums.

A letter from Henrietta Leslie this morning says: "We are very upset by the departure of that darling revue. I cannot understand it. It was so much more charming and intelligent than any of the other revues running in town. Really, people *are* stupid. Will you tell Bertie that we feel personally insulted. I'm afraid it will have meant a great loss and even greater disappointment to both of you."

Except for you, I am not much disappointed, not in a way that affects my feelings of any importance to me. The course of things has made me fairly indifferent to certain sorts of disappointments that years ago would have affected me a great deal; one does change, perhaps one's instincts grow deadened with experience, or perhaps because they have changed their values a bit. One also changes one's fears – I had most of them as a girl, I can think of almost nothing I wasn't afraid of, but I think it is true that I have sloughed a great many fears; though I may flatter myself when I think I wouldn't be very much afraid of the (jumping) pepperpot. I would certainly be surprised, I would certainly be startled, and I would possibly be alarmed; but not being able to explain a thing that is a material manifestation is not what creates sensations of fear in me; honestly I think this, and may one day be proved quite wrong. I doubt if any jumping pepperpot could create the sensation of fear I felt in passing through the trees on Blackcap when, without any manifestation at all, or any preconception, I simply felt appalled. As to what I may declare that I believe in the power and force of hate, and the power and force of love, and that the first is the nearest I can come to meaning the Devil, and the second is the nearest I can come to meaning God; and that these two forces, with their power to affect the course of things, are not things of the brain or reason, though the reasonable brain may do its best to apprehend them. Perhaps this doesn't get us very far. But after our burgundy-type discussion the other night, I wondered why you thought I *must* be afraid of a jumping pepperpot because you would be, but could not understand why I

240

might be afraid of black magic because you wouldn't be. Your brain and reason get you to a certain point. So all other persons' differences from that point seem illusion to you? That may be one of your illusions, mayn't it? I'm not saying I haven't lots of illusions of my own; I'm sure I have, though I'd be hard put to it to sort them out from such small wisdom as may come near a truth or two. But since we are strange and imperfect mixtures, I think even the illusions need not matter much if they do not defeat character and undermine one's powers.

Argal: I hope you will shed as soon as possible the illusion that you are not going to write for the theatre any more.

Your eternally devoted and loving
   Nellie


The war went on. There was a sense of dogged, rather dreary determination in the country. Since the first blitz on London, children had started queuing up outside the tube stations at four in the afternoon, loaded with family blankets, in order to get a safe night's lodging on the underground platforms. They would be joined by their parents at six, after work. And every night in the blackout those who travelled by underground, found it difficult to get to the trains without tripping over the feet of the huddled bodies which encrusted platforms to their very edge. Children slept on the concrete like grubby angels, adults like grubby ghosts, grey with anxiety and work, queuing, lack of sleep and the endless discomfort of life in the broken city. Grime from the tumbled buildings had got into everything and everybody, but the camaraderie of these extraordinary circumstances broke down the English reserve; people were wonderfully friendly.

Of course, Eleanor still smiled and talked to strangers as she had always done. She still walked down to her brother Harry in Fellows Road on her bad feet to bring him food and cheer. He was ill with Parkinson's disease and had a stone in his bladder. A new pupil meeting the musician for the first time said her immediate thought had been, "Oh you poor little man!" But after the first lesson she never thought it again.

Earle was becoming more difficult. He had developed a mania for heating pokers in the coal fire and bending them when red hot. This had nearly resulted in disaster, and Eleanor was terrified that he would set the house on fire while she was out. She used his clothing coupons to buy Lampel a pair of shoes.

PEN Club committee meetings occurred about every two months, and these Eleanor attended regularly with J. B. Priestley, H. G. Wells, Hugh Walpole, C. V. Wedgwood and Rebecca West among the notable members. With enthusiasm and energy she helped raise funds for writers in trouble all over the world, a number of whom became lifelong friends. She devised a PEN Club game for the famous, to which Shaw responded, 'Sorry, too old for these games, and no time for them. G.B.S.' while Osbert Sitwell wrote, 'Believe me it is no spirit of mere *unwillingness* that makes me refuse – but sheer inability. I hide in a corner – and have done so all my life – whenever a game is mentioned.' Noel Coward and J. B. Priestley also refused, among others, while Arthur Koestler was one who amiably accepted the challenge. Nothing came of it in the end. She laughed when H. G. Wells stormed out of a committee after accusing the PEN of becoming a tool of the British Council; she was host at grand luncheons, but was also ready to spend days organising in the office and sticking stamps on hundreds of letters.

Meticulousness over money marked all financial dealings, whether big or small. When anybody did the shopping, each item had to be gone through with the pennies, halfpennies and farthings added up to make sure that the change was correct. Bad shopping made her quite cross. A page of accounts at the back of her diary gives an insight into the weekly cost of living for an elderly couple and three cats in 1944. [See facing page.]

2 Perrins Court (whose lighting and heat cost £1. 12. 7, which must have covered far more than a week) was a tiny slot of a cottage which had been bought at the end of 1943. It was in the lane across the wide Fitzjohn's Avenue, opposite Perrins Walk. A pair of cottages had been acquired for £500, but one had an old couple in residence, and this must have been resold at some time. The money came out of Savings Certificates, in advance of an insurance policy which was to mature in November 1944.

The empty cottage, now furnished, was intended as a free lodging for some couple, the woman to help in Eleanor's house, the man, perhaps, in the garden. For legal reasons there was to be a peppercorn rent of one shilling a year. When this was advertised in *The Times* there were thirty-seven replies. From a second advertisement

| | £ | s. | d. | |
|---|---|---|---|---|
| Baker and Confectioner | | 3 | 1 | |
| Dairyman | | 5 | 1 | |
| Butcher | | 3 | 4 | |
| Grocer | | 8 | 8 | |
| Greengrocer | | 3 | 6 | |
| Charity and Gifts | 11 | 3 | 3 | (Annabel's Wedding cheque: £11) |
| Draper | | 8 | 11 | |
| Furniture and Repairs | 8 | 2 | 6 | (Chesham for carpets and moving) |
| | 9 | 6 | 0 | (Geary's bill for 2 Perrins Court) |
| Garden, Flowers | | 4 | 2 | |
| Lighting and Heating | 1 | 12 | 7 | (2 Perrins Court) |
| Cats | | 10 | 5½ | |
| Stationery, Books and Stamps | | 10 | 5 | |
| | 34 | 1 | 11½ | |

in the *Hampstead and Highgate Express* there were also many answers, one from Teresa Dodds, who explained that she had a small baby and needed a home badly. Eleanor liked the letter and asked her to call. At the cottage door the applicant found herself pressed to an ample bosom, and welcomed with the words, "If you'll take me, I'll take you!" Her new employer then stood back to add, "And Mr Earle and I will have a baby too!"

This was one of Eleanor's impulsive appointments which she never regretted. The following letter to Mrs Dodds shows how determined she was, whether in seeking out cats or telephone numbers.

*August 10th, 1947*

Dearest Tess,

Just a follow-up of my 'phone call – I was so excited that I forgot to tell Godfrey that Smokey came back too! I could have cried for joy when Gert rang me up at 10.30 to say Pip had been hidden way back in the coke-cellar all the time, and wouldn't come out for anybody. He was terrified of everything and everybody, and wanted to fight his own brother, and wouldn't eat. Gert was going to twelve o'clock Mass, and Kearton had a midday job, so I wolfed breakfast, told Winnie Ferris, and bowled down to No. 24 by 11.10. Kearton went down with the basket and presently he and Gert appeared empty-handed to say that there was no sign or sound of Pip, and the coke-cellar was impossible to search properly, because of all sorts of boards. Gert thought I must leave the basket and wait till they could get hold of him sometime and let John bring him up; but I couldn't bear the uncertainty, and insisted on having a try myself, though Gert and Kearton both swore he wouldn't come for anybody. I got as far into the cellar as I could, and spoke to him in Cat-Language, and presently heard a little scrabble – then Gert whispered, "I can see his eyes!" and soon the rest of him came out and ran towards me – he knew I was from his own home-ground, and was I conceited? Yes! We got him quick into the basket, and in the motor all the way home he rubbed his chin hard against my fingers, and told me all about it; he wanted me to know he'd had a hell of a time. When we got near Perrins Court, up went his little nose to sniff. Winnie and I took him into his own room, and let him out, and contentment set in at once; Mickey Ferris ran to the doorstep, and Pip met him from below, and they kissed like long-lost brothers; Win went for milk and I ran back for fish and meat, and the last I saw of him was his behind in the scullery while his in-front gobbled fish ravenously. He had two days rations to make up.

I shall have a word with him every day, and see there's plenty for him, and though he'll miss you I think the relief of being back, and in touch with humans he likes and a cat he's not afraid of, will keep him serene till your holiday is over. Oh Tess, I felt so light-hearted that the only thing to do was to ease your still-heavy hearts by a trunk-call. Of course the first one was a misfire, and the Shiplake girl could only give me the name of the Sandbourne, but not its telephone number. So I had to get on to Trunk Inquiries, and first they wanted the proprietor's name, and then swore there was no such hotel, but eventually found it; and assured me the exchange I wanted was Westbourne. Then the Trunk Girl assured me there was no such exchange, until she agreed it was so;

and when I got on to the Sandbourne it was a long time before I could persuade the man there that there was any Dodds staying in the place; but after having plunged into the depths of the coke-cellar I wasn't going to be put off by any other obstacle, and to my joy got Godfrey in time to save one day of misery for you. So now enjoy your holiday to the full, darling.

I wrote ten letters in bed, between 5.30 and 7.30 this morning, posted up my diary, and did my accounts; then got tea, fed cats, fed humans, and after the Pip-Saga typed my play (beds were made and slops emptied, perfunctorily); now lunch is over and I shall shell peas and do Crosswords with Pod till one Mrs. Roberts turns up about the flat. Another one comes at five. But last night I saw a very very possible applicant, who may be excellent, and I find the Nursing Mirror was really the place to go to all the time; my 'phone has gone like mad and I feel very hopeful.

However, this is all stodgy London news – forget it. Go and make sandpies. My love to all four.

Your affectionate

Eleanor Farjeon

P.S. I am happy!

P.P.S. I AM happy!

P.P.P.S. Oh, by the way, I'm happy!

Smokey is *lovely*, and very friendly. He merely turned up quite coolly, but couldn't leave Gert's heels. He may be the sort of adventurous cat who *likes* to roam now and then.

It was also in this year that Eleanor ordered Joscelyn, now married to the singer Ernest Frank, to make her a great-aunt by next January; which command was conscientiously obeyed.

One morning Frank himself, on leave from the army, came down the cobbled yard in battle dress, and, standing beneath Eleanor's bedroom window, burst into Don Giovanni's serenade:

*"Deh, vieni alla finestra, o mio tesoro . . ."*

*Oh come to the window my treasure,*
*Oh come and console my grief,*
*If you refuse to give me comfort*
*I shall die before your eyes . . .*

At this the casement was flung wide and Eleanor leaned out to respond with one of Donna Elvira's arias.

Even though now over sixty and fat, Eleanor remained unshackled by normal conventions. One day a window cleaner arrived and went up his ladder to do the front windows, but he soon came hurrying down and into the kitchen to Teresa Dodds.

"I can't do the bedroom," he exclaimed. "There's a naked woman in there!"

"You carry on, Miss Farjeon won't mind," Mrs Dodds urged.

"But how can I go through the room to do the inside panes with her like that? I won't!" he announced.

So Teresa Dodds had to go and persuade her mistress to put on a dressing-gown before the young man would venture up his ladder again.

Nor was Eleanor troubled by an affair Earle had with a school mistress. To explain her tolerance she said, "You see, I am not a very good lover."

All sorts of people came up and down that cul-de-sac. There was witty bitter Doris Thompson,[1] who amused with her gossip and massaged away Eleanor and Earle's aches; there was kindly Roland Watson, who would sit with Earle to discuss pubs and Keats or go out to lunch with Eleanor: special Fridays were kept for Watty. There was her friend and agent, David Higham. There were Sally and Stephen Thomas[2] who lived in Church Row, and Sally had only to run down her garden and through the back gate to the cottage to pour out her troubles or read her poems after tea. There were the two Guthrie boys, Robin and John, who arrived in uniform to be received as sons, or Clifton and Yoma Parker: Clifton had composed for Bertie's revues and Yoma had been the leading dancer in *Big Top*. Later little Piers Plowright, son of Eleanor's doctor, would go down his garden with his sister and climb over the wall into Eleanor's world which was, he said, like a Christmas treat, whatever the time of year. Americans, strangers, soldiers, sailors, relatives and beggars all turned up, each to be treated as though he or she was the most valued friend. And every so often Margaret Radford, ragged and hungry, would knock on the door: she must be fed and her wild talk listened to for hours.

1. Doris Thompson, sister of Hugh Popham, Rosalind's second husband.
2. Sally Thomas, actress; Stephen Thomas, stage director.

Eleanor loved the intimacy of these tête-à-têtes, but in them there was the very element of which Edward Thomas had complained in his relationship to Godwin Baynes. For the time each individual was made to feel the most important person in the world, and for the time this was probably true: there was no trickery, no disloyalty in the emotional response between the protagonists. Yet to the fastidious there was the knowledge of being one of a crowd.

Many many friends lived happy in the illusion that they were Eleanor's best beloved, as she threw herself heart and soul into their personal problems. Settled opposite one another across the table in the tiny kitchen, the confidences would be presided over by one of the cats, centrally placed between them on the bread board. After such emotional heart to hearts, Eleanor would emerge drained of strength, while her confidant went away up the yard restored.

# The End of the War

IN 1943 BERTIE received a letter with a new suggestion from the film star and actor-manager, Robert Donat. 'I wondered if I dare approach you and your sister with the idea of writing the First Real Children's Pantomime.

'I have always felt that a lovely job could be done in the theatre for children and children only, with no distortion of the story, no inclusion of snappy modern songs, no jokes about beer and mothers-in-law; just a simple and honest concentration on the story and its faithful telling with all the great traditions and glamour of the theatre to help it . . .'

Donat wanted to put on the show for his young sons.

Eleanor and Bertie were delighted with the idea – there was no more talk of never again writing for the theatre from Bertie – and they at once began work on *Cinderella*, with a Christmas production in prospect. Clifton Parker was their chosen composer. Eleanor shelved the novel she had started so that the play might be ready in time. However, towards the end of October, Donat's secretary casually informed Bertie that there was no chance of a production this year, the proposed theatre was booked.

There was consternation. Eleanor wrote one of her rare almost stern letters to the agent, Aubrey Blackburn, expressing dismay. She explained that she and her brother were carrying on steadily with the work, so that the original impetus of friendly and enthusiastic feelings with which they had begun should not be dissipated. 'But I do feel that at this point the business side of it must be dealt with promptly and effectively, if the creators are not to feel that they are up against a certain pleasant slackness of attitude, due to the family-party feeling of all concerned, in which you are the liaison officer. We are still waiting for the contract . . .' She also said that had it been clear the show was not to go on this year she would have written her novel first, and so gained income both from it and the play next year. The agent was ticked off for his dilatory behaviour.

Response was immediate. Donat did not wish to lose the pantomime. A contract was signed and the advance of £75 shared out.

For freelance artists such delays can be disastrous, since a flow of commissions must be relied on for income. Bertie and Eleanor were established and could find other work, but for Clifton Parker the situation looked bad and he was lent money.

Eleanor kept up her 1944 diary, more or less, to the end of August, and although it is never very detailed her movements and feelings are made clear.

> *January 1st.* Morning to Otto to buck him up after finding him very low on the telephone. He went down on his knees and kissed my feet. Then to Bertie – long talk, very good, with him and Joan. Settled last details of *Cinderella*. Feeling much better.

> *January 3rd.* Tried to discuss financial position with Pod; messed it thoroughly, upset him and was ill for the rest of the day. Mustn't try again, must just pay out. Money makes things so mean.

> *January 4th.* A better day after a bad night. Pod seems well. I hope I didn't hurt him. I love him so much and sometimes find it so hard to manage without trying to discuss things.

January 12th has nothing to report except that she was able to buy ten pounds of cats' meat. This was an event, for by now food was scarce and people were having their pets killed. The adult allowance each week was – 1s. 2d. worth of meat, 2 oz. butter, 2 oz. cheese, 2 oz. tea, 8 oz. sugar, 2 pints of milk. In one year there was an allowance of 30 eggs, while only children were given a sweet ration. Cauldrons of cods' heads were boiled in Eleanor's kitchen, the eyes and flesh being carefully separated from the bones so that there would be no danger of a cat choking. Joscelyn was sometimes sent out to buy the best steak which had to be minced for an elderly toothless cat. Or Eleanor would trudge out in her plimsolls carrying two huge shopping bags, leaning forward so that her front coat tails trailed the ground. There was a pets' meat shop at the bottom of Arkwright Road where she would queue for an hour and a half if necessary, sticking it out once through an attack of diarrhoea.

Now Eleanor and Bertie were working simultaneously on three musical plays. *Cinderella*, renamed *The Glass Slipper* to avoid confusion with conventional pantomime, a one-act operetta *Phryne* with music by Geoffrey Wright, and another full-length operetta *Aucassin and Nicolette*, with music by Parker once again. For this it was planned that Yoma Parker should take the role of Nicolette, although the fact that she was a dancer and could not sing set the authors a serious problem. However, this was solved in the following manner: Nicolette, imprisoned, was to take a vow of silence until she should be reunited with her Aucassin, which lasted the length of the play. Such a solution gave scope for the dancer's talent in movement and mime; yet Bertie was never happy with it, for to have a dumb heroine while everybody else was singing their heads off seemed to him to upset the balance.

In her May diary Eleanor reported that Bertie was stuck with *Aucassin* and her feet were bad.

It was about this time that Yoma Parker took the place of Elizabeth Myers as Earle's favourite 'nymph', this being the term he used for favoured and pretty young women, although the tubercular Myers had once written to Eleanor, 'Well, I am a poor specimen to a cold eye.' Earle was now happy to teach the dancer about English literature, setting poems to be learned by heart, instructing her on meaning, pronunciation, and where to put the stress in a line. His portrait was painted that year by Anthony Ayrton and shown at the Academy Summer Exhibition. It was an excellent likeness, the pipe in mid air, just removed from lips which can be heard propounding: "The light that lies behind is the light that shoots ahead – the story of the past is the story of the future." Or, "Slang is the safety valve of the passing generation. It is the tilting ground or playing field of youth of every class." Or his favourite theme, "A word is in itself a metaphor, and language nothing but a web of metaphor – life's a metaphor."

Eleanor took her old lover to the Academy opening and they both felt proper pride to find him hung on the line. It was not like a previous portrait of Earle, a bust by the sculptor, Janko Briovitch, cast in plaster. This was so disliked that during the war Eleanor gave it to Doris Thompson with instructions that it be destroyed. Mrs Thompson buried the head at the end of her garden, and for years after complained that bits of Earle would keep coming to the surface.

Now the German aerial attack changed. There were no more heavy bombing raids on London, but single buzz-bombs. These were launched from the French coast and buzzed their way across the Channel, often chased and blown up in mid-air by Spitfires. Next came the Doodlebugs, which flew faster, while their engines roared spasmodically on and off. Lastly came rockets, which made no sound at all till the gigantic explosion on landing. With this last onslaught many people became hysterically anxious. But not in Perrins Walk. Eleanor wrote a postcard to her friend Roland Watson:

We go on all right here; Pod quite unalarmed, too much so, sometimes. He takes Alerts for All-Clears, Doodlebugs for our bombers, and their explosions for our gunfire. So for him everything's for the best in the – worst? – of all possible worlds. I don't mind them either, personally, but I do H A T E feeling relieved as they pass over our heads and go somewhere else; it is so hard for the somewhere else, yet the sensation of relief is unavoidable. We sleep in the shelter again; it is very comfortable, and we sleep quite as well there as here. A neighbour has a third bed in it. Before she comes, about 10.30, Pod reads to me, for he won't have his pet habits disturbed for any Doodlers. I find I can't work much, but I think that was so before this phase set in – a sort of restlessness with the end of the war, very distant perhaps, but still the end, looming nearer from News to News. I like your story, and feel its application strongly when we lie snug in our little brick box across the yard; it really is very hard to find. Much love, dear Watty; and we are here when you want us.

Eleanor

By autumn Donat had acquired the beautiful St James Theatre (so wantonly torn down in 1957) for *The Glass Slipper*. Hugh Stevenson designed exquisite décor, the actors were perfectly matched to their parts.

The plot follows the traditional story, that strange balance between the fairy world of ideal princes, princesses and magic, and the grim reality of jealous sisters, not enough to eat and dirty-washing up. The play was linked by songs which enhanced both the unearthly and the domestic. There was a flow to this collaboration, which seems to have been one which Bertie enjoyed as well as his sister. In the opening scene Cinderella is discovered in her cupboard bed at the back of the kitchen, rubbing her eyes and grumbling:

> *"Oh! Oh!*
> *Silly old rooster!*
> *Crow, crow!*
> *Shrilly old rooster!*
> *Every morning*
> *Crow, crow!*
> *'Time to get up!'*
> I *know!*
> *Fire to light,*
> *Kettle to boil,*
> *Lamp to polish*
> *And fill with oil,*
> *Ashes to sweep*
> *Up in a heap,*
> *Oh dear!*
> *I'd ever so rather go back*
> *To*
> *Sleep!"*

But the Things continue to badger: the Clock ticks, the Tap drips, the Chair creaks, all demanding attention. And as she begins to polish and dust and oil her much loved kitchen objects, Cinderella continues with her very human little complaint about scrubbing and scouring. When the Stepmother appears she is properly nasty, when the Ugly Sisters come down in their dressing gowns they are properly comic and spiteful, while the Prince is perfectly handsome in every feature and feeling.

At Christmas the show was a triumph. Beverly Baxter's review in the *Evening Standard* stood out as fulsome as any author or composer greedy for praise could wish:

And now I come to one of those unexpected experiences which happen to men who undertake the responsibility and hazards of theatre criticism. I could not go to the opening performance of *The Glass Slipper* at the St James's this week. One knew beforehand that the piece would have pointed humour, for are not the authors the talented brother and sister, Herbert and Eleanor Farjeon? What is more, it was certain to have taste, since it was presented by Robert Donat.

Yet I was wholly unprepared for what I found. The notices had been kindly and encouraging, not more.

In my opinion, *The Glass Slipper* is so completely enchanting, so compelling a work of imaginative art that it will be a classic, and will be played for years in every civilised country in the world. It ranks as a theatrical event of the utmost importance.

Let us first take the music of Mr Clifton Parker. Without plagiarism at any point it contrives to blend the mysticism of *The Immortal Hour* and the felicity of Sullivan with the charm of *Rosenkavalier*; and it is so brilliantly scored that the orchestra of 22 sounds as if it is of symphonic proportions.

Who is Mr Parker? He is a young man in his middle thirties who was almost completely disregarded until a couple of years ago. With our quaint attitude towards the arts, the classical composer is left to beg or starve.

This much I will say. I have never heard a young composer with such a sense of theatre in his music. The effects he produces when Cinderella heard the midnight strike were worthy of Strauss at his best. He has the stuff of great opera in him.

Robert Donat was so confident of *The Glass Slipper* that he spent £8000 on the production – and with exquisite result. What is more he has cast it perfectly. The herald of Mr Geoffrey Dunn, the Cinderella of Audrey Hesketh, the father of John Ruddock and the stepmother of Elliot Mason are things to be seen and remembered . . .

The final paragraph runs: 'If we have left the authors to the last it is only because they deserve a final award. They have contrived to combine wit, phantasy and charm with unerring taste. *The Glass Slipper* is something no one who loves the creative theatre should miss. After many vicissitudes the lordly St James's has found a piece worthy of its past.'[1]

On a May evening, five months later, the phone rang in Eleanor's cottage. The call was from Joscelyn. There had been an accident. Bertie was dead.

Eleanor, unable to find a taxi or stop a car, ran in the rain almost all the way from Hampstead to St John's Wood. She found that Bertie, working alone in his study, had stumbled and, falling, hit his head on the mantelpiece. Unconscious, he had choked on blood from his nose and died. Whether he had had a heart attack simultaneously was never clear.

Years later Eleanor wrote a piece *For Bertie's Joan* in which she compared her own and her brother's manner of composition.

> If Bertie never sounded in his work certain depths that were in him, which might have been sounded but for his too-soon death, I think this was because the critic in him made writing a sort of torture. He could not, he told me, enjoy writing a single line that was not born perfect. The quality he attained in his revues set a standard still remembered and often quoted: he had to struggle for it. With the inception of a new idea he would sit at his typewriter tapping out first and last lines painfully, variations of a couplet, a refrain, a rhyming scheme. He could hardly get on with it for going back on it, he was like a cyclist continually puncturing his tyre with thorns in the road. The end was near-perfect, and worth the pains, but he hadn't enjoyed the journey. He wrote direct on to the typewriter, and once showed me a sheet of typescript saying with a wry smile, "This is how I do it, Nellie." His lyric-in-the-making looked like a headache, a trayful of mosaic splinters, to be composed at last into a small bright picture.
>
> On the other hand, I *do* enjoy the journey inordinately, perhaps too much. I can only create in manuscript, and self-criticism does not block my road until the faults glare out at me from the first typing. Bertie's torment and my enjoyment, his fine etching and my splashing with the paintbrush, made us a curious complement of each other.

1. *Evening Standard*, December 1944.

# 31

# Aftermath

*LOVE AFFAIR* is a novel based on an operetta which had been planned before the war, and which was about to be recommenced at the time of Bertie's death. It was known as the 'Manet Opera', because two Manet paintings had been at the root of Bertie's original idea. One was the café scene where a young man in a straw boater gazes eagerly across the table into a young woman's face, the other the picnic scene, 'Déjeuner sur l'Herbe', where a naked model lies between two artists in black suits, while behind another nude female rises from a lake. The story they had concocted was about a French girl, living in the Paris of 1876, who had left home and was struggling for independence as a governess. Having suddenly won money in the National Lottery, she goes to a café and there meets a charming but feckless artist. The prim plain virgin responds to his pleas and they go off to live together until her money runs out; then they quarrel and part. She returns to her family to bear his child.

The hero of Eleanor's novel turned out a mixture of the two admirers to whom she had been so attracted during the last six years : charming, ardent Tony Kraber, and effusive, cheeky Otto Lampel. The heroine was a mixture of Eleanor and her governess, Miss Newman. The settings portrayed a good deal of Trilby's Bohemian Latin quarter and Marguerite Gautier's country hide-out, sun-flecked woods, sitting out of doors in cafés, the heart's disillusionment and the spirit's resilience. In this book the different states of love were more fully and more readily discussed than ever before, revealing the author's own experience.

'It was one of those times when, in the mysterious rhythm of love, she was on top of the arc while her lover swung to its base. The power is to those on top, and just now she was strong with love. At other times she was beset with unaccountable weakness, she ran like molten wax in the flame of his mood; and the weak times were secretly more precious to her than the strong ones, because they were strange to her, and called into being a woman she had not known was part of her.'

Here was no longer the affirmation made in her thirties that 'dreams are as near the truth as we can come'. For although *Love Affair* is a lightweight romance, it expresses a variety of attitudes to money and social failure, to lying in bed resentful beside an oblivious lover.

Michael Joseph published the novel in 1947. Before it came out eight thousand advance copies had been sold.

In this year Joseph also published *First and Second Love*, those sonnets written before the end of the First World War. There are thirteen to the unknown love, an interim of seventeen, and then the fourteen to Edward Thomas. In this century sonnets have gone out of fashion, the problem of their strict form seeming out of key with the mood of poetry. Yet, despite the basic Elizabethan pattern from which the sonnets never quite escape, Eleanor's moods have their own character and do not strike one as archaic. The yearning sentiment is delicately slotted into words which have the ring of a young heart.

### XIII

*I marvel now in what exalted state*
*Love's truth I fitted to an unfit case.*
*Only one face of love I knew – too late*
*I learned that he possessed another face.*
*I know that when eternal things I sang*
*Between myself and you, I was misled*
*By my prevision of a love that sprang*
*From moods we had not both inhabited.*
*Lost friend, it was a mood I could not teach.*
*I dreaded to be quick to learn a tongue*
*That offers love the common coin of speech*
*And leaves the heavenlier air unsung.*
*Not that I loved too much requires my tears,*
*I loved too little and love stopped my ears.*

But it is in the final sonnets to Thomas that the poet's individuality stands out and makes it a lasting regret that she never again struggled to be what she called 'a real poet'. Surprised critics gave good reviews. In a letter de la Mare called them 'sovereign sonnets, full of truth and beauty . . . I am glad you've shared them with the world at large'.

The previous summer Earle's wife had died. Eleanor wrote of this matter to Watson: 'The odd thing is that his daughter and my friends all seem to take it as an axiom that he and I will get married now – but why spoil a good thing? This has been a success for twenty-six years and neither of us can feel any reason for changing it. Pod says it would upset all our friends, and I couldn't look my tradesmen in the face.'[1]

During the war, when visiting Eleanor for the first time, Leslie French had been surprised to find an old gentleman sitting by the fire smoking his pipe. "Oh," he exclaimed, "I didn't know you were married!" To which she replied, "We haven't been, not for the past twenty years." The meeting came about because she wished French to act the young Napoleon in her play *Recamier*, which for a long time was on the verge of being produced by Leon M. Lion. "It was an excellent play," Leslie French said. "But such a big cast, so many scene changes."

There came the death of Eleanor's old friend, the matriarch Bunny. Putting down the cats was always a tragic occasion, to be retailed in full detail over the phone to sympathetic friends. This going-over relieved some of the misery and was a method of reassuring herself that the right decision had been made. She was an excellent nurse, whether of animal or human being, insisting on proper Victorian standards of comfort. To her friend, Roland Watson, she wrote:

Darling Watty,

We both want and need you on Friday. One or two things you'd better know first. Yesterday I sent for Brian Cartland and quickly and quietly he put our little Bunny to sleep. Her tumour had burst overnight; she wasn't in the least pain, even then. She sat on my bed (I've got bronchitis again) all the morning purring in an

1. Letter from E.F. to Roland Watson, 13.8.46.

ecstasy, as she always did before a great experience. A little while before Brian came she walked firmly to the door and went to Tess. He came – and that was all. Pod didn't know anything till it was over, but when I told him he was knocked right out. I've been anxious for him, but tonight he seems much better. I've talked lots about Bunny and so has he – it doesn't do to sit on an emotion in his case, though I've sat on mine. I could sob and sob, but I promised myself after Honey's death not to endanger my lungs again. So when you come talk about her too. The others – Coney and Nonny – are very subdued today, lying on my bed as usual. Well, she really never had a twinge of pain, and I wish I had the right to spare my Harry in the same way. It is, though, tremendous and awful to have the right of life and death.

Harry is in a strange state – teaching and collapsing by turns – things are going to be very hard soon, and when I'm ill most complicated. Pod and I drove to Felpham on Thursday for what was to have been a week's holiday. I was overtired when we started after a queer night earlier with Harry when I couldn't come home, and when I got to Felpham I wasn't well enough to make it wise to stay, so we drove back on Sunday. Since then I've stayed in bed, under the doctor, and it might have been a lot worse, and I'm thankful to have been here for Bunny's crisis. But I'm becoming a little stupefied by what I must face, endure, and be responsible for. I need so much at this moment to relax and not have to think and do things which never get settled from week to week. And I *don't* know how to get on with any work at all, yet so much more must be earned to meet Harry's tragic case. We won't talk of *that* before Pod on Friday. Tonight he still feels strange in the head, and won't take the cachet prescribed for this feeling. Well well, I must let it slide after doing what I can. But how long can I go on, Watty? Honestly, I begin to wonder.

All my love, darling, Eleanor

Harry's condition was worsening. His hands shook so that dressing had become a long drawn-out agony. No one was allowed to help, and Eleanor would watch for an hour while he struggled to put a back stud into his shirt neckband and then through the collar. In the morning, Bertha must bathe his eyes with warm water before they would open, eating became difficult, his speech more and more slurred. Yet even though his hands had to be lifted for him and placed on the piano by pupils, he still taught at the Academy. He had worked there for forty-seven years.

With feet that were giving almost constant pain, Eleanor bought a car, a black Hillman saloon. She decided it would be cheaper and more convenient than taxis. The car was kept a few doors away in Kearton's Garage, with Mr Kearton acting as chauffeur when a friend or relative was not handy. Eleanor was inordinately proud of her motor car: she and Earle would sit up together in the back with the conscious air of royalty.

Joe, with his sweet jolly jokes that covered an anxious melancholy, was always ready to help with Harry, to read and talk to him. But like all the Farjeon brothers he was not practical: for any job about the house they would announce, "We'll get a man in." But the men who had done jobs so handily before the war were now a scarcity. Eleanor, with Bertha and her husband as aides, took responsibility for 137 Fellows Road.

In his last years the child Harry adored most of all was Bertha's daughter, named Margaret after Maggie Farjeon. He and the six-year-old girl would go out together walking slowly up Primrose Hill, where the old musician would sit on a seat, always the same seat, while the child played for a little nearby. Then she would lead her shuffling half-blind companion home. He told her stories, gave her treats and at her birthday party would go down to the basement and sit in a corner, listening to the children's play, and holding his hands together so that their trembling might not be noticed.

He was growing weak and apathetic. As Eleanor wrote to Watson: 'He has entered one stage nearer the mysterious end which is hardly more mysterious than his being here now.'

In 1948 he slipped and broke his thigh. He was taken to hospital and died within a few days.

Eleanor wrote to Joe: 'The greatness of Harry's living, locked into me since childhood, is locked in me till I die.'

In the Golders Green crematorium, a Church of England service was arranged at which the priest informed the congregation that Harry was being 'borne aloft on angels' wings'. The astonishment of his nephew and nieces, who had never seen any sign of Christianity in their uncle, although none would have disputed his otherworldliness, was not expressed to their aunt. Doubtless she was quick enough to sense that they felt the service to be a piece of humbug. One obituary commented: 'In many ways he seemed to attain that rare selflessness which transcends personality altogether.' Which amounted to the same thing as Harry's childhood announcement: "I am not a Boy. I am a Being."

After the cottage in Sussex had been sold, one of the post-war delights was the acquisition of a new bit of garden in Hampstead. An old lady died in No. 16 Church Row and there was an auction of her goods at which Eleanor got to know an architect who wished to buy the house. However she was £2000 short. So Eleanor lent the money with the lower part of the garden as security and, when the loan could not be repaid, became its owner. As this garden abutted on the pathway beside Eleanor's property, there was easy access through a door in the wall. The new land was planted with flowers, apple trees, roses, Royal Sovereign strawberries and an asparagus bed. It was a charming plot which turned Eleanor's end of the lane into a tiny estate over which she could show visitors, expatiating on its beauties. A brick shed was rebuilt into a solid square room, to which the stacks of books that littered the floors and chairs of the cottage were removed. Besides lining the walls with shelves, a bed and desk were installed, so that it became possible to work or rest there in summer weather looking out on to greenery. This retreat became known as the Garden Room.

The rebuilding work was done by Mr London, over whose talents Eleanor became wildly exultant. At the height of her enthusiasm she took him to the Stratford-on-Avon Shakespeare festival. Mr Kearton was another whose brilliance as chauffeur and mechanic was unrivalled. Such infatuations came not singly, for others were always filling the roles of The Finest Young Writer, The Most Hopeful Composer, The Most Intelligent Actor. In fact, it was still necessary for Fate to supply Farjeons with The Best.

But it was also a time of trouble and death. Another cat had to be killed and many friends applied for help in a variety of dramas. Earle had another stroke.

Roland Watson became one of the great comforts now. He would sit with Eleanor's old man, allowing her to attend a PEN Club committee or theatre. He was calm, he could listen, or tell of the doings of Helen Thomas and her daughters, with whom Eleanor had never lost touch, helping Helen financially when things were difficult. The list of those to whom she gave considerable sums of money is long, and some part of every cheque she received was given away. The extent of her generosity will never be known, for a condition of charitable gifts was that they remained anonymous.

In November 1949 Earle came home from a little walk carrying a fuchsia in a pot. He stumbled on the cobbles outside the cottage and fell heavily. His frail body was carried in by the men from the garage, with blood streaming from a deep cut in his forehead. As Eleanor ran forward to meet him, he exclaimed, "Oh Nell! I've had another nasty fall. The worst moment was when I knew it was coming, and that *magnificent* line from *Hyperion* flashed through my mind: 'Earthquakes jar their battlements and towers!'"

Earle died peacefully in his own bed, and for three days afterwards Golden Coney sat on the shelf overlooking the dead man, refusing to eat. When he was gone she ate a large meal, slept three days and returned to her usual habits.

Although Earle never wrote anything long or lasting, his phrases ring in the memory with the resonance of a church bell. His devotion to the English language was absorbed by Eleanor to feed her own knowledge. She wrote down some of his sayings: 'Every impression which falls on the sense or the mind must be exchanged into a word before it can live.' His tongue could be sharp enough speaking of a dull woman: "It is hard to imagine any company in which she would prove an asset." Or the pronouncement made on emerging from a bad film: "We would have been better employed, Nell, in downright iniquity."

For Eleanor it was something of a relief, though she missed his strong intelligence and learning for the rest of her life; but he had become most difficult and demanding at the last. Her determination to make the best of every experience is in this letter to George Benson.

20 *Perrins Walk, N.W.* 3.
*Nov.* 18*th*, 1949

Oh darling George,

'a made such a good end.[1] I shall always have it as one of my most wonderful and most perfect experiences, I am not unhappy – I am really happy, and scarcely ever tired. I shall see you soon and tell

1. A misquote from *Henry V* on Falstaff's death.

you everything. Joan may have told you something, but George there are even touches in it of the sweet funniness in him that was so lovable. I can't imagine a more unshadowed death. He held you dear, you know. So does

Your Nellie

The Irish writer, Arland Ussher, wrote to her from Dublin:

Though I have been able to see so little of him in recent years, he was always much in my thoughts and I can truly say that I have had many imaginary conversations with him, and composed many letters to him which, alas, I never got down to writing. It is a wonderful memory to have had his friendship, in my boyhood and youth, and he influenced me perhaps more than I knew – greatly though I felt the fascination of his mind and his conversation. Indeed I owe more to conversations than to all the books I have read – and yet I cannot but feel it is a misfortune that he never had time to leave this thought to us in writing; for he had insights such as I have never met with in any other man, though joined to a culture which is becoming more and more rare in the world.

# 32

# Denys Blakelock

THE URGE TO WRITE remained constant when the three power-ful characters in Eleanor's life, Harry, Bertie and Earle, were gone. She finished a children's play, *The Silver Curlew*, which was pro-duced in Liverpool's Playhouse for Christmas 1948. The story was based on the Norfolk version of *Rumpelstiltskin*, with music by Clif-ton Parker. There were fey additions: a man-in-the-moon bewitched into a loony fisherman, and a lady-in-the-moon bewitched into a silver curlew. The heroine turned out a greedy, lazy, dreamy cabbage-rose of a girl, who gobbled dumplings, leaving none for her hungry brothers. The dumpling song was very much better than the good food song for the 'Poor of London' in the Soyer operetta.

King Nollekens of Norfolk, who marries the lazy girl, on the understanding that she will spin a roomful of flax once a year, turned out to be a man with a double nature, wilful, affectionate and weak. There is much foolery and fun in this play, which alternates between the coy and charming. It was back to a Martin Pippin style of badinage, whimsicalities which would never have passed through the net of Bertie's criticism. The moral is cleverly overlaid by happy fantasies. The dialogue whisks along and there are good homely songs, such as when Nanny loses her bag just as everyone is about to set out late for the royal christening.

> *Everyone knows what bags are.*
> *Nanny has lost her bag,*
> *All of us know what the snags are*
> *When Nanny loses her bag.*

263

*Bags are prone to displacement,*
*Bags refuse to be static,*
*You leave 'em down in the basement*
*And find 'em up in the attic.*

At the christening four gifts are presented to the baby: a kind heart, happiness, magic and beauty. Eleanor herself had been given the first three, which is more than can be expected for most of us.

Once again she sat in the stalls watching rehearsals, once again the cast gazed in surprise at the blowsy pebble-spectacled old lady, wondering who she was, if not one of the theatre cleaners, and once again the moment she spoke the first words of eager friendship they were enchanted.

The show went so well in Liverpool that it was given next year at the Arts Theatre in London, again directed by John Fernald. Parker's orchestral score had been rearranged for two pianos, and this perfectly balanced the small stage production. The actor now engaged for the role of King Nollekens, since Cyril Luckham of the Liverpool Repertory Company was unavailable, was Denys Blakelock, one who knew all about a double nature.

This player, son of a clergyman in Muswell Hill, North London, had been brought up with great severity by his mother, and would be beaten and locked in a cupboard when rules were broken. He developed into an exceedingly nervous, appealing man, whose claustrophobia may have started with his terrifying experiences in the cupboard: anyway, from the age of twenty he never ventured into an underground tube train. Gradually the disease so constricted his career that he was at last driven to give up acting altogether. In his book *Eleanor, Portrait of a Farjeon* he wrote that a strict religious upbringing had left him 'with a highly-trained, not to say over-developed, conscience about sex'. He was a homosexual, he turned Catholic. 'It was hardly to be wondered at that by the time Eleanor Farjeon and I met up with one another I, approaching forty-nine, was an established victim of dark moods of depression and anxiety, and subject to irrational fits of anger and resentments.'

Eleanor appreciated his nature, one side of which was so gay, intelligent and sweet, the other so racked with egotism, spite and guilt. She might have written the part of King Nollekens for Blakelock, who described the character he had to play with amused

264

Denys Blakelock

sympathy. 'Nollekens was a cry-baby King of indeterminate age, who went about with his Nanny, and had a double nature of which he was inordinately proud. When he was horrid he would stamp his foot and cry and chop off people's heads, which delighted the children in the audience.'[1]

Of course Eleanor willingly took on the role of Nanny, and was to enjoy the wit, see to the comfort and struggle with the temper tantrums of her middle-aged monarch for the next fourteen years.

It was not all one-sided though. When they became friends Eleanor was in great need of companionship, for Earle had died ten days before the London rehearsals of *The Silver Curlew* commenced. And Earle was the one who had helped to keep her level-headed when emotion threatened her reasonable spirit, while his quiet basic wisdom seemed unassailable. Although revelling in drama, Eleanor could grow fearful of her own reactions, which became obvious even on the phone, when the voice in which a conversation was commenced would give her away immediately: for whatever state predominated was expressed with heart-felt fervour.

Having to support Blakelock through the early days of rehearsal was in itself a discipline which took her mind off personal sorrow: he needed much clever handling until panic subsided and confidence prevailed. The manner in which Eleanor lightened the humdrum and put fears to rest was gratefully received by the jittery actor.

> Never did I appreciate this side of her character as much as I did then, during the rehearsals of *The Silver Curlew*. I had made a very shaky start and, in fact, did my utmost to withdraw from the engagement, a thing I was guilty of doing all too frequently in my professional life in the theatre. Eleanor did her successful best to make ways as smooth for me as possible, with her gay spirit and her genius for organising and dealing with the problems of creature comforts and anticipating one's every need.
>
> "This is the Perrins Walk Catering Department," she would cry down the telephone without preamble. That was an offer to bring thermoses of coffee and sandwiches to rehearsal. She knew that I leaned on these things at that time, but was too disoriented to prepare them before the day's work. Or, "This is

1. *Eleanor, Portrait of a Farjeon.*

the Perrins Walk Electrical Engineering Department," when the heating in my dressing-room had broken down. An electric fire, bought in Hampstead, was on its way for the evening performance.[1]

An early visit to his flat fell on a Friday, so Eleanor was reminded that, as a Catholic, this must be a meatless day, for she was supplying the meal. Thursday morning brought a postcard:

> *Tomorrow*
> *I'll be there*
> *With Friday fare;*
> *Things in tins*
> *That once had fins,*
> *Cheese and eggs –*
> *But nothing with legs;*
> *And none of the things*
> *That once had wings.*

It was through Eleanor that Blakelock began to learn the lesson of coming to terms with his temperament, and began to understand the disastrous effect of his double nature with 'the ruin brought about by vengeful ragings and resentments, the scorings off, the hittings back, the writing of angry letters'.[2] His book is more concerned with himself than with its subject, but it gives a clue, many clues, as to how Eleanor was able to help so many neurotics, and why she was so adored.

For many years Denys Blakelock had been accepted in the theatre as a fine actor, not a top actor, for he lacked the powerful personality that must go with a heroic performance. But within his own range there were few who could better the delicate, humorous and poignant originality of his stage and radio performances.

The friendship between actor and author developed at top speed. In June 1951 they went on what Blakelock called their 'honeymoon' holiday to Cornwall. Although of course no sex was involved, there was a great deal of love and laughter in getting to know one another. Blakelock wrote: 'There is nothing like a holiday to reveal a friend's foibles and funny little ways. Eleanor discovered several of mine, I am sure; and I uncovered many of hers.

1, 2. *Eleanor, Portrait of a Farjeon.*

'There was the affair of the Single Egg, for instance. At Marazion we ordered fried eggs and bacon. They brought me bacon and two eggs. Eleanor was given bacon and one egg.

"Why two eggs for Mr Blakelock and only one for me?" she asked. "A gentleman's portion, Madam," the waitress replied. But Eleanor would not accept this inequality of the sexes, and before many moments had passed she was tackling her second egg with enthusiasm.'[1]

Then there was the matter of clothes. By the age of seventy, so long as she was comfortable, Eleanor hardly cared how she looked. But her companion was extremely conventional and self-conscious about appearances. He could not bear the way Eleanor came down to dinner in a rather smart hotel at Looe with old white plimsolls on her ungainly feet and a shabby dress, while all the women round had changed into gowns for dinner. Her hair was another bone of contention between them, but only once did he get her to the hairdresser, much later, when the Queen Mother attended a performance of *The Silver Curlew* at the Royal Academy of Dramatic Art. Then he thought she looked charming, even though she sat down to supper with the Queen Mother *without gloves*. But of course the ladies got on splendidly.

"You're vain, I'm conceited," Eleanor remarked to her new love, proving a superior confidence in true Farjeon style. She mocked his personal vanity gently, especially that quiff of silky brown hair in front.

> *When your hair is uppity*
> *You are just my cup o' tea!*
> *But you are not my drop o' tea*
> *When your hair is floppity!*

The actor lived in central London, but now began to spend every weekend in Hampstead, sleeping in Earle's bed in the sitting-room. He did not like the cottage, it was too dim and cluttered for his nerves and taste, yet they had so much fun together life in Perrins Walk was irresistible. Besides, Eleanor's spiritual welfare had become a concern.

1. *Eleanor, Portrait of a Farjeon.*

After the Cornish holiday seventy-year-old Eleanor was received into the Catholic Church, as she said, "A very old baby." The letter written to her brother, Joe, explains the event just as though she was excitedly telling it by word of mouth.

20 *Perrins Walk, N.W.3.*
*August 20th*, 1951

Darling Joe,

I have some lovely news – I know you will think it is, for me – and I was going to write to you tomorrow, I wanted you to be the first of the family to be told; but Joaney rang me up this morning, and wanted me to come for a day and night to 137, and I told her why I couldn't come before Friday. On Wednesday I am being baptised at 5.30 at the Catholic Church in Spanish Place. Only Denys will be there with me. When I come in September we can talk our hearts out, but I can't talk much now; I've got tired with a great pressure of comings and goings here, and two silly falls which jolted, but haven't injured me, and the next two days I want to be quite quiet, so that my body can feel as serene as my spirit does. When I told Joaney she said in her fresh lovely voice "I'm not surprised – I feel it is so right for you now." And she seemed as joyful for me as I hope you will be. Denys is coming tonight after his rehearsal, will be with me on Wednesday, and here again on Saturday night, to take me to my first Communion on Sunday.

I have been reading tremendously all this year, not only the Bible in a living way I've never tried to read it before, all sorts of things, simple and abstruse – I get most illumination I think from St. Augustine and a wonderful 13th Century mystic who wrote *The Cloud of Unknowing*; writings in which I find things which match my own spiritual thoughts and feelings for many years. I have prayed more and more, night and morning, and indeed at constant moments through the day, for prayer and the thought of God and love can't be pigeon-holed in one's being for use at stated times, but must be the air one breathes spiritually as unconsciously as one breathes the air one's body lives by. You and Fan and Joaney are always part of the prayer, and one of the things I have prayed deeply for you always is that your days should have happiness in them while you are here to live them. I've prayed for other things for Denys which seem to have been answered when a certain darkness needed lifting from him. And in much confusion of thought I've gone into the little Catholic Church near by and prayed with all my heart to God for myself, and always afterwards found myself in a state of extraordinary peace. Since January I've been going to Farm Street to talk with a fine priest – Father Mangan – and have "Instruction" from him. I left long intervals between the first three times and the last four, reading and clearing out my own confusions before I felt ready to go again. He never exercised, or seemed to exercise, any spiritual power in our talks, only explained things in the Catechism, answered my questions ('I can't promise you that I know all the answers' he wrote before we met) and gave me *The Cloud of Unknowing* to read when he found that was the sort of thing that 'clicked' (his word) with what I already felt. He is a Jesuit, the order which contains the greatest minds, not necessarily the greatest mystics, in the Church. I was supposed to have at least Twenty Hours Instruction before Baptism, if I wished for Baptism eventually. (I have intensely since the beginning, but there had to be much else as well), [before it] could be contemplated, and I was astounded when last Thursday, the seventh visit, he laid down the Catechism and said, "Well, Eleanor, that's as far as *I* can take you." "Then where am I now?" I asked rather blankly. He smiled and said, "You're ready." "But what about the Twenty Hours that must be filled in the form?" (a form must go to Cardinal Griffin or somebody to get his imprimatur for my baptism on my Instructor's guarantee). "Oh you've had more than that; all you've read for yourself, all you've learnt from Denys, and the services you've attended, and your prayers on the rosary, can be counted. I shall put down Twenty-five hours," he said, calmly, drawing the form towards him. "Well," said I, "if that's a lie it's *your* responsibility." I asked how soon it could be, because of Denys's being there before his tour; and all day he is rehearsing. "It should be arranged next week," said Father Mangan. "Tell him to ring me up and give me a time." I came out in a daze, and when I spoke to Denys that night he was as dazed as I was – and we both still are. He arranged the time that night with Father Mangan, and asked me what name I would take (one has a new name on becoming Catholic – his is Peter, and he asked if I would like Mary, one of whose special days next Wednesday is). I have chosen Mary. On Friday morning I went to the lovely little church in Holly Place, with my rosary, where two weeks ago I'd gone to pray and be quiet; I wanted to say Thank-you to God. In the porch I stopped to tie a scarf on my head as I had no hat. Just as I finished I put my hand on the door and felt the handle turned very softly from the other side. The opener was a very little boy, not more than four I think, with a wonderful grave and innocent face and solemn eyes. We looked at each other for a moment and he held the door for me to go in as he went out. I stooped and said, "Thank you. What's your name?" He whispered, "Peter. What's yours?" I said "Eleanor" and he closed the door. Then I suddenly wished I'd said Mary, and opened the door to tell him – and uphill and down there wasn't a sign of him. Isn't that a nice story – whatever you make of it? He reminded me of the tiny Bambino in Fiesole, where I was lost at midnight on the night of my arrival trying vainly to find Rosalind's villa in the dark; and this three or four-year-old-baby came through a little door and grabbed my finger in his fist and led me through some bushes to a step – lisped "Villino Ada, Signorina," and disappeared. Any child with innocent eyes can seem to be the Child. That's twice for me.

I didn't mean to write so much, but it came. There could be infinitely more. What I have learned, and shall come to learn more and more, is that nobody thinks I wouldn't go to heaven if I weren't a Catholic (that's all a mistake) – but that's not why I'm going to be baptised. No, nor is it for love of Denys, though he is the cause. One thing I asked myself some time ago was : "If Denys died today, would I go on with this?" And I knew I would. And all this year he said, "You mustn't ever feel, if you don't become a Catholic, that it can make any difference to my love for you." But it does, of course, make a great difference to his sense of joy for me, and so for himself. A very few people know. I'll tell Cliff and Yoma and the family on Thursday. I didn't want this time to be disturbed by a sense of criticism or noncomprehension from anyone who, loving me, would still be unsympathetic. Joaney's sunlit delight made me feel quite radiant this morning. I don't expect the same response from Joscelyn!

God bless you, darling.

    For ever your

      Nellie

The romance of Christianity, with its emphasis on Mother and Child, was something she had responded to always. The Christmas festivity, birth, pity and generosity, brought out strong feelings to be expressed in poems flecked with a dry realism which kept them from becoming too sentimental. But until now the birth of Christ had been no more than a moving story which might have been incorporated into TAR. A letter to Gervase three days later has a more persuasive and anxious tone than the one to Joe. Anyway, Eleanor was well aware that Bertie's children were a tougher proposition where religion was concerned.

*August 23rd* 1951

Dearest Gervase,

Last night I would have told you what Violetta[1] has already told you, and what I want all my beloved family to know, but it wasn't a clear moment to speak in. Scarcely two hours before, I had come from my Baptism and reception into the Roman Catholic Church. This may be a surprise, and even a shock, to some of you who are so close and dear to me. Strangely enough, although many of the loveliest things in life have been part of our family experience, love of people, and of beauty in many of its forms – the natural beauty of the world, the creative beauty of art and words and music – the experience of religion in a positive shape has not been, or seemed to be, among them. It is mine now, and the hope I have is that this new wonder won't seem to divide me from you all if it happens to be one you can't share or even talk about. (But I hope you can, if you want to.) To me, it makes all I love more mine, and I don't believe it will make me less yours in your hearts and thoughts. I don't think you'll find me any different from the Nellie you've always known and been able to come to now and then in difficulties. This last year has been a strange one for me, and what it has ended in is less, I believe, a Conversion, than a progression to a form of faith towards which my own sense of spiritual life has been moving for the last thirty or forty years. One has to be 'converted' from one faith to another – and I've never had another to be converted from. I have had an always increasing sense of the

---

1. Violetta Farjeon, Gervase's wife.

immortal spirit from a source I could only think of as God, and in our first talk I told Father Mangan, the priest who baptized me yesterday, that I didn't think I was going to have any difficulty about the Holy Ghost. And I haven't. I wrote to Joe on Monday, and yesterday morning began with a beautiful letter from him. The day was a lovely one for me. Denys joined me at the Church and came back with me afterwards. He will be here on Saturday and Sunday nights, to take me to my First Communion. That's why I can't come to supper that day, darling. But I wanted specially to write at least a little of this, to tell you how *very* dear you are to me, and how much I love you for never letting time go by without seeing, or wanting to see me. When I can't come it is only for the reasons that don't count. What does count is that, especially since one day in 1938 during a rehearsal at the Kingsway of *The Elephant* and still more since that terrible night of Daddy's death, you have been a true part of life for me, little though we may say, and seldom though we may see each other.

This all sounds more solemn than I feel. I never can be solemn for long at a time, but there are moments when I want to show my heart to those who have it, and this is one of the moments and you are one of those. And I am

Always your Nellie

The ceremony of baptism had been marked by humorous interpolation from Father Mangan himself who, to Blakelock's amazement, suddenly broke into unexpected English taken from Eleanor's ballad about a destitute old woman who rescued starving animals and hestitates to venture through the heavenly gates – "There's room for another, Mrs Malone," he quoted.

From this remarkable event, retailed fully by Eleanor at the top of her voice next June on the Centre Court at Wimbledon during a wait for the next game, there developed a group of Catholic friends consisting of priests, writers and actors, all of whom now held a particular place in Eleanor's wide range of loved ones. She gave up nobody, and outwardly religion made little difference; but the fact that she had taken on so exorbitant a category of ideas did make a difference : she no longer seemed the same free agent, able to develop her own opinions, and a vast area of spiritual adventure was barred, her pattern of thought fixed by pious convention.

# Catholics

SOON AFTER Blakelock became attached to Eleanor he introduced her to a friend and fellow actor who was also an anxious Catholic, John McBennet. Like Blakelock, he had homosexual tendencies and was a lonely man. It was to him that Eleanor was able to talk over the difficulties of Blakelock's most difficult character. Another important bond, which the loved one could not share, was their mutual appreciation of music. McBennet would come to the cottage for an evening concert on the radio or gramophone and, after an elegant supper eaten in the kitchen, they would settle upstairs to listen to some opera or symphony. The telephone receiver removed, they were safe from interruption as if they had been sitting in a concert hall or theatre.

One of Eleanor's invitations to McBennet for a production of *Uncle Vanya* at the Arts Theatre was sent in the following rollicking terms:

> *An can ye spree*
> *Alang o me*
> *Ma Lee-Land Laddie, can yer?*
> *Come Wednesday fort*
> *night wall ye sport*
> *Wi' Nell at "Uncle Vanya?"*
>
> *At six we'll greet*
> *In Cranbourne Street*
> *Tae take a modest peck of*
> *Whatever fare*

*We fancy there*
*Before we feed on Tchekov.*

*And we will sup*
*A kindly cup*
*An' pray the Powers Eternal*
*That this produc*
*tion may brung luck*
*And gowd tae Jockie Fernal!*

*An' when the play*
*Has said its say*
*We'll join the throng that trickles on*
*The stair, tae blast*
*Or kiss the cast –*
*An' we'll kiss Nora Nicholson.*

*Then hame we'll reel,*
*Twa comrades leal*
*An' loving, blithe and bonnie –*
*Gin ye will spree*
*Along o' me*
*As stated. Wull ye, Johnnie?*

Nelly Burns

A second Catholic introduced by Blakelock was a young man at Oxford, James Roose-Evans. Having taken a degree in English, he came to London with a theatrical career in mind and found that Eleanor was able to expand his knowledge of literature and the theatre. Her descriptions of great artists she had seen, Nijinsky most especially, fired him with an interest in dance as a medium of expression to be combined with traditional acting. They were soon great friends. "She bewitched me from the start," he said.

For a time she and Blakelock looked on Roose-Evans as their son, and he was given the Perrins Court cottage to live in with his friend, David March. In return for the usual peppercorn rent, the young men made themselves free to be called on for errands or shopping and general help when other assistance failed. Roose-Evans was another who accompanied Eleanor to the theatre and, while she sat absorbed, would be himself distracted by the continual rattle of rosary beads in her lap or the click-click of raised opera glasses as they met the surface of her spectacles.

Friendship with the Meynell family was re-established. A long standing invitation to Greatham was accepted, for now Eleanor felt that the old intimacy could be renewed with the added satisfaction of a mutual faith. Alice and Wilfrid were long dead, but their children, grandchildren and great-grandchildren had multiplied in biblical fashion. Numbers still lived on the estate, in and around the big house. The invitation was for a weekend when kinsfolk were accustomed to gather, this time to be blessed by the presence of Monsignor Mathew. I drove her down. In the June evening the wide valley of the Arun looked beautiful as ever, long shadows stretching across the water meadows, where patches of kingcups glistened like the 'golden isles' of the poem about the floods of Amberly Wildbrooks. The brick house, the gravel courtyard and outbuildings looked just the same, Eleanor remarked. In the living-room stood the big table at which Alice and her seven children were once wont to sit, each writing a poem. Now through glass doors at the far end other generations could be seen spread like a herd on the lawn.

When we entered the long room a startling male figure rose from a wide Windsor chair. On either side sensibly shod, grey-haired Meynell ladies attended him and introduced 'Monsignor Mathew'.

The Monsignor wore a voluminous black cassock with purple buttons all down the front, around his expansive waist was a purple cummerbund, on his high head a black skull-cap with purple piping, while a purple flap the shape of a paint scraper appeared below his collar. He held out a hand and on one strong finger gleamed a huge mauve amethyst.

Eleanor at once dropped on her knee and kissed the ring.

I shook hands stiffly enough and was then introduced to a second man, dressed in clerical black, "Father Gervase Mathew – Monsignor's brother."

The brother's eyes shone with amusement, whether at Eleanor's enthusiasm or my queasiness it was impossible to tell.

On the whole the weekend was a success, although Eleanor was quieter than usual under the bishop's spell. But she remembered and noted everything to do with the Meynells: names, relationships and places. Next day, in the sunny afternoon, we watched the children bathe in the swimming pool, "Some screaming to come out, others screaming to go in," as she said. She was a little jealous of my walks with Gervase Mathew, for we indulged in more lively conversation than seemed possible with his distinguished brother.

In a speech of acceptance for the Regina Medal[1], Eleanor described how she wandered over the croquet lawn as evening fell. "The sound, of laughing children, screaming children, jeering children, thinned away to their suppers. The hammock was empty – oh no! the little girl's doll lolled in it, forgotten till somebody remembered it. But I knew that it had always lolled there, and would loll forever; and forever under the apple tree a spotted toy horse would stand, when the children now sitting at their suppers came out in their latter years to sit on a seat in the evening sun.

"I knew – I know – that childhood is one of the states of eternity, and 'in that state we came we shall return.'"

The intimacy with Blakelock remained of first importance, and their mutual religion gave Eleanor more understanding and influence over him. Certain of his friends were upset that he was kept so snug under her maternal wing, for during weekends in no circumstances could anybody intrude. The actor's rest time, his chair, his cushion, his meals and his peace were inviolable. Talk was incessant: 'We shall never be done with talking, you and I' was the opening of a poem Blakelock wrote to Eleanor, and during those early years a nightly telephone call was the rule when they were not together.

In 1954 Eleanor recalled in a letter a scene from their first familiarity:

'When you asked me yesterday if I remembered your weeping in that chair (as if I could forget) it was like a picture out of the past – I sat on the chair-arm, holding you, with your dear face bowed into your hands and the tears trickling through the fingers, while you whispered, "I feel so dried up." You have come a long way since then, darling, into a prospect of happiness out of one of sorrow. You did have bursts of happiness that relieved the sorrow, and you will have, no doubt, moods of sorrow to shadow the happiness – we are all so full of weather, it can hardly be otherwise – but oh the difference in your outlook, under any sky!' And farther on: 'When friends have entered that part of each other completely, we cannot

1. An American Catholic award for children's literature.

277

come out from it alone as we were before, for he whom we entered is now some part of oneself. And that is why, I believe, we must enter Christ through His Passion; it is only after we have been with Him in Gethsemane that we can have Him in Heaven. I can't regret whatever humble reflection of Gethsemane here has been mine through suffering, and still less (because you are more to me than myself) can I regret yours for you. Not after seeing you yesterday smiling in the chair where I saw you weep.'

Blakelock needed the support of religion to keep him sane, he was a very devout mystic Catholic, and religion remained a great bond between the two of them. It certainly helped Eleanor to help him.

As Blakelock's claustrophobia worsened, travel by train became impossible, for the train would not stop at the moment he was overwhelmed by terror. Thus touring with a theatrical company seemed out of the question, until Eleanor arranged that Kearton should chauffeur him in her car from provincial town to town. However, the expense of this soon became insupportable, so the actor bought his own three-wheel Minicar. It used little fuel and never went fast, both of which seemed advantages, but it would break down, and journeys ended in far distant, last minute appeals to Hampstead for help. From Newcastle Blakelock wrote that his poor Minnie was 'little more capable of doing these long drives than her owner'. His nerve failed and next day he telephoned. "Leave it to me!" Eleanor cried. An hour later a telegram was delivered: 'ARRIVING FRIDAY COMING BY NIGHT WITH HANDSOME GIANT DRIVER'.

Eleanor and her escort left Hampstead at two in the morning. They drove all through the night, picnicking on the way, got ahead of the rush-hour in Doncaster and were in Newcastle by 11 a.m. In his *Portrait* Blakelock wrote: 'Eleanor enjoyed every minute of this nocturnal adventure. She stayed for the rest of the week with me, and the handsome giant took the Minicar back to London. As he drove into his garage in Hampstead the steering wheel came away in his hands. So Eleanor Farjeon and her handsome giant had probably saved not only my reason but my life.'

For the next two days, after her dramatic arrival, Eleanor became to the cast of *White Sheep* what she had been to that of *The Two Bouquets*. 'She stood smilingly at the front door of the Newcastle "digs" to see us off in Fixer (her Hillman); the stalwart John Paul in the driver's seat, Derek Blomfield by his side as the navigator, and myself sitting complacently in the back.

'How different from the previous Sunday, thanks to Eleanor's organisation and unselfishness. I was soon *en route* for Manchester in comfort with the anxieties smoothed away, while she was travelling by train back to London and home.'

Three years later John Gielgud offered Blakelock the part of Firs in his production of *The Cherry Orchard*. Rehearsals began in a mood of optimism, then confidence failed and one morning at four o'clock, after a sleepless night, the actor wrote a letter of resignation, walked down to the Haymarket Theatre and gave it to the fireman at the stage door. He never worked in the theatre again, but settled down to teaching at the Royal Academy of Dramatic Art and acting in radio plays. He discovered that he had to learn to teach, and here Eleanor took a special interest, providing him with material for dramatic studies and advising from her wide knowledge and long memory.

The course of their friendship seemed set for life till, all of a sudden, Blakelock fell in love. He wrote: 'It is enough to say that in August 1955 the pains and perplexities of an infatuation took hold of me: that sickness that turns a middle-aged man into a fool, without will-power, reason or dignity. There is no antidote, no antibiotic. The fever has to rage until it is spent.'

It raged for seven years and seriously disrupted the friendship, for Blakelock imagined he could confide everything to the woman who loved him so dearly. Yet for all her generous sympathy, Eleanor was jealous and suffered badly. Her instinct for self-preservation kept the balance and, when the infatuation had worn itself out, they returned outwardly to their old relationship.

In a way those, like Eleanor, who give sympathy rather than take it, those who exhaust themselves identifying with another, are more acclimatised to bear emotional pain when it strikes: by proxy they have grown a little accustomed to bear sorrow in a way the egoist finds impossible. Yet the old relationship with Blakelock was never quite the same: each had grown more critical of the other.

## 34

# The Last Book

IN OLD AGE the author had acquired a good number of ailments and illnesses which were bravely borne. There were cataracts, for which she was sent to Moorfields Hospital and operated on by Mr Stallard, for whom she conceived a passion, assuaged by writing a grotesque paean on his name allying him to the stag family. His letter of thanks on receiving one of the privately printed copies was a comical mixture of courtesy and embarrassment. There was bronchitis on and off, and always the threat of it. The attacks were exhausting, especially as they made talking difficult, although from the bed a gasping voice would still manage lengthy phone conversations. There were the bunions which had been forcing her toes out of alignment for years, till walking became a most awkward and painful process: ultimately one toe had to be amputated. There was a gall bladder operation of which she wrote to Tony Kraber, 'On April 1st I came back from hospital leaving something like the Stone of Scone behind me. I was told it would take me six months to get over it. Six months and two weeks have passed, and as I am a nice obedient girl I've got over it.'

During the 1950s new editions of old works for the young were republished by Michael Joseph and Oxford University Press. *Silver Sand and Snow* and *The Little Bookroom* are still her finest collections of poetry and prose, lively, imaginative and varied, works which are more complex than they appear and support her maxim that children grasp more than they can understand.

There was also a revival of *The Two Bouquets* at the St Martin's Theatre. This time Eleanor took little part in the production, but after the first night wrote an emotional letter to George Benson, who had played the original Edward in the operetta.

20 *Perrins Walk*, *N.W.* 3.
*May* 14*th* 1953

Oh my darling George-Edward! how I was thinking of you all night – and of Bertie – even before I opened your telegram somewhere around midnight. The feeling in the St Martin's was the Ambassadors 1930 all over again – bewildering and dazzling (and very chokey for me) – and the Press has been as Ernest Irving wrote to me afterwards, 'a paean'. There's plenty of delightful acting and singing (the real star of this show is the singing of the marvellous chorus); and Hugh Paddick is a born comedian, and from now on will be on his way up. The remarkable thing is (for your private archives) that the better he is, the more I know that for me and everybody who saw him there can never never never be another Edward Gill than young Mr. Benson. I remember Lady Mount Temple saying to me: "Tell him I was miserable whenever he wasn't on the stage." Thank you, darling, for all you did for *The Two Bouquets* in 1936 to make it a hit in 1953.

Your loving
Nellie

Joe, the last brother, had always been the one to whom Eleanor could abandon herself to the limits of sentiment, he was so tender and fond, so tolerant that he could hardly bring himself to criticise, although now and then he might laugh gently at his sister's whims and fancies. His wife had died of cancer in 1950. Now, five years later, he was found to be suffering from the same disease. He was taken to a nursing home in Hove, near his home. Eleanor went down to spend days and nights at his bedside, from whence the following letter to Roland Watson was written in April 1955.

| Helen [Thomas] might see this letter. | 3 *Eaton Gardens*, |
|---|---|
| She knew Joe was ill. | *Hove, Sussex* |

My dearest Watty,
On April 11th Joe, who had been X-rayed for strange pains, was operated on in Hove for a minor trouble, and cancer of the

liver was discovered. He was not told. Since then I began going up
and down from London to see him; but as he became much weaker
I came to Sussex so that I could be with him constantly, and take
charge of his affairs for him. His darling Joaney is stuck in
Cambridge on a big job which has to be done – till the rail strike
she made strenuous efforts to come and go from Cambridge, and
now of course she can't. The production will release her next
Tuesday and then she must come by car at whatever cost; but I am
not sure he will live as long as that. His weakness is so great that he
can't turn his head on the pillow, and lies there still and
unmurmuring and accepting all as it comes. During his illness an
overwhelming sense of God has come on him completely – not in
any named Faith but God himself – and six weeks ago today he
asked me to baptise him. It was one of the strangest moments of
my life. Since then we pray together every day, but now he is
almost too weak to speak, so I say *Our Father* for him and he thinks
it. He is in the most wonderful nursing home I've ever known –
everybody in it from the cleaners to the Matron is loving, tender,
and happy, and their sweet ways with him keep him happy too. I
am in a nice room with nice people just across the road, and can be
with him as much as I like, and when I come everybody looks after
me too. Yesterday the doctor said he thought Joe couldn't live *more*
than two weeks, and I feel it won't be so much. The love between
us has never been so strong and we give each other infinite things.
Also, I am very near my Church, and go to early Mass every
morning before breakfast . . .

I am writing this by his bed. While I was in London I tried twice
to ring you up but wasn't lucky. Don't be troubled for me. I have
peace and strength in me every day.

Your loving
Eleanor

In the early fifties her religious feeling was strong: she had not yet
settled down to a calm acceptance of God and of course revelled in
dramatising her relationship with Him. Here is a paragraph from
another letter, half incoherent with excitement, to Watson, sent
from London in August 1954.

'Amazing things seem to be happening under this roof; it has
always been a place for friends, in a way, but more and more come in
love and need as though it was the source of something – a way of

282

living they are groping to find for themselves; I don't mean only religion, though the only answer to the disillusionments and losses and dissatisfactions that so many of them come to after the unfulfilled shocks of human experience, the darkest and most bitter with endurance, *and* to be joyful, must be possible, or there would be no joy in the world; to love completely; whether one is loved or not, giving, not having, love – women and girls and young men come oftener and oftener with their burdens of anguish and of bliss; I feel this place is being used by God sometimes, and hardly know how to contain myself for humble gratitude, and all that is given and taken.'

The cottage, or rather its owner, had always been a refuge for those in trouble. As the emotional egotism of youth and middle age diminished, Eleanor had grown more and more able to help others with sympathy and wisdom. Grace Hogarth, children's editor for Oxford University Press, explained "Eleanor could never resist an alley cat in need, no matter how bedraggled. Not only the four-legged, but the two-legged ones. Indeed all cats and humans were individuals to her, and we all felt that her love was special to each one of us."[1]

Certainly the necessity to support others in order to support her own ego became more pronounced, and she would sometimes show a smug conceit, expecting deference and praise due, as it were, to a notable old lady. At other times she was modest enough, as when she said to me with quiet sadness, "All my life I have tried to use what little talent I have to the full." In this moment of confidence, she saw her talent as 'little' and only appreciated the dogged hard work which had achieved results.

In 1953 a BBC radio programme about Edward Thomas was recorded. In it there was a suggestion that Eleanor had been his mistress, and that, with his wife, there had been a ménage à trois. Eleanor was upset, and wrote the producer a letter of protest at this unfounded suggestion. After a long while an answer was received with a very side-stepping evasion and no apology. Then she was angry. The following is Walter de la Mare's gently consoling response to a cry for sympathy after a repeat broadcast was given.

It's quite incomprehensible to me how it came about that Patric Dickinson should have made any statement which could be

1. BBC Radio Broadcast, 10.2.81.

283

misconstrued in that way. And hardly less so, that anyone in authority who has seen the script, (and script there presumably was) didn't question it. Its utter want of truth is bad enough, and perhaps, still more, that it should be possible to make such statements, true or otherwise, without complete verification. In the repetition was any reference made to the original broadcast, I wonder. Surely this could have been done with due caution against any exaggeration of further misrepresentation coming of it. And didn't Helen herself know anything about the broadcast until it was given? . . .

Oh how much I wish you could have been spared such a worry, and how much I hope that all goes well otherwise. Only the other day I was reading one or two reviews of mine of Edward's poems; of all that time ago, in the T.L.S. Indeed I reviewed many of his books. A selection of these ancient things are being published in a volume soon.

Since I have every now and again found peace and delight in the copy of your poems for children which you gave me when last we met I cannot possibly have expressed my delight in them. Beautiful things and solely your own. Have you ever given a B.B.C. reading of these?

All blessings always

W.J.[1]


The misrepresentation weighed heavily on Eleanor's mind and most likely impelled her to consider publishing Thomas's letters in a manner that would put the matter straight. In September she told de la Mare that she had begun to write about their friendship.
to spend days and nights at his bedside, from whence the following 1958. It contained the Thomas correspondence from 1913–17, interspersed with explanations and descriptions of Eleanor's own emotions at the time, especially her feeling for the man who had been so loved. It is a great loss that her replies do not exist. To admirers of Thomas's work she wrote that his letters 'help to reveal something more of the least self-revealing of men: a man whose central evil was "self-consciousness carried as far beyond selfishness as selfishness is beyond self-denial". He could write this of himself in 1913, only two

1. Letter from Walter de la Mare to E.F., 5.3.53.

284

years before the torturing self-consciousness was transformed into the poet's self-expression.' In dealing with Thomas she never pretended romance where none existed, and wrote frankly: 'He counted on me for friendship; and I loved him with all my heart. He was far too penetrating not to know this, but only by two words in one of his last letters from France, did he allow himself to show me that he knew.'

So in old age Eleanor pursued her first great love. The writing had a clear cool quality now, uncluttered by the hither and thither of the first nursery memoir.

# 35

# The End

CATHOLICISM satisfied the ideal longings of this enthusiastic convert, satisfied her innocence and her ripeness with the promise of bliss in a perfect hereafter. Father Benignus became the most important figure in Eleanor's religious exercises, and under his tutelage she went to retreats at St Joseph's Church on Highgate Hill. A set of notes on his talks in her handwriting remain, when he spoke of Heaven and Hell, beginning: "Now my dear children I am going to leave you with some happy thoughts to go to bed with. I am going to talk about Death. It is good to think sometimes about Eternal Truths, and we can only think about them with Christ. I know that when I die I have come to the end of something for ever – and to the beginning of something for ever."

Later in these notes Eleanor made her own comments and reflected on Purgatory and 'the purgation of Self which stands between us and God', concluding: 'Only the choosers of, and rejoicers in, mortal sin, are those who need to fear because they have pushed Him away. If this were not so, where is the hope He holds out to us millions of poor imperfect sinners? For how many can go perfect to Heaven?'

There is also a description of confessing to Father Benignus with too little to confess, and of being truly sorry for the things she could not think of. 'I said my Penance and then one more for him with tears of joy in my eyes. You see – I know it is not he, but Christ in him, that makes him what he is, to be loved beyond anyone I've ever known because he is the brightest shadow that reflects God's love.'

The problem of confession was often on her mind. She would

boast that, old and untempted, there was nothing to confess. Plainly she felt pretty sure of salvation. But she told me that one time, in desperation, she had owned up to living in sin with a man. "Poor Pod!" she said with warm laughter. "It seemed a shame to bring him in, and really, as I told my priest, it all happened before my baptism, and so didn't really count. But I had to say something. He gave me some Hail Marys and that was all. But I knew it was a cheat, for at that time I was unborn so far as the Catholic Church went."

So Harry's strict rule of Fair and Unfair impinged on religion: the priest had not played the game properly. But the inconsistencies and peccadillos of this new faith did not seriously worry Eleanor: she seemed a true Catholic in this, as in her wholehearted acceptance of the holy creed. Naturally the superbly produced theatrical ceremonies were entirely to her taste.

Blakelock was too taken up with his own moral dilemma to think much of his friend's. And this is how she liked it, having all her life listened to the details of other people's perplexities. If she did expose some vexation it was from the past and came as a counterweight to balance another's confidence. To God alone she probably unburdened the sorrow which hangs over those who have outlived their generation. Yet it would be no surprise to know that even with God there was a check or two, for Harry's discipline was a force to rival the Almighty's. In defence of her own psychological privacy, she once told my husband with some severity that psycho-analysis was like tearing the petals off a rose to find the worm at the centre.

Catholicism brought friends in the publishing world who otherwise might have remained on a business footing, although it was almost impossible for Eleanor to write a letter without some show of personal interest, or some smiling sentence to alleviate its formality.

The collection of stories in *The Little Bookroom*, brought out in 1955 and then in Penguin paperback by Kaye Webb, won her new friends and three medals, which formally recognised the importance of her work for children: The Carnegie Medal from the British Library Association, the Regina Medal from America and the international Hans Andersen Award. But the personal publicity involved was not to the author's taste and a photographer who pestered her for a picture was determinedly refused admission. At length he telephoned.

"Would you please tell me, Miss Farjeon, what you look like?"

"Like a cheerful suet pudding."

"Well, your hair, I suppose, is silver?"

"No dear, it's gunmetal."

In an interview on the occasion of being given the Carnegie Medal, she said, "I am at the end of a long career. I have enjoyed every phase of it from my Victorian childhood to this atomic old age. I would go back on none of it. I am impatient to enjoy what comes next."

*The Little Bookroom* was illustrated by Edward Ardizzone, the finest and most understanding of all the artists who ornamented her work. His drawings express more nearly than any others Eleanor's especial sense of the cosiness, dreaminess, and strangeness of childhood. In a letter to Grace Hogarth she wrote: 'My big thrill was the Ardizzone drawings for my autumn book of tales. John Bell[1] told me they were the best things he'd ever done, and he thought so too; and when they were dropped in on me, last week-end, I turned them over, one after the other, with a lump in my throat. All I feel about childhood is in them, and I shall have two joys to look forward to this year; the *Slipper*[2] is adorable, but the autumn book goes deeper, and may remain for me the happiest book of my life, so far as collaboration is concerned.'

Soon Ardizzone was a personal friend and received the following verses of appreciation:

*When all the fairy tales are told*
*And young and old go bedward,*
*Oh, what a debt both young and old*
*For ever owe you, Edward.*

*In darkness lit by dreams come true*
*The years revive their embers*
*And what the child's eye saw, through you*
*The ageing eye remembers.*

*The phoenixes of infant joy*
*And woe and all-desiring*
*Which time endeavours to destroy,*
*Arise from their first firing,*

1. John Bell, editor, Oxford University Press.
2. *The Glass Slipper*, a story written from the play.

*Reborn in images once born*
*Ere the dull brain retarded,*
*Picturing still our earliest morn*
*When words were unregarded.*

*So with my Picture book I lie*
*Among the old ones bedward*
*Knowing the unpaid debt which I*
*For ever owe you, Edward.*

To Ted from Eleanor, September 1956

Because Eleanor lacked courage for public speaking, and had the excuse of ill health, Ardizzone was sent to accept the Carnegie Medal in her place, while for the Regina Medal presented in 1959 she was able to make a record of her acceptance speech and send that over to America. It began:

> At this moment, when one of the most wonderful things in my life as a writer is happening to me, I do not seem to be there. Believe that I am. Try to believe, all of you who are responsible for the moment, that I am among you *now*, speaking to you in my own person, however impossible this may seem.
> Everything is possible to people of faith and imagination. The Red Queen was able to believe Six Impossible Things Before Breakfast. I am asking you to believe only One Impossible Thing After Lunch.
> Believe then, dear Madam President, and everyone else here present, that a very shy and overwhelmed old lady is looking at you rather blindly, with some difficulty steadying her voice while she thanks you for the honour you have done her today.

Although accepting the three literary awards, Eleanor refused a more conspicuous honour, that of Dame of the British Empire, saying to her nephew that she did not wish to become different from the milkman.

It was the admired playwright and friend, Christopher Fry, who brought Kaye Webb, the children's editor, to Perrins Walk. "It was a formal and rather special occasion," Kaye Webb recorded.[1] "When

1. BBC Radio Broadcast, 10.2.81.

we arrived she was sitting in her downstairs sitting-room with a beautiful and elaborate tea. I remember the china had roses all over it, and there were little sandwiches and little cakes and we were all rather polite to each other and at one point I was a bit nervous and dropped something, probably a sandwich, I don't remember – and I do remember she said, "Oh, no, no no – leave it where it is, because Denys will pick it up when he comes – he owes me a stoop." And apparently they'd got this arrangement, she and Denys Blakelock, whereby as they both had aching backs whoever felt the most agile did the active work – and she reckoned that he owed her some stoops at this time."

The game of fair exchanges was extended to notabilities, for when Eleanor took her friend to visit de la Mare, he responded by introducing her to Laurence Olivier.

To Kaye Webb, Eleanor, a year before she died, wrote one of her determined letters of refusal, having been asked to contribute to a special series of books for children.

*September 24th* 1962

Dearest Kaye,

Ring me up and let's arrange to kiss and talk next week. I'd rather explain off my tongue than out of the inkpot why I don't feel able to produce what you'd like for this series – which is a cute idea as a selling series for aunts and uncles and will probably result in quite charming gift-books, but the basic idea for me is flawed by my life-long experience and conviction that there is no such thing as the mass-produced Child of Eight— or Nine— or Ten or God help them of, above all ages, Eleven; at which age to-day's conception of Education[1] is to stamp them all with the same mental demand, and grade them with their superiorities and inferiorities for many years to come. In fact, not to admit that all children *are* different, and need to grow differently, without strain or self-consciousness, from the first conscious moments. What would little Mills or little Mozart make of a birthday book for Five-Year-Olds? Go to, Kaye! – and then go to it, and produce a delightful series which its possessors will enjoy – but oh, don't impose on them an artificial adult notion of the thrill of becoming

1. The Eleven Plus exam was at this time in vogue.

curly-figured 8 after being straight-limbed 7. Don't be twee with children, Kaye, respect them. We adults have forgotten too much to be able to tell children what to think or feel or be at any age. There is Childhood. The stages they reach within it differ in time and depth and development for each of its inheritors.

Oh dear! The Inkpot leaves the Tongue at the Starting-point. Forgive me, and come.

Your rebellious, most-loving
Eleanor

In 1959 there began a voluminous correspondence with Stanley Scott, a whimsical devotee whose admiration had just been aroused by reading *The Soul of Kol Nikon*. Eleanor no longer felt satisfied with this early work and, referring to Thomas's gentle mockery, explained that she was 'not as able then, as I am today, to appreciate the fineness of the surgeon's knife which divided the immaturities of fancy from the reality of imagination'.

Nevertheless an admirer was always welcome and a flirtatious kind of waggery at which both were adept was carried on. 'Are you a Leprechaun too?' she demanded. 'No, you needn't tell me. I do not like knowing things. One has so much more leeway.'

The following letter written to an admirer some years previously is a good example of how appreciation was received.

Dear Mrs Harrison,

What a delicious fan-letter! I am so glad that my final sorting out of my verses has given you pleasure, and I shall keep your letter to wave at people who imagine I write for Children; when the truth is I write for anybody who will be kind enough to like it. I am, of course, only a child compared with you, a mere seventy-one next week; but I shall grow up in time and perhaps write something really adult when I am eighty-five.

The Collins book you speak of was published in the Twenties, and has been long out of print; and I was glad of this chance to salvage a lot of things out of it that even I had almost forgotten.

My dear, I do hope you are happy living in Yesterday Street. That Street depends so entirely on what happened in it when it was Today, and if the happenings were largely happy, and if, as one grows old one is wise enough to learn how to lose them with sorrow but not with bitterness, then that street can become the loveliest of playgrounds. My own Street is filled with the loveliest memories, I had, and have, wonderful friends, and a sweet family, though no children of my own – my one great miss. However, I took that out in joy in other people's children, and whatever else happened the work I love doing went on. I am among the very lucky ones.

But I do think you ought to have a copy of the book yourself, and I shall at least send you a little copy of *Mrs Malone* all on her own. She has been much loved by a lot of people, but one little boy reserved his opinion until I promised him that the Animals went in too. As if she would have gone without them! At present I have only one little cat to convey me to the Gate; I had been a year and a half without one, and a month ago a beautiful little golden stray walked in on me, needing food and shelter. So of course he got it, and was straightway christened *Mr. Malone*. He is called Benny, however, his middle name being Benignus, for reasons of my own. Thank you so much for writing. Benignus sends you his blessing, and so does

Yours affectionately,
Eleanor Farjeon

1959 was a busy year. James Roose-Evans had arrived one day with a shoe-string found in the Perrins Court cottage saying, "Hampstead must have a theatre." Eleanor gave a party in the Garden Room to which well-known residents and others gathered to listen to the Roose-Evans scheme. Everybody offered help, some with money, some with secretarial services, with material for curtains or costumes, others were ready to post circulars through doors. When finances got low, Roose-Evans would spend an evening busking outside the Everyman cinema to collect a few more half-crowns. So the Hampstead Theatre was launched.

The Garden Room was lent for rehearsals although, after a while, Eleanor was not pleased with the displacement of her things. Books being taken from the Garden Room without leave by those allowed to use it created another problem. On one occasion, when she was in bed unwell, I was sent down for a certain volume of memoirs situated, my aunt said, on the passage wall, one shelf up from the bottom, five or six along from the end nearest the door – she was almost certain it was six along, a blue book. I went to fetch the memoir, but it was not there. I searched every shelf round the room from floor to ceiling and at last returned empty-handed. My aunt looked grave when I told her and, for the moment, somewhat upset. Then she smiled at me. "Ah well, at least people who take one's books want to read them. And that is what books are for."

The problems with Blakelock were confided to John McBennet: there were even positive complaints. In a letter to him in April 1959 Eleanor described trying to help her neurotic love by serious discussion:

> He listened and I think accepted a lot of what I said, though I took care not to make it too critical of him. The theatre party was *very* gay and happy for us all, but I felt very tired, and felt rather ill and dreadfully astray in the cold Church at 10 o'clock Mass. I prayed hard for forgiveness for everything and asked specially for help in eradicating all the sore feelings which I too often tell you about. After the afternoon rest Denys began unexpectedly to talk about the state of the world and his feelings of fear – not emotionally but with a face of such suffering that I saw a different man, in need of the utmost charity, and I loved him more than ever. The day ended with a tender phone call at 11, to thank me. That's all.
>
> Yours Eleanor

In turn Blakelock grumbled about Eleanor, and on one occasion when the phone was continuously engaged, exploded to McBennet, "Oh, I suppose it's that damned music again!"

McBennet wrote a short memoir of his friendship with Eleanor, and records their visits to theatres and concerts. As an actor he was keenly interested in her appreciation of Vanessa Redgrave as Rosalind, Alec Guinness as Hamlet and Edith Evans, who she rated higher than Irving, Gielgud or Olivier.

In the summer of 1959 one Sunday morning when Blakelock was staying the weekend, Eleanor spotted an advertisement in the paper: a delightful studio house, just up the way on Windmill Hill, was for sale. There had been many complaints about the box-like flat in an ugly block on the sunless side of Tavistock Square in which the actor lived. Eleanor suggested they might just look at the studio and so they walked up. There stood the neatest smartest little residence with a fountain and pool in the patio garden. It was the perfect place for a bachelor. The studio seemed right for teaching and entertaining, there were small rooms upstairs, the garden was paved, so that no hard work would be needed to keep it in order. It was ideal.

Eleanor phoned family and friends in a state of euphoria to tell them of this stroke of luck. Denys would be near her now, with no tedious journeys to spoil the beginning and end of his visits – yet he would not be right in her lap. If he grew lonely he could just run down to the cottage for comfort. Private pupils and actors who wanted coaching had only to take a taxi or the tube to Hampstead. Doubtless she saw that she would be better able to keep an eye on the loved one and, perhaps, wean him from the sin which weighed so heavily on his conscience.

In a remarkably short time the studio was bought. Eleanor was abuzz with plans for furniture, curtains and cutlery. Blakelock, almost equally excited, hired builders, decorators and upholsterers. His life was about to expand. He had become a householder.

The move complete, a grand house-warming party was given for around one hundred guests: theatrical friends and relatives. Eleanor, just out of hospital after one of her cataract operations, sat in a chair in the middle of the crowd, a little dazed and weak, but very happy and proud that her plan had worked out so well. Guests presented domestic implements to aid the housekeeping, with laughter and congratulations at this marvellous find. Blakelock tripped back and forth, smiling his nervous charming smile, the sun shone, the fountain tinkled and his friends looked well dressed.

Then the party was over and he was alone. The newly painted little house seemed unfamiliar and unfriendly, the road outside was silent, fearful terrors assailed him. He could not bear his gilded cage.

For three appalling weeks Blakelock stuck it out and then fled down the hill, back to the ugly flat in Tavistock Square.

In a remarkably short time the studio was sold. The actor reverted to Perrins Walk weekends, when a notice would be hung on the front door knocker: 'Do Not Disturb'.

Grace Hogarth was one of the few to whom Eleanor turned when Blakelock's disordered mind got the better of them both. One day she phoned asking Mrs Hogarth to come at once: she was in great trouble, being in bed ill and unable to cope with her friend's distraught state. He was found weeping on the floor, but managed to go out for a long walk on Hampstead Heath, when he talked of his anguish in an uncontrollable flow. However the suicidal depressions passed and the couple were happy again, full of jokes and sayings, little games and rituals.

Another woman with whom a lasting friendship developed late in life was Eileen Colwell, the children's librarian for the borough of Hendon. Miss Colwell was herself an expert story-teller – not a story-maker – who would gather children in her library and relate stories to them. She travelled all over the English-speaking world in order to foster the telling of tales. In 1955 she asked Eleanor's permission to retell some of her work in the United States, and so began a friendship sealed by their mutual empathy with the youthful imagination. They appreciated too the wise child within the adult, this union which makes Eleanor's humour so sure and simple, as when King Nollekens tries to bribe the wicked Tom Tit Tot: "Here's my crown! Here's my sceptre! Here's my penknife with three blades!"

On the old lady's eightieth birthday a letter to John McBennet gives a picture of her childlike excitement at the occasion.

*February* 17th 1959

Dearest John,

I meant to ring you up at the week-end, but somehow things didn't work out that way. So here's my loving thank-you for the splendid card, the first opened on Friday morning. Before I had time to open all the heap of cards and letters, the telephones and parcel postman and callers started in spate. My car to take me to Denys was ordered for 4.10. At three fifteen, as I was putting the last flowers in a vase, I realised I hadn't eaten or even read all my letters – I opened a tin of sardines and crammed two sardines between two bits of bread and munched – more flowers came (my room is breathtaking) – I did my best while munching, changed my dress, never touched my hair, fell into the car – and finished reading my mail at midnight. It was all lovely, and has been a crowded time since, with water going wrong, plumbers, piano tuners, masseuse and nieces. But I'm feeling wonderful. We'll talk soon.

Your Eleanor

In November she was trying to write a Postscript for the reprint of *A Nursery in the Nineties*, and ended up unsure as to whether it was good enough, having torn up two or three hand-written efforts and five typescripts. The result was sent to John Bell of Oxford University Press with a letter to say that if he felt it was only half-right it should be omitted. Then she pressed on with her overseas Christmas cards, about three hundred of which involved little annual letters. There was also a visit to the doctor.

"Do you want to look at what I've got inside me or ask me questions?" she began.

"I know what you've got inside you and I want you to tell me how you are," he replied.

The consultation ended satisfactorily with his order to ring up at once if there was any trouble, and what a great pleasure it was to know her. So she presented him with *The Little Bookroom* for his children and went home.

The sending of hundreds of personal letters every Christmas, let alone during the rest of the year, was a feat. On the greeting card some old or new verse would be printed. In the cottage reciprocal cards would be strung in festoons and crammed collapsing on every ledge, as thick as autumn leaves. But, after the age of eighty all this correspondence became too much. With typical practicality the following handout was printed, to be sent all over the world.

20 *Perrins Walk, N.W.* 3.,
*Hampstead* 2429
*Date as postmark*

Dear Friend, Acquaintance, or Stranger,

I hope to answer your letter in due or undue course.

Advancing years, increasing infirmities, faults of method and temperament, plus chronic secretarialessness, make my accumulating correspondence a burden beyond what any of you would wish for me. Lawrence of Arabia shovelled his unopened letters on the fire. Bernard Shaw wrote postcards. This is what I do.

You will hear from me This Year, Next Year, Sometime, or Never.

Love to Friends, greetings to Acquaintances, and apologies to Strangers from

Eleanor Farjeon

To within a few weeks of her death Eleanor planned and cooked meals for her close friends. She remained both gourmet and gourmande. The actor, David March, was one of many who would enviously watch the preparation of specialities for Blakelock, who was generally resting upstairs in his special chair, cuddling his special cushion and waiting for his hostess to carry up a delicate glass of sherry at the right moment. Droppers-in were never invited to join the party, but were welcomed into the kitchen to be tantalised by succulent smells with a disquisition on the pleasures to come.

A letter to Kaye Webb in 1963 relates how the day suddenly teemed with business letters, in between cooking for Denys today and tomorrow. But by now Eleanor was not strong and decided to put the cottage in Perrins Court to the use for which it had been intended. A projected advertisement worked out on the back of an envelope shows many scratchings out and emendations. It was almost certainly intended for the small ads in the *Hampstead and Highgate Express*.

'Hampstead Authoress, 83, needing part-time companion help offers newly furnished cottage, 3 little rooms 3 beds, plus £52 per annum to responsible intelligent elderly woman with good references write fully.'

She was now immersed in plans for the next book of memoirs, to be devoted to Bertie. A few bits and pieces were already written, but she found him difficult to describe, as have others, for his reserve, his wit, his kindliness and nervy determination were all marked by a delicate sharpness that was not easy to catch. However, press cuttings, articles, obituaries, letters and odds and ends had been collected ready for the serious start.

This year there was the delight of a visit from Robert Frost, who had come to give lectures in England. The two poets had not met since 1914. From those days of insignificance both had become literary figures. Frost was the only man left with whom Eleanor could talk of Edward Thomas as a mutual friend, and whose memories accorded with her own.

On a summer afternoon her plump shining smiling face, with the thick glasses glinting in the bright light, welcomed the American poet at her door. With a stick for support, she showed him round her gardens, the strawberry bed, the roses, the fig tree, and they talked of the past and the present as though the fifty years between their last

conversation were nothing. "My!" he said, looking at her shelves and the 80 volumes of work, "what a lot you've written! Do you know how much I've written in 60 years? Six hundred pages." "Yes, but every one will live," she replied. "So much of mine will go in the waste paper basket."

Frost did not want to leave, but a car was waiting and, always a stickler for punctuality, Eleanor made him go at last, only a little late for the next appointment. Accompanied by her old friend, Helen Thomas, Eleanor attended his lecture at University College.

But every winter the attacks of bronchitis grew worse and lasted longer, till in May 1965 the illness developed into pneumonia. Eleanor was firm in her determination to stay in her own home, so day and night nurses were engaged. Benignus, the only cat now, sat on her bed and she often grew anxious as to whether he was being provided with the food he liked. Once, in a mood of despair, she cried out for her brothers, "I want my boys." But generally she was quiet, clutching her rosary.

In the garden cherries glinted pinkly between the leaves of the cherry tree and a grey squirrel sat on a branch eating the half ripe fruit from his paws. When I described this, she exclaimed with delight, "Good – he is enjoying himself!" She never gave up wanting life to be a glorious feast of love and enjoyment, and never gave up the struggle to make it so, with remarkable success.

On May 21st the nurse reported in the Patient's Book: '6 pm Pressure Points attended to. Light diet taken. Gum-boil is better, the dear lady is more settled today.' But by June she was breathing with difficulty and her colour had turned yellowish grey. Although her voice was faint she could still joke, for one day taking my hand she felt a large ring, which she raised close to her face for inspection. With a faint smile she whispered, "Ah, like Edith Sitwell I see."

She was given the last rites by her priest and died on June 5th.

Eleanor was buried in the romantic little churchyard which spans the side of Hampstead Hill between the Protestant church in Church Row and the Catholic church in Holly Walk. Her grave is generally smothered by a big rambler rose and is hard to discover. She was never keen on personal publicity.

# BENNY

❧ ❧

INSTRUCTIONS *left for Mrs Elsie Palmer to look after the cat, Benny;*

Pig's liver:
½ to ¾ lb
at a time

Cod's Tail:
4/s to 5/s
boil about 12
minutes in fish
covered pan.

Fresh Lean Meat,
according to what
is best at the
Butchers: Stewing
steak, skirt.
Chuck steak,
Top Shin, etc.
½ to ¾ lb
at a time.

Liver about ¾ lb, sliced, covers three to four days. Cod's tail, boiled, 4 to 5 days (be VERY careful about the bones on the sides of the fillets; waste some of the side-pieces rather than risk it).

First meal between 10.30 and 12. Generally liver. Bring water to boil in the little saucepan, drop a slice of liver into it, remove in about 6 to 7 seconds, cut very fine on board, mashing it a little with the back of the knife, or a fork, and leaving it in moist little masses on the plate so that he can lick it up easily.

Second Meal is usually before 4 o'clock, and is generally fish, flaked with the skin cut up.

Meat last thing at night, very finely minced and arranged on the plate in little lumps. His gums are very tender, and he can't chew much.

When he is left alone in the house his special window on the right must always be left open a little so that he can come in and out, and the door at the foot of the stairs always shut, so that Black Jack can't get downstairs.

Fresh water every day, both in the kitchen and the upper room.

# ELEANOR FARJEON BIBLIOGRAPHY

*❧ ❧*

1  *Pan-Worship, and other poems*, Elkin Matthews, 1908
2  *Dream-Songs for the Beloved*, Orpheus Press, 1911
3  *Trees*, Batsford, 1914
4  *Nursery Rhymes of London Town*, illustrated by MacDonald Gill, Duckworth, 1916
5  *More Nursery Rhymes of London Town*, illustrated by MacDonald Gill, Duckworth, 1917
6  *All the Way to Alfriston*, illustrated by Robin Guthrie, The Greenleaf Press, 1918
7  *Sonnets and Poems*, Basil Blackwell, 1918
8  *Gypsy and Ginger*, illustrated by C. E. Brock, Dent, 1920
9  *Tomfooleries*, The Daily Herald, 1920
10  *Moonshine*, The Labour Publishing Co. and Allen & Unwin, 1921
11  *Martin Pippin in the Apple Orchard*, Collins, 1921
12  *Songs for Music and Lyrical Poems*, illustrated by John Aveten, Selwyn & Blount, 1922
13  *Tunes of a Penny Piper*, illustrated by John Aveten, Selwyn & Blount, 1922
14  *The Soul of Kol Nikon*, Collins, 1923
15  *All the Year Round*, Collins, 1923
16  *The Country Child's Alphabet*, illustrated by William Michael Rothenstein, Poetry Bookshop, 1924
17  *The Town Child's Alphabet*, illustrated by David Jones, Poetry Bookshop, 1924
18  *Mighty Men and Poems*, Basil Blackwell, 1924
19  *Faithful Jenny Dove and other tales*, Collins, 1925
20  *Tom Cobble*, illustrated by M. Dobson, Basil Blackwell, 1925
21  *Young Folk and Old*, The High House Press, 1925
22  *Nuts and May*, illustrated by Rosalind Thornycroft, Collins, 1926
23  *Joan's Door*, illustrated by Will Townsend, Collins, 1926
24  *Come Christmas*, illustrated by Molly McArthur, Collins, 1927
25  *The Wonderful Knight*, illustrated by Doris Pailthorpe, Basil Blackwell, 1927
26  *A Bad Day for Martha*, illustrated by Eugenie Richards, Basil Blackwell, 1928

60 *The New Book of Days*, illustrated by Philip Gough and Meredith W. Hawes, Oxford University Press, 1941
61 *Cherrystones*, illustrated by Isobel and John Morton-Sale, Michael Joseph, 1942
62 *Golden Coney*, Michael Joseph, 1943
63 *The Fair Venetian*, Michael Joseph, 1943
64 *Ariadne and the Bull*, Michael Joseph, 1945
65 *The Mulberry Bush*, illustrated by Isobel and John Morton-Sale, Michael Joseph, 1945
66 *Dark World of Animals*, illustrated by T. Stoney, Sylvan Press, 1945
67 *Love Affair*, Michael Joseph, 1947
68 *First and Second Love*, Michael Joseph, 1947
69 *The Two Bouquets: a novelette based on the operetta*, illustrated by Reginald Wooley, Michael Joseph, 1948
70 *The Starry Floor*, illustrated by Isobel and John Morton-Sale, Michael Joseph, 1949
71 *Mrs Malone*, illustrated, Michael Joseph, 1950
72 *Silver-Sand and Snow*, Michael Joseph, 1951
73 *The Silver Curlew: a story based on the children's play*, illustrated by Ernest H. Shepard, Oxford University Press, 1954
74 *The Glass Slipper: a story based on the children's play*, illustrated by Ernest H. Shepard, Oxford University Press, 1955
75 *The Little Bookroom*, illustrated by Edward Ardizzone, Oxford University Press, 1955
76 *The Children's Bells*, illustrated by Peggy Fortnum, Oxford University Press, 1957
77 *Elizabeth Myers*, St Albert's Press, 1957
78 *A Puffin Quartet of Poets*, illustrated by Diana Bloomfield, Penguin Books, 1958
79 *Edward Thomas: The Last Four Years*, Oxford University Press, 1958
80 *Italian Peepshow*, illustrated by Edward Ardizzone, Oxford University Press, 1960
81 *Mr Garden*, illustrated by Jane Paton, Hamish Hamilton, 1966
82 *Invitation to a Mouse*, illustrated by Anthony Maitland, Pelham Books, 1981

## MUSICAL WORKS

83 *Singing Games for Children*, illustrated by J. Littlehohns, Dent, 1919
84 *Nursery Rhymes of London Town*, four books, Oxford University Press, 1919–26
85 *Morning has Broken and two other hymns*, Songs of Praise, 1923
86 *Songs from 'Punch' for Children*, J. Saville, 1925
87 *Singing Games from Arcady*, Basil Blackwell, 1926
88 *Songs of Kings and Queens*, Arnold, 1938

89  *Filoretta: an opera in 2 acts*, music by Harry Farjeon, Royal Academy of Music, 1899
90  *The Registry Office: an operetta in 1 act*, music by Harry Farjeon, Royal Academy of Music, 1900
91  *A First and Second Chap Book of Rounds*, music by Harry Farjeon, Dent, 1919
92  *Kings and Queens*, with Herbert Farjeon, illustrated by Rosalind Thornycroft, Gollancz, 1932
93  *Heroes and Heroines*, with Herbert Farjeon, illustrated by Rosalind Thornycroft, Gollancz, 1933
94  *The Two Bouquets: an operetta*, libretto with Herbert Farjeon, S. French, 1938
95  *An Elephant in Arcady: an operetta*, libretto with Herbert Farjeon, Ascherberg, Hopwood and Crew, 1938
96  *The Glass Slipper: a fairy tale*, music by Clifton Parker, words with Herbert Farjeon, S. French, 1945
97  *The Silver Curlew: a fairy tale*, music by Clifton Parker, C. P. Chappell, 1950
98  *Aucassin and Nicolette: a lyric drama*, music by Clifton Parker, libretto with Herbert Farjeon, C. P. Chappell, 1952
99  *A Room at the Inn: a masque*, music by Harry Farjeon, words with Herbert Farjeon, S. French, 1957

Prefaces and literary journalism are not included, nor are the six masques written for broadcasting with Herbert Farjeon, or the songs and sketches Eleanor Farjeon provided for his theatrical productions. The works listed in this bibliography are first editions only.

# INDEX

Abercrombie, Lascelles 104, 105, 106, 177

Adelaide Road homes, London
life at 14–24
Little Bookroom 22
No 13. 16, 17
No 196. 20

Adrian, Max 238

Albery, Bertie 231, 232

Albery, Bronson 229, 231, 232

Albery, Wyndham 'Button' 25, 26, 56, 161

*All the Year Round* (periodical) 8, 9

*Answers* 83

Antonietti, Aldo 86

Ardizzone, Edward 22, 288
accepts Carnegie medal for EF 289
illustration for *The Little Bookroom* 23

Aumonier, Stacey 85

Australian gold rush, 1850s 3–4, 6

Ayers, Ann 206

Ayrton, Anthony 250

Barrie, J. M. 66
*Peter Pan* 75

Battersea Library, London 177n

Bax, Arnold 85, 86, 96

Bax, Clifford 85, 87–8, 177
cricket weeks 96, 179
publishes book of EF's poems 92

Bax, Ridley 85

Baxter, Beverly
enthusiastic review of *Glass Slipper* 252–4

Baynes, Chloe
receives literary criticism from EF 181

Baynes, Godwin 85, 89, 94, 247
marries Rosalind Thornycroft 89

romantic paganism of 91
treats Edward Thomas 93, 96–7

Baynes, Rosalind 89, 142, 198, 271
illustrates *Kings and Queens* verses 158
invites EF to Italy 142, 143–4
parts from Godwin Baynes 144
second marriage 246n

Beerbohm Tree, Sir Herbert 39, 224

Bell, John 288, 288n, 296

Belloc, Hilaire 93

Benignus, Father 286

Benson, George 164, 183, 261, 281
pictured 163

Bernhardt, Sarah 75

Bettesworth, Bertha 170, 218, 259

Bettesworth, Margaret 259

Birrell, Francis 117

Blackburn, Aubrey 248

Blackwood, William
prints EF's spoof Elizabethan poet 80–1

Blakelock, Denys 269, 270, 271, 273, 287, 290, 293, 297
acting ability 267
Catholicism 278
contradictory nature 264
*Eleanor: Portrait of a Farjeon* 264, 266n, 267n, 268n, 278
friendship with EF 264, 266–8, 274, 275, 277, 278–9
pictured 265

Blau, Bela 186, 196, 199, 206, 216

*Boy's Own Paper, The* 45, 50

British Broadcasting Corporation (BBC)
radio programme linking Edward Thomas and EF 283

Bulwer Lytton, Edward
*Rienzi* 32

307